Encountering GOD'S HEART for YOU

Encountering GOD'S HEART for YOU

365 DEVOTIONS FROM GENESIS THROUGH REVELATION

DIANE STORTZ

a division of Baker Publishing Group
Minneapolis, Minnesota

Published by Bethany House Publishers
11400 Hampshire Avenue South
Bloomington, Minnesota 55438
www.bethanyhouse.com

Bethany House Publishers is a division of
Baker Publishing Group, Grand Rapids, Michigan

Printed in the United States of America

Library of Congress Cataloging-in-Publication Control Number: 2019019121
ISBN 978-0-7642-3218-3

Cover design by LOOK Design Studio

Author is represented by Books & Such Literary Agency

19 20 21 22 23 24 25 7 6 5 4 3 2 1

In keeping with biblical principles of creation stewardship, Baker Publishing Group advocates the responsible use of our natural resources. As a member of the Green Press Initiative, our company uses recycled paper when possible. The text paper of this book is composed in part of post-consumer waste.

For every woman
of the Word.

—DS

As You Begin . . .

The Bible tells a big story . . .

about the creation of the universe and the first human beings,
about the disobedience of those humans and the consequences they unleashed,
about a special nation and a Redeemer for the world,
about a day of restoration when all will be put right again.

But mostly the Bible tells us about a big God with a big heart . . .

a powerful God who spoke the universe into being out of nothing,
a loving God who would not abandon His fallen humans to themselves,
a just God who sent His Son to be the Savior of the world He loves so much,
a sovereign God whose kingdom of love and righteousness will never end.

May you be blessed as you follow this little guide to the Bible's big story and encounter God's heart for you. And in response may you also discover a heart of love for Him!

Diane Stortz

All Scripture is God-breathed.
—2 Timothy 3:16 NIV

Encountering GOD'S HEART for YOU in the OLD TESTAMENT

The Books of Law

In His Image

GENESIS 1–2

So God created mankind in his own image, in the image of God he created them; male and female he created them.—Genesis 1:27 NIV

Right from the start, God's written Word, the Bible, invites us to know our Creator.

The Hebrew word for God in Genesis 1:1 is *Elohim*, which has the sense of "the highest, no one better." The first two chapters of Genesis tell us God created the heavens and the earth and everything in them, in six days, out of nothing, by His mighty power. Creation culminated with the first human beings—a man and a woman, Adam and Eve.

God formed Adam with His hands, and Adam took in his first breath directly from God. God formed Eve from Adam's rib! Individually and together, male and female bear God's image: we think and feel, plan and work, protect and nurture, imagine and create. We desire relationship. We love.

Do you sometimes feel "less than," or doubt your worth? Remember that God—who hung the stars and carved the mountains—created you to bear His image. Wouldn't it be wonderful to know your Creator better? He wants you to know Him, and He has much to tell you about himself in His Word, right from the very beginning!

Heavenly Father, I do long to know you, my Creator, so much better. Thank you for showing me who you are in your written Word. Amen.

2

Thinking of You

GENESIS 3

> "I will put enmity between you and the woman, and between your offspring and her offspring; he shall bruise your head, and you shall bruise his heel."—Genesis 3:15 ESV

Adam and Eve walked and talked with God in Eden. Yet when Satan came on the scene in the form of a serpent, they chose to listen to him instead. Satan got them thinking God was holding out on them. Rejecting the authority of what God had said, Eve and then Adam ate the fruit from the Tree of the Knowledge of Good and Evil.

Suddenly they knew they had made a terrible mistake. For the first time, they felt fear and shame and the need to blame someone else.

Their sin had consequences. Eve would know physical pain during childbirth and struggle in her relationship to her husband. Adam would work longer and harder to grow food in ground affected by a curse. Then . . . they would die, as God had warned. Sin had entered the world and all humanity would be affected.

But God also expressed compassion toward Adam and Eve. Satan's scheming wouldn't be allowed to prevail forever. One of the most amazing verses in the Bible tells us that God planned "from before the beginning of time—to show us his grace through Christ Jesus" (2 Timothy 1:9).

Even before creation began, God knew what would happen and planned to send Jesus. He was thinking of you and me! He knew we would need a Savior.

Father God, your goodness astounds me! Thank you for planning to send our Savior, Jesus, even before you made the world. You know me so well. Thank you for your love. Amen.

Beginning Again

GENESIS 6–9

The LORD regretted that he had made man on the earth, and it grieved him to his heart. . . . But Noah found favor in the eyes of the LORD.—Genesis 6:6, 8 ESV

Humanity's evil grew and filled the earth with violence. God felt great sorrow and planned to begin again, with Noah, the one man on earth who walked closely with Him.

Can you imagine receiving Noah's instructions? To escape the flood that was coming in judgment, he was to build a box-shaped boat—longer than a football field, about half as wide, and more than four stories tall. Inside, the ark would house Noah, his wife, their three sons and their wives, a zoo-sized menagerie representing all the animal kinds God had created, and food for everyone.

Crazy, right? But "Noah did everything exactly as God had commanded him" (Genesis 6:22).

When everyone was inside the ark, God closed the door and the rain began. Noah's cooperation with God's plan—his obedience to God's commands—saved his family and allowed humanity a fresh start.

Does beginning again sound good to you? Do you need a fresh start? Today and every day, you can reap the rewards of cooperating with God's plan: "Now he commands everyone everywhere to repent of their sins and turn to him" (Acts 17:30).

Dear Lord, your ways are good and right! Thank you for Jesus. Thank you for your offer and your command to turn to Him, to begin again, to be saved from sin. Amen.

4

Planning with Purpose

GENESIS 11

> Then they said, "Come, let us build ourselves a city, with a tower that reaches to the heavens, so that we may make a name for ourselves; otherwise we will be scattered over the face of the whole earth."—Genesis 11:4 NIV

Are you a planner? A list maker? Do you scour websites and Facebook groups for the best deals in town? Do you rely on a network of sitters and mothers' helpers to keep your family's busy life on track? Do you choose a word for the year or create a five-year life plan?

The Bible approves wise planning, with the understanding that our focus should be on God's will for our lives. And that's exactly where Noah's descendants went wrong after the flood. God had told them, "Be fruitful and multiply. Fill the earth." Multiply? Fine. Fill the earth? Not so much. The descendants of Noah's sons thought staying put and building a ziggurat—a multistoried tower with a shrine on top—was a much better idea.

But it wasn't God's plan. They didn't know best. He did, and He took action to point them in His direction again by giving them different languages instead of one.

So make your plans, but be sure to line them up with God's. Ask for His wisdom and seek out His will.

Dear God, you've given me the ability to dream, plan, and achieve. But help me keep my eyes on you and your will for my life, today and every day. Amen.

5

Faith Is What Matters

GENESIS 12, 15

Abram believed the LORD, and the LORD counted him as righteous because of his faith.—Genesis 15:6

When you were a girl, did you fill a sash with Girl Scout badges or bring home a report card with straight A's? Or maybe you struggled to earn just a badge or two and never saw an A. In Abraham's life, God shows us that neither our accomplishments nor our failures make any difference when it comes to our relationship with Him.

More than two thousand years before Jesus was born, God promised Abraham that he would become the father of a great nation and that his family would bless the entire world. Abraham and his wife, though old and childless, would have a son to kick things off, and Abraham's descendants would be as innumerable as the stars. Incredible, right? But Abraham believed God would do what He said, "and the LORD counted him as righteous because of his faith."

God has made promises to us too. We can't earn ourselves a place in heaven and our sin won't keep us out—if we have responded to God with faith. God says we're counted as righteous when we believe His Son, Jesus, is the Savior He has sent. We can't earn the status that says we're right with God. It's His gift.

Have you been counted as righteous?

Heavenly Father, forgive me for striving to earn your love. Faith is what you've always wanted. Thank you, thank you, for Jesus! Amen.

6

The God Who Sees Me

GENESIS 16

> She gave this name to the LORD who spoke to her: "You are the God who sees me," for she said, "I have now seen the One who sees me."—Genesis 16:13 NIV

If you've ever felt invisible or cried out to God in frustration over circumstances that seemed unbearable, then you need to know Hagar.

God had promised Abraham and Sarah a son, but when year after childless year went by, Sarah devised a plan of her own—Abraham could father a child for her through her Egyptian servant, Hagar (a common practice in those days). But when Hagar became pregnant, she began to treat Sarah with contempt. Perhaps she felt elevated, not voiceless, and more than a slave.

Sarah blamed Abraham, who took Sarah's side and reinforced Hagar's slave status. Sarah then began to treat Hagar harshly and she ran away, maybe to try to make it back to Egypt.

But God found Hagar near a spring in the wilderness and spoke with her. He told her to return to Sarah and to name the son she carried Ishmael, which means "God hears," because He had heard her cries of distress. He gave her promises about her future.

Hagar's circumstances didn't change, but her view of God did. Her son's name would be a constant reminder that God hears us in our need. And Hagar began to call God "the god who sees me."

Whatever you're dealing with today, remember this: He hears and sees you too.

Father God, let me learn from Hagar today! You do indeed hear and see me in the situation causing me distress. Help me trust you to care for me and show me what to do. Amen.

7

Laughing with God

GENESIS 18, 21

Sarah said, "God has brought me laughter, and everyone who hears about this will laugh with me."—Genesis 21:6 NIV

Sarah couldn't believe it when she heard God telling Abraham that she would bear a son within a year. She and Abraham hadn't gotten any younger waiting all this time for God to fulfill His promise. Abraham would soon be one hundred, and she was nearly ninety. Finally, a baby? How could it be? Sarah laughed, silently she thought, but the Lord heard her.

God kept His word, of course. Sarah conceived and gave Abraham a son. Abraham named him Isaac, which means "he laughs," perhaps because, as Sarah said, "God has brought me laughter." After all, who *doesn't* smile and coo and giggle at a baby? And the story of this baby made everyone laugh with delight, right along with Sarah.

What about you? What impossible possibility has you silently laughing with disbelief? If God is in it, you just might find yourself laughing out loud soon. He is, as He told Abraham, *El-Shaddai*—"God Almighty" (Genesis 17:1)—and nothing is too hard for Him.

Dear Lord, I want to laugh out loud at your goodness over and over again. Help me see and believe! Amen.

8

Salt

GENESIS 19

> When he hesitated, the men grasped his hand and the hands of his wife and of his two daughters and led them safely out of the city, for the LORD was merciful to them.—Genesis 19:16 NIV

Abraham's nephew Lot had settled with his family in Sodom. At Abraham's prodding, God promised He would change His plans to destroy Sodom if just ten righteous people could be found there. Sadly, there were not.

The behavior of the men of the city toward Lot's guests (who were actually angels) tells us much about the city's immorality, as does the reaction Lot received when he tried to warn the men his daughters were betrothed to marry. Lot himself elevated hospitality over the safety of his daughters. Without the angels' intervention, the scene would have turned even more ugly.

Lot delayed leaving the city until the angels finally led him and his family out by the hand and instructed them to run and not look back. Lot's wife turned to look, however, and she became a pillar of salt.

Why were Lot and his family so reluctant to leave Sodom? Perhaps they had grown accustomed to the sin all around them and viewed it as normal, and I have to wonder how much we might be like them today. Jesus calls us to be salt to the world around us—not salt like Lot's wife, but salt that preserves the good. What kind of salt are you?

Dear God, where I am complacent about the sin plaguing my city, my state, my country, wake me up and show me how to respond as good salt. Amen.

9

Totally Trusting

GENESIS 22

"Now I know that you truly fear God. You have not withheld from me even your son, your only son."—Genesis 22:12

God asked Abraham to sacrifice his son Isaac as a burnt offering; that's a fact. But God always acts consistently with His own character, and Scripture tells us in other places He abhors human sacrifice. So why did God make this strange request?

Think about someone, or something, you hold most dear. Maybe you waited years for that relationship, that child, that home, that bank account, that position. Now, tie it up and place it on an altar. Prepare to give it over to God forever, just because He told you to.

Would you do it?

Abraham obeyed the strange command, trusting God. He didn't need to know the reason because he trusted God's promises. God would provide a lamb for the sacrifice instead of Isaac, or God would bring Isaac back to life (Hebrews 11:19), but He wouldn't break the promises He had made.

A ram appeared in a thicket. Abraham called the place of the sacrifice *Yahweh Yireh*, which means "The Lord will provide." And many years later, God provided a Lamb for another sacrifice, on a cross outside Jerusalem. That time, it was God himself who didn't hold back His only Son.

Heavenly Father, Abraham's trust in you astounds me. May I trust you as my Yahweh Yireh to provide for me in every way, all the days of my life. Amen.

10

Family Matters

GENESIS 24–35

"Your name is Jacob, but you will not be called Jacob any longer. From now on your name will be Israel."—Genesis 35:10

Isaac and Rebekah's story began beautifully but veered off into conflict, as our own family situations often do.

Abraham had sent a trusted servant to find a wife for Isaac from among his relatives. God led him to Rebekah, who agreed to journey to Canaan to marry Isaac. Rebekah eventually gave birth to twins, Jacob and Esau.

They should have been a happy family. But as the brothers grew, Isaac favored Esau, and Rebekah favored Jacob. Esau acted rashly; Jacob acted with deceit. Rebekah schemed for what she wanted, and Isaac allowed himself to be manipulated.

With his brother threatening to kill him, Jacob left home and traveled to Haran, hoping to find a wife among Abraham's relatives as his father had done. And he did—two wives and two concubines. A new family chapter of favoritism, trickery, and jealousy began.

When Jacob returned to Canaan years later as the wealthy patriarch of a large family, God appeared to him and repeated the promises He had given Abraham and Isaac. He also changed Jacob's name to Israel. Eventually Jacob's descendants would be known as the Israelites.

Despite all the family turmoil and trouble, God had a plan. There was hope for the family of Abraham, Isaac, and Jacob, just as there is hope for your family and mine.

Father God, you care about my family even more than I do. Restore us wherever we have need of your mercy and forgiveness. Lead us so your plans can prevail. Amen.

11

Living Above Circumstances

GENESIS 37, 39

But the LORD was with Joseph in the prison and showed him his faithful love.—Genesis 39:21

Long days and nights caring for little ones. Marriage stresses. Financial pressures. Illness. Prodigal children. Caring for aging parents. What difficult road is facing you today? Let Jacob's favorite son, Joseph, encourage you to persevere. You don't know where your challenges will lead, but you do know that God is with you.

Cocky at seventeen, Joseph bragged to his brothers about his dreams. That only increased his brothers' jealousy, and soon Joseph found himself at the bottom of a cistern, then sold to traders passing by, and then on his way to Egypt to be sold again as a slave.

As a servant in the house of Potiphar, the captain of the guard for Pharaoh (the title of the Egyptian king), Joseph excelled because God was with him. Potiphar noticed and made Joseph his household manager. Potiphar's wife noticed Joseph too, but Joseph's steadfast refusals to sleep with her landed Joseph in the king's prison, falsely accused of attempted rape. Even as a prisoner, however, Joseph excelled, because God was with him. The warden soon put Joseph in charge of everything in the prison.

Joseph worked hard and chose to do right, but it was God's presence and faithful love that sustained him, prospered him, and prepared him for what would come next. Joseph journeyed from young man of privilege to slave to prisoner, but with God he lived above his difficult circumstances. We can too!

Dear Lord, when circumstances would crush me, remind me that I'm not alone and that you have a plan. Guide me and guard me, I pray. Amen.

12

Tamar

GENESIS 38

When the time came for Tamar to give birth, it was discovered that she was carrying twins.—Genesis 38:27

You might expect the illegitimate sons of a woman who pretended to be a prostitute and her father-in-law to be outcasts. Instead, one of them is found in the genealogy of Jesus.

Tamar had been married to Judah's oldest son, Er, and when Er died, his brother Onan married Tamar, but Tamar remained childless, a serious disgrace in that culture. According to custom, Judah should have allowed Tamar to marry his youngest son, Shelah, when he came of age, but he did not. When Tamar saw an opportunity to have a child by tricking Judah into sleeping with her, she took it.

Both Judah and Tamar manipulated circumstances and people to achieve their goals. Neither acted morally, but Judah acknowledged his mistreatment of Tamar when he said, "She is more righteous than I am, because I didn't arrange for her to marry my son Shelah" (Genesis 38:26).

I love that Scripture records people's stories truthfully; we see faith-filled choices as well as actions that miss the mark. Still, we might wonder why Tamar's story is recorded for us. One reason could be to show us God's understanding of Tamar's plight. Despite her actions, she received a role in the lineage of Jesus—through Perez, one of her twin sons by Judah (Matthew 1:3). God planned to send His Son through the family of Judah. How good to know that the plans of our compassionate God always succeed despite our human sinfulness!

Dear God, thank you for the encouragement in Tamar's story, showing us your leading and your compassion. Amen.

13

Tapestry of Life

GENESIS 40–50

"Don't be angry with yourselves for selling me to this place. It was God who sent me here ahead of you to preserve your lives."—Genesis 45:5

Corrie ten Boom, who told her WWII survival story in *The Hiding Place*, also is known for a poem she often quoted. Our lives are like the messy underside of a beautiful tapestry, she tells us in the poem. Events confuse and sadden us because we see only the tangled threads, but God is weaving the tapestry of our lives. He knows how beautiful the upper side will look when the tapestry is complete.

Through all his ordeals, God was with Joseph and showed him His faithful love (Genesis 39:21). But even after Joseph interpreted Pharaoh's dreams and began a new life as a high-ranking Egyptian, he gave his sons names that told of his trouble and his grief.

Then Joseph's brothers arrived in Egypt, seeking to buy grain to see them through the famine. Joseph recognized them immediately but didn't reveal his identity until he had tested their character. Had they changed over the years? Ultimately, the entire family joyfully reconciled with Joseph and moved to Egypt to live with him.

The underside of Joseph's tapestry showed more than twenty years of trouble and heartache. Yet Joseph told his brothers, "You intended to harm me, but God intended it all for good" (Genesis 50:20). Both sides of the tapestry of Joseph's life had finally come into view.

Heavenly Father, when I question what is happening, when I wonder why, remind me that you're the master weaver and you're creating something beautiful. Help me trust you! Amen.

14

Brave

EXODUS 1–2

> But because the midwives feared God, they refused to obey the king's orders.—Exodus 1:17

Would you be willing to go to jail or face death to stand up for what is right?

Afraid of the number of Hebrews—Jacob's descendants—in Egypt, the king made the Hebrews slaves. When their number continued to grow, he ordered the Hebrew midwives to kill all the newborn Hebrew baby boys at birth. They refused to sin against God in this way, and God honored their reverence for Him with families of their own.

But Pharaoh ordered all Egyptians to kill Hebrew baby boys by throwing them into the Nile River. And under that order, a Hebrew woman named Jochebed gave birth to a baby boy. She saw that he was special (Exodus 2:2) and hid him as long as she could. Then when the baby was three months old, she floated him on the Nile in a basket covered with tar to make it waterproof.

God honored Jochebed's actions too. Pharaoh's daughter found the baby, and in a beautiful twist of circumstances, she gave him back to Jochebed to care for him until he was old enough to be weaned and live at the palace. Pharaoh's daughter named the baby Moses.

Did Jochebed know the role she played in God's plan? Did the example of the midwives influence her decisions? We can't know, but we can be thankful for their examples and pray to learn from them.

Father God, lead me and guide me to always honor you in my decisions. I want to do what's right, and I want to be a woman who bravely trusts in you. Amen.

Yahweh

EXODUS 3

"I AM WHO I AM. . . . This is my eternal name, my name to remember for all generations."—Exodus 3:14–15

Whenever we meet someone new, the first thing we usually do is smile, introduce ourselves, and ask, "What's your name?" Even in a group where several women have the same first name, knowing one another's names sets us apart as the unique individuals we are.

God has many descriptive names, such as *Elohim*, "Creator," and *El Shaddai*, "God Almighty." But in the wilderness of Sinai, Moses asked God for His personal name, because he knew that the Israelites—the people God wanted him to lead out of slavery—would want to know. (After Joseph's death, Jacob's descendants had been enslaved in Egypt for more than four hundred years.)

God told Moses, "I AM WHO I AM," or *Yahweh*. This personal name tells us that God is ever present and unchanging, like the bush from which He spoke, on fire but not burning up. The Israelites could be assured of His constant presence, care, and power.

In English Bibles, when you see the word *LORD* in large and small capital letters, the actual word is the name *Yahweh*. We're reminded, just like the Israelites, that our unchanging, powerful, loving God—Yahweh—is with us, for us, and wants us to know Him in a personal way.

Dear God, you are the same today as you have always been and the same as you will be forever. May I remember your name and your presence with me today and all the days of my life. Amen.

16

Who Am I?

EXODUS 4

> But Moses again pleaded, "Lord, please! Send anyone else."—Exodus 4:13

God chose Moses to lead the Israelites (the Hebrews) out of Egypt and toward a new home in the land He had promised to Abraham, Isaac, and Jacob. But standing near the burning bush in the desert, listening to God's instructions, Moses was having none of it. Who was he to go and talk to Pharaoh or even to the Israelites?

A Hebrew adopted as a child by Pharaoh's daughter, when he was grown, Moses had killed an Egyptian for beating a Hebrew slave. To save his own life, he fled to Midian and lived there as a shepherd for forty years, away from the Egyptians and from his own people. Words weren't his strength; he felt clumsy and tongue-tied.

God patiently but firmly directed Moses' focus off himself and onto Him: "I'm the one who made your mouth. I'll be with you and I'll even tell you what to say." And finally, God offered to send Moses' brother Aaron to go along with Moses as his spokesperson.

What task has God given you today? You might be mothering littles or teens, leading a department at work, or starting a ministry to your community. What causes you to feel inadequate? Past sins have been forgiven. Confidence comes from the God who made you and is with you. Real or imagined disabilities are overcome by God Almighty. If the task is from the Lord, He will help you accomplish it day by day.

Dear Lord, when I don't feel confident to face the tasks you've given me, thank you for your reassurances, forgiveness, prodding, and strength. Amen.

When I See the Blood

EXODUS 7–12

"The blood on your doorposts will serve as a sign. . . . When I see the blood, I will pass over you."—Exodus 12:13

When he was five, my grandson loved the animated story of the ten plagues in a children's Bible app on my phone. But the image of the Israelites painting lamb's blood over and around their doorposts puzzled him.

Pharaoh repeatedly refused to let the Israelites leave Egypt, and each time God responded with a plague that showed His power over the so-called gods worshiped by the Egyptians. The last plague would demonstrate God's power and judgment. To protect the Israelites, God told them to paint their doorposts with the blood of a sacrificial lamb or goat. That night, when the firstborn son of every Egyptian family died, the death angel passed over the Israelites' homes.

God instructed the Israelites to keep a Passover ceremony yearly to remind them that the blood of a lamb kept them safe from death on the night He brought them out of slavery in Egypt. Hundreds of years later, another Passover lamb—the Lamb of God—was slain. The blood of that Lamb causes God to free us from our slavery to sin.

"The blood on the doorposts kept the Israelites safe," I told my grandson, "and Jesus' blood saves us." To a five-year-old, the connection was too abstract to be meaningful, but someday he will understand.

Heavenly Father, your promises and your power astound and humble me. Thank you for the blood of Jesus that covers all my sins. Amen.

18

Just Stay Calm

EXODUS 14–15

> "Don't be afraid. . . . The Lord himself will fight for you. Just stay calm."—Exodus 14:13–14

In *Mrs. Oswald Chambers*, author Michelle Ule describes the unflappable faith of Oswald Chambers' wife, Biddy. Whether facing wartime deprivation or the untimely death of her husband or later financial disasters, Biddy remained calm. How did she do it? Perhaps she lived by the same "secret" Moses had discovered.

Stuck between Pharaoh's army and the Red Sea, the Israelites panicked. How quickly they had forgotten God's power! And Moses' response? "Don't be afraid. Just stand still and watch the Lord rescue you today. . . . The Lord himself will fight for you. Just stay calm."

Stand still? Stay calm? Right. I always respond like that when circumstances terrify me, don't you?

Moses held his staff out over the sea as God told him to, and a strong wind divided the sea so the people could go across on dry land. But as the Egyptians followed after them, they rightly shouted, "The Lord is fighting for them against Egypt!" (Exodus 14:25) before the walls of water came crashing down and destroyed them all.

The world can be a scary place. Satan and sin see to that. As moms and grandmothers, we're afraid and we worry. But God tells us not to fear. If we will let Him, He will fight for us. We *can* stand still and stay calm.

Father God, the evil forces of this world are frightening, and I am often afraid. Help me, please, to look to you, trust you, and let you fight for me. Amen.

19

Sabbath Rest

EXODUS 20

"Remember the Sabbath day, to keep it holy."—Exodus 20:8 ESV

We don't want to disappoint, so we rarely say no to anyone—our employers, our kids, our husbands, our friends, our churches. We're always in motion; *stop* isn't part of our vocabulary. But it should be.

God rested. Not because He was tired. God "does not faint or grow weary" (Isaiah 40:28 ESV); no, God rested on the seventh day of creation because He had finished the work of creation. The word for *rested* in Genesis 2 actually means God ceased, or stopped, working.

The Sabbath as a day of rest, a complete break from working, became a law for Israel. On the Sabbath, everyone—servants and animals included—could recuperate from labor and honor God, who had set the pattern of six days of work followed by a day of rest. For us, however, the idea of Sabbath rest is not a commandment but a wise pattern to follow.

I can hear you now, saying, "But my work is never done!" Still, you need rest—physically, mentally, emotionally. Taking a Sabbath rest, regardless of the day or time, means acknowledging what's up to us and what is not. It's giving God priority and depending on Him to provide for us and care for our concerns while we take time off from getting things done.

Are you tired today? Schedule a Sabbath rest.

Dear Lord, forgive me for thinking that getting things done is all up to me. Help me rest and be renewed. Amen.

20

Substitutes

EXODUS 19–20, 24, 32

When the people saw [the calf], they exclaimed, "O Israel, these are the gods who brought you out of the land of Egypt!"—Exodus 32:4

In the wilderness the Israelites continued to learn about God's desire and ability to care for them. Then near Mount Sinai, God made a covenant, or agreement, with the Israelites: He would take them as His special treasure and make them a holy nation and a kingdom of priests. The people's part of the covenant was to obey God, to live His way, following the laws we now call the Ten Commandments.

God again called Moses to come up the mountain, to receive the Ten Commandments on two stone tablets, and while Moses was away, the people became fearful and lost faith. They clamored for Aaron to give them an idol to be their god, and he complied by making a golden calf. The Israelites sacrificed to the idol and held a drunken feast.

The Israelites wanted a substitute god. You and I don't bow down to golden statues, but we can turn to any number of other substitutes—shopping, overeating, social media, decorating, sports, working, to name a few. I know I sometimes do. We usually choose our substitutes to bolster us where we feel weak or anxious, but God deserves to be our source of strength and joy. The next time your favorite substitute beckons, what will you do?

Dear God, how thankful I am for your mercy and for my Savior! Amen.

Fully Known

EXODUS 33–34

Inside the Tent of Meeting, the LORD would speak to Moses face to face, as one speaks to a friend.—Exodus 33:11

Spending so much time in God's presence seems to have changed Moses. After the Israelites leave Egypt, we don't hear any more about his problems speaking. Just the opposite, in fact; Moses became quite articulate as he led the people and talked with God. Then after spending time with God on the mountain or in a meeting place, Moses' face took on a heavenly glow. And the more time he spent with God, the more he desired to know Him.

Is God your treasured friend, someone you want to spend time with, someone you're comfortable talking to freely? God told Moses, "I look favorably on you, and I know you by name" (Exodus 33:17). Moses knew he was safe in his relationship with God.

Do you guard your relationship with God? He wants to be our focal point. "The LORD, whose very name is Jealous, is a God who is jealous about his relationship with you" (Exodus 34:14).

Are you different because of your relationship with God? What changes do others see in you since you took Jesus as your Savior?

Friend, focal point, change agent. Spending time with God by reading His Word and meditating on what He says, talking with Him and obeying His instructions—that's what changed Moses, and that's what changes us.

Heavenly Father, how wonderful to be your friend! Help me care for my relationship with you. I love you. Amen.

22

Tabernacled

EXODUS 40

> The cloud of the LORD hovered over the Tabernacle during the day, and at night fire glowed inside the cloud so the whole family of Israel could see it.—Exodus 40:38

The overarching story of the Bible is God working out His plan to make it possible for Him and humankind to dwell together again.

On Mount Sinai, God gave Moses detailed instructions for the construction and furnishing of the tabernacle, a beautiful tent that could be taken down and put up again as the Israelites traveled through the wilderness and into the Promised Land.

The Israelites willingly provided the materials, and those gifted by God with the needed skills and artistic ability led and directed the work. When all was ready, God's glory, His presence, filled the tabernacle in the form of a cloud and fire that stayed over the tabernacle day and night. The Israelites could never question God's presence with them again.

How do you recognize God's presence with you? In a radiant sunrise? In the night sky? In the smiles of loved ones—human beings made in God's image? In the talents God has given you? In the promises you find in God's Word? In all these ways and more, because Jesus' death on the cross allows God to declare you right with Him—so His Spirit can come to live in you and assure you of His presence every day.

Father God, as your presence in the tabernacle could be seen by your people in the wilderness, may I be as aware and sure of your presence with me today. Thank you for Jesus, my Savior. Thank you for being tabernacled with me.

A Covenant Community

LEVITICUS 11

"Be holy, because I am holy."—Leviticus 11:44

Throughout the book of Leviticus, it's clear God's people were to be different. God gave them a system of offerings and sacrifices, rules for ritual purity, festivals, and dietary rules. Living out God's laws as a community would show the world the holiness—the perfect rightness—of the Lord. God's laws were never intended to create holiness but to reflect it, to demonstrate the people's relationship with a holy God in a covenant community.

As the Bible's story continues, we'll see the Israelites break their covenant agreement with God many, many times. But God never broke His end of the covenant. He remained faithful to His people and His promises. The old covenant ended when God replaced it many years later with a new one based on the death, burial, and resurrection of Jesus. So the church, the worldwide body of believers, is a covenant community also. The church is meant to show the world the Savior.

How do we do that? Holy living still matters. And the love believers have for one another and the good works we do for all people show others that we are Jesus' disciples (John 13:35, 15:5).

How will your life help others see Jesus today?

Dear Lord, I so want my life to shine for Jesus, bringing others into His light. Today may I love and serve others as a woman set apart for you. Amen.

24

The Day of Atonement

LEVITICUS 17

"This is because the life of the body is in the blood. . . . It is the blood that removes the sins from your life so you will belong to the Lord."—Leviticus 17:11 ICB

I stopped scrolling because the social media post was so unusual. A friend confessed she had lost her temper and acted badly toward someone else. "Today I failed as a Christian but I will make it right with God and tell the other person I'm sorry. . . . I'm actually glad this happened so I can begin praying about my attitude and what I need to do."

She took her sin seriously. Too often we don't. But God does.

God gave the Israelites a system of sacrifices and offerings to deal with individual sins. Laying one's hands on the head of a lamb or goat and slitting its throat surely had an impact. Then on the yearly Day of Atonement, in addition to animal sacrifices for himself and for the people, the high priest performed a ritual that carried away the sins of the nation on the head of a live goat sent into the wilderness—a scapegoat.

Long before Jesus came, the animal sacrifices and the Day of Atonement pictured what He would accomplish on the cross, and after the cross, those things were no longer needed. What a price was paid to carry our sins away from us—the precious blood of Jesus!

Father God, I brush off my sin so easily so often. I take for granted the grace you gave at the cross. Forgive me and help me. Amen.

25

Love Your Neighbor

LEVITICUS 19–20

"Love your neighbor as yourself. I am the LORD."—Leviticus 19:18

Are you surprised to find this command in the Old Testament, when we usually associate it with Jesus' teaching in the New Testament? And later the apostle John would write, "If someone says, 'I love God,' but hates a fellow believer, that person is a liar; for if we don't love people we can see, how can we love God, whom we cannot see?" (1 John 4:20). The more I study God's Word, the more I learn about the surprising connections between the testaments.

God not only had requirements for how His people as a nation would live in relationship with Him, but for how they would live with one another. What kind of personal conduct toward one another did God require of the Israelites? Showing respect to family members, the elderly, and those with disabilities. Honesty. Fairness. Willingness to get involved when lives were threatened. Willingness to confront. Forgiveness. Care for the poor and foreigners. Sexual morality. Refusing to participate in pagan and occult practices such as idolatry, fortune-telling, and consulting mediums. At all times, honoring God.

Where do you do well with the expectations on this list? Where do you struggle? With Jesus we are never left without mercy or hope!

Heavenly Father, I want to live a holy life because you are a holy God. I want to love others because that has been your goal for me from the beginning. Help me act in ways that please you. Amen

26

A Family Blessing

NUMBERS 6

"Whenever Aaron and his sons bless the people of Israel in my name, I myself will bless them."—Numbers 6:27

Some families eat pizza and play games every Friday night. Some parents pray with each child as he or she goes out the door to school every morning. Some grandparents love to tell stories about the pranks they pulled when they were kids. We all have traditions that help to hold us together and make our families unique.

For the twelve tribes of Israel, one of those binding traditions was a special blessing from the Lord prayed over them by the priests.

God had assigned the tribe of Levi to serve Him as representatives of the firstborn sons of Israel whom He spared during the final plague in Egypt. The role of priests went to Aaron and his descendants; the other Levites took care of the tabernacle, transported it, and camped around it.

God gave Moses this special blessing for the priests to pray over His people:

> May the LORD bless you and protect you.
> May the LORD smile on you and be gracious to you.
> May the LORD show you his favor and give you his peace. (Numbers 6:24–26)

Did you know that if you are a believer in Jesus, the Son of God, then you are also a priest (Revelation 1:5–6)? Why not make praying this special blessing one of your family traditions?

Father God, thank you that I can come to you and ask for your blessing on my family, friends, fellow believers, and even those who don't know you yet, because you care. Amen.

27

Enemies

NUMBERS 10

And whenever the Ark set out, Moses would shout, "Arise, O LORD, and let your enemies be scattered!"—Numbers 10:35

Two years after the Israelites had left Egypt, the cloud of God's presence over the tabernacle lifted and the people set out from the wilderness of Sinai, headed toward Canaan, the land God had promised. They followed the orderly plan God had given them for breaking camp by tribes and for transporting the tabernacle and all its furnishings. The beautiful, boxlike ark of the covenant (the seat of God's presence in the tabernacle) led the way, carried on poles by the Levites, with the cloud of the Lord hovering over it. When the cloud over the ark stopped, the Israelites camped; when it rose, they set out again. And as they did, Moses cried, "Arise, O LORD, and let your enemies be scattered!"

Who are your enemies? Are they clearly known, or are you unsure you have any? The Israelites had been their own worst enemy so far, but Moses knew they would face many more as they moved into Canaan. Sometimes we fight against ourselves, sometimes others do attack, and always we have an enemy in Satan, who wants only to kill and destroy.

Moses also knew God was the one who would fight for the Israelites and rescue them when necessary. How might things change for us if we depended on God to lead our battles? Make Moses' shout your own prayer today and see what a difference it will make.

Dear Lord, lead me today and fight for me. Make me strong against my enemies as I depend on you. Amen.

28

Wavering

NUMBERS 11

Moses heard all the families standing in the doorways of their tents whining. . . . And Moses said to the LORD . . . "What did I do to deserve the burden of all these people?"—Numbers 11:10–11

I'm not sure how I would have taken to living in a tent in the desert for two years, eating mostly manna and traveling toward an unknown land. God's loving presence, power, and provision should have been enough for anyone, but among the Israelites, human sinfulness sometimes won out over obedience and trust. This time the Israelites were fed up with their limited diet—and Moses was fed up with them.

God heard all the complaining, and He told Moses to tell the people that their whining was a rejection of Him. As a consequence, they would receive and eat what they had clamored for—meat—until they couldn't face it another day.

Moses cried honestly to the Lord about his need and his frustration. And although God was angry with the people, He moved to help Moses bear his burden. Perhaps the difference is that Moses turned to the Lord for help but the people had turned away from Him.

Where are you wavering today? What situation seems unending or unbearable? Will you respond like the faithless Israelites or like their faith-filled leader?

Dear God, I do get tired, overwhelmed, worn down. I do waver and complain. Forgive me and help me turn to you for help instead. I want to trust you more. Amen.

29

Like Grasshoppers

NUMBERS 13–14

"We seemed to ourselves like grasshoppers, and so we seemed to them."—Numbers 13:33 ESV

God had promised the Israelites the land of Canaan. He had told them to push out the pagan peoples living there and that the battles to do so were really His. Now, from the Israelites' camp in the wilderness of Paran, Moses sent twelve men to go into Canaan to explore the land.

They discovered it to be as beautiful and as bountiful as they had been told. They also saw large, fortified towns and, in places, people they called giants. Ten of the twelve spread word among the Israelites that the land could not be taken. Only Caleb and Joshua kept their faith and continued to trust what God had promised. But despite their urgings and encouragement, the people rebelled.

Their decision brought disaster. Because they had doubted and refused to trust God, only their children—those under age twenty—would enter the Promised Land, and not for another forty years. Instead, the entire nation would live as wanderers in the wilderness until everyone twenty and older had died. Caleb and Joshua would be the only exceptions.

Do you ever feel small compared to the challenges of your life? Does your ability to believe and obey God seem feeble? Remember, as Caleb and Joshua did, that God is with you and His plans always succeed. With His power and presence, you are the giant, not the grasshopper.

Heavenly Father, forgive me for forgetting your power and presence with me! Help me stop seeing myself as a grasshopper, and help me believe and obey you instead. Amen.

30

A Plan for Difficult Times

NUMBERS 14, 20

Then Moses and Aaron fell face down on the ground before the whole community of Israel.—Numbers 14:5

When other people's behavior breaks your heart or makes life difficult for you, what's your first response? So often I'm tempted to try to fix it, even though I know I can't change anyone but myself.

But when the Israelites cried out against Moses and refused to obey God and go forward into the Promised Land, what did Moses do? He didn't cajole, or criticize, or wring his hands, or sit and worry, or look around for someone to try to talk some sense into them. He and Aaron went immediately before the Lord. God would know the answer.

Then Moses moved to intercession for the rebellious Israelites, and prayed, "In keeping with your magnificent, unfailing love, please pardon the sins of this people, just as you have forgiven them ever since they left Egypt" (Numbers 14:19).

God honored that request. He also gave the Israelites a hard consequence, and Moses calmly accepted the changes that consequence brought into his own life. Think of all he'd been through with the Israelites, and now he would be leading them in the wilderness for another forty years!

Moses wasn't perfect. He didn't always respond to troublesome situations in this manner. But when he did, he modeled a good plan for us: going first to God, asking for what's best, and accepting the outcome with humility and trust.

Father God, keep me from trying to manipulate situations or change other people. Show me where I need to change instead. Help me humbly walk with you and trust you always. Amen.

31

The Star of Jacob

NUMBERS 22–24

"I see him, but not now; I behold him, but not near. A star will come out of Jacob; a scepter will rise out of Israel."—Numbers 24:17 NIV

As the Israelites neared Canaan, the people living nearby grew afraid of their strength and the stories of God's power that traveled ahead of them. When the Israelites camped near Moab, the king of Moab tried to enlist a pagan prophet named Balaam to come and pronounce curses over them. In a story that always makes me smile, God used Balaam's donkey to show Balaam He was serious about blessing the Israelites instead.

In his final prophecy, Balaam spoke of the coming of one we now know to be Jesus. Jacob himself had made a similar prophecy when he blessed his sons before his death: "The scepter will not depart from Judah, nor the ruler's staff from his descendants, until the coming of the one to whom it belongs, the one whom all nations will honor" (Genesis 49:10).

In years to come, God would promise King David that one of his descendants would always rule over Israel. David was from the tribe of Judah, and Jesus was his descendant. God always keeps His promises. All nations *will* honor Jesus someday. And we can trust that our lives and our loved ones are just as firmly held in the hands of our loving, sovereign God as well.

Dear Lord, help me understand what your sovereign rule over all things means for my life, and show me how to give you the honor you deserve. Amen.

32

People of the Land

NUMBERS 25, 31

The LORD spoke to Moses, saying, "Avenge the people of Israel on the Midianites. Afterward you shall be gathered to your people."—Numbers 31:1–2 ESV

It happened in Moab, but it would become a familiar and repeated story in the history of the Israelites. Men of Israel became involved with pagan women from the people groups and nations living in and around the Promised Land. Enticed and invited by those women, the men joined in feasting and worshiping the women's gods and idols, breaking the Lord's commands. This time, the neighboring Midianites joined in the seduction.

God did not allow the Israelites to engage the Moabites in war, perhaps because they were descendants of Abraham's nephew, Lot. But God did instruct Moses to attack and destroy the Midianites for what they had done. His similar commands to push out the pagan people in the Promised Land would be repeated again and again. He would no longer tolerate their sinful practices, including child sacrifice. The time for His judgment had begun.

Have you ever said to a child, "Don't do that again. If you do, I will have to punish you"? As mothers, we do our best to know when the right time is to teach, to forgive, or to discipline, but sometimes we make mistakes. God's judgments are never wrong, however, even if they seem harsh to us as we read the history of the Israelites. We can trust Him.

Heavenly Father, you are indeed king over all the earth, and your purposes and judgments will prevail along with your love and mercy. Help me honor you for all you are. Amen.

33

The Daughters of Zelophehad

NUMBERS 27, 36

"If a man dies and has no son, then give his inheritance to his daughters."—Numbers 27:8

International Women's Day, celebrated on March 8, recognizes the accomplishments of women regardless of national, ethnic, linguistic, cultural, economic, or political ties. I think the daughters of Zelophehad would have enjoyed the day! Their names were Mahlah, Noah, Hoglah, Milcah, and Tirzah. Their father, Zelophehad, was a descendant of Joseph.

In the patriarchal cultures of Old Testament times, property passed from father to son. Zelophehad had died in the wilderness, but his son would have received his portion of the land assigned to their tribe in the Promised Land—if he had a son. Instead, Zelophehad had only daughters, and they came before Moses, Eleazar the priest, the tribal leaders, and the rest of the community with a request: "Give us land along with the rest of our relatives so our family name will not die out."

God honored their request and made it part of Israel's civil law: the inheritance of a man who left no sons would pass to his daughters. In Numbers 36, we read that Mahlah, Noah, Hoglah, Milcah, and Tirzah did receive their land.

In the future, God would act again and again to honor and elevate the status and rights of women alongside those of men. It seems He meant what He thought at the end of the sixth day when He had created both man and woman to bear His image: It was very good.

Dear God, thank you for the ways you uphold and honor women. Help me use my voice to speak out for what is fair and right. Amen.

34

Near to Us

DEUTERONOMY 4

"For what great nation has a god as near to them as the LORD our God is near to us whenever we call on him?"—Deuteronomy 4:7

Moses died in 1406 BC, forty years after leading the Israelites out of Egypt. Knowing that the nation would soon enter the Promised Land without him, Moses retold the story and reminded the people of their history with God. Throughout the book of Deuteronomy, we hear Moses' pleas and urgings for the people to respond to God with more than only outward obedience.

God had proven His love and care for Israel and His power with the wonders He worked in Egypt, "right before your eyes" (Deuteronomy 4:34). And what other nation, Moses asked, "has a god as near to them as the LORD our God is near to us whenever we call on him?"

Even more, Moses said, although a day would come when the Israelites would turn from God, they would also turn back and search for Him. And when that happened, "if you search for him with all your heart and soul, you will find him" (Deuteronomy 4:29).

Have you ever "lost" your keys, glasses, or phone and then found what you were looking for right where you'd left it—and in plain sight? God is always near, always ready to be found, always right in plain sight, whenever you are ready to look sincerely with the eyes of your heart and soul.

Father God, thank you for your power, your love, and your desire to have a relationship with me. Thank you for always being near. Help me keep my eyes on you, I pray. Amen.

One God

DEUTERONOMY 6

"Hear, O Israel: The Lord our God, the Lord is one. You shall love the Lord your God with all your heart and with all your soul and with all your might."—Deuteronomy 6:4–5 ESV

The concept of the Trinity is one God as three Persons—Father, Son, and Holy Spirit. But Moses emphasized to the Israelites that God is one. Why? He wanted them to understand the utter uniqueness of their God.

All the nations and cultures surrounding them, including Egypt, worshiped multiple gods and goddesses—but these were deities that didn't exist. Not only was Israel's God the one true God, there simply were no others. Throughout the book of Deuteronomy, Moses seems to take every possible opportunity to praise Him, reminding the Israelites of the beautiful character of their awesome, powerful God.

Is the God of the Old Testament the same God we meet in the New Testament? The answer is yes! His love, faithfulness, compassion, mercy, power, and judgment are on display in all His actions recorded throughout the entire Bible. We find references to the Spirit and to the Son throughout the entire Bible too.

Our one-and-only God deserves our wholehearted, focused love. What difficulties do you have with this command, and how can you begin to obey it more fully today?

Dear Lord, forgive me for allowing distractions, worries, issues, and cares to keep me from loving you with my whole heart. I want to know you, the only God, so much better. Amen.

36

Teach Your Children

DEUTERONOMY 6

"In the future your children will ask you, 'What is the meaning of these laws, decrees, and regulations that the Lord our God has commanded us to obey?'"—Deuteronomy 6:20

Do your children or grandchildren ask you questions about your faith? If they don't, why not?

As Moses encouraged the Israelites with final instructions before they entered the Promised Land, many of those listening to him had not experienced life as slaves in Egypt, or the amazing rescue God performed to lead His people out of Egypt, or the miraculous crossing of the Red Sea. Many would have been born in the wilderness after their parents or grandparents refused to go into the Promised Land as God commanded.

No wonder, then, that Moses emphasized the importance of talking with children about loving and respecting God and obeying His commands—talking with them not just on special occasions but every day, at every opportunity. Behind the talk, however, had to be commitment. Moses expected the Israelites to live out their love for God in such a way that their children couldn't miss it and would ask questions to understand the reasons why they did so.

Which causes me to ask, what does *our* faith look like to the children who are watching *us*?

Dear God, where my life and teaching have fallen short, forgive me. Help me make today a new beginning, obeying and trusting you openly before my children or grandchildren and talking about your ways. Amen.

Chosen

DEUTERONOMY 7–9

"Of all the people on earth, the LORD your God has chosen you to be his own special treasure."—Deuteronomy 7:6

On the playground standing alone as teams line up, in the middle school lunchroom longing for a place at the "right" table, in the high school auditorium watching the musical instead of performing in it—the sting of not being chosen can last for years. Aren't we good enough? Don't we matter? But when we *are* chosen—as a cheerleader, for the soccer team, for that promotion, by the man we've come to love—we feel valued. We belong.

God chose Abraham's descendants to be a nation He would bless and sustain who would in turn bless the entire world; Moses wanted them to understand why they had been chosen.

It wasn't their size or strength. "The LORD did not set his heart on you and choose you because you were more numerous than other nations, for you were the smallest of all nations" (Deuteronomy 7:7).

It wasn't their goodness. "You must recognize that the LORD your God is not giving you this good land because you are good, for you are not—you are a stubborn people" (Deuteronomy 9:6).

God chose the Israelites because of His faithful love and because of His covenant promises to Abraham, Isaac, and Jacob (Deuteronomy 7:8). It wasn't about who the Israelites were, but about who God is. He was working His plan to make it possible for Him to dwell with humankind again as He had with Adam and Eve. Today He chooses as His children all who have faith in His Son, Jesus. It's still all about who He is.

Heavenly Father, thank you for making a way for me to be your child. Thank you that I am chosen! Amen.

38

Every Word

DEUTERONOMY 8

"People do not live by bread alone; rather, we live by every word that comes from the mouth of the LORD."—Deuteronomy 8:3

One of the most important lessons for the Israelites and for us is that God is our source. He created and sustains our lives. He provided manna for the people in the wilderness and kept their clothes from wearing out. But more important than providing for their physical needs in these ways, God was teaching them to depend on Him and follow His ways—His laws and His promises. His Word is what gives us life.

Reading the entire Bible and discussing it weekly with a women's group impacted my life in so many wonderful ways. For one, I learned the value of reading the Bible daily. But sometimes I still struggle, not simply to take time to read God's Word, but to *want* to.

Too much going on? Health issues in the way? Seemingly unending cold winter days devoid of sunlight? All of the above.

But I'm *starving*. And there's only one solution. I need the life-giving nourishment and power He spreads out for me in the Bible every day. How about you?

We have an enemy who wants us weak and hungry.

But we have a Father who makes us strong and full.

Father God, forgive me when I look at your Word as a side dish and not the staple of my life. Help me and guide me to spend time meeting you in your Word every day. Amen.

Inside Out

DEUTERONOMY 10–11

"Be careful to obey all these commands I am giving you. Show love to the LORD your God by walking in his ways and holding tightly to him."—Deuteronomy 11:22

Have you ever caught yourself just going through the motions, doing whatever was expected or required but not being committed with your whole heart? Throughout his long history with God, beginning at the burning bush, Moses had learned that obedience brings blessings, but just going through the motions leaves us open to deception and falling away.

The generation that refused to go into Canaan years earlier had all died. Moses wanted their children—who had experienced God's power and care as He led them out of Egypt and through the wilderness—to remember what they had seen and to choose to obey God fully in their new land. Even more, perhaps, he wanted them to understand what their motive for obedience should be—to show God their love for Him.

We can slip into outward-obedience-only mode at any age or circumstance of life, from being busy with family and career to feeling lonely and left out in our later years. The solution is what Moses prescribed—remember who God is and how He has shown His power and love to you. Then begin again to show Him love by walking in His ways, obeying from the inside out.

Dear Lord, I never want my relationship with you to become stale. Forgive me for the times I've just gone through the motions of obeying you, and help me learn to let love be my motive instead. Amen.

40

God's Economy

DEUTERONOMY 14–15

Be sure to set aside a tenth of all that your fields produce each year. . . . so that you may learn to revere the LORD your God always.—Deuteronomy 14:22–23 NIV

As part of the ceremonial law they would follow in the Promised Land, the Israelites were to set aside a tenth of their harvest and a tenth of the increase of their flocks and herds each year and bring them to the central place of worship for a feast.

Every third year, the tithe went to the Levites, who had no land of their own, and to orphans, widows, and the foreigners living among the Israelites. Every seven years all loans to fellow Israelites would be canceled, and any Israelites who had sold themselves as slaves would be set free.

In God's economy, He is the giver, and we, the recipients of His gifts, are generous stewards who think of others' needs as well as our own. Tithing is not a New Testament command but remains a valuable principle.

Besides celebrating God's provision with their tithes, setting the tenth aside had another purpose—teaching the Israelites to respect the Lord and put Him first. Have you ever experienced the gut-wrenching exhilaration of writing a check for a tithe you'd rather keep for yourself—but you give it to acknowledge God's priority in your life? If not, maybe your next payday will be the day to give it a try. He will take care of you!

Dear God, I know you are good, and I want to trust you with my finances. Help me honor you and put you first. Amen.

True Justice

DEUTERONOMY 16–17

> Do not pervert justice or show partiality. Do not accept a bribe, for a bribe blinds the eyes of the wise and twists the words of the innocent.—Deuteronomy 16:19 NIV

Sitting on a jury for the first time, I thought that once we delivered our decision to the court, our job was done. Officially that's true. But I was surprised to learn it's customary for the attorneys for both sides to visit with the jury right after the trial to learn what factors led to their decision. They're interested in learning how to do the best possible job they can the next time to secure justice for their clients.

God cares about justice. He "shows no partiality and accepts no bribes" (Deuteronomy 10:17 NIV), and He gave the Israelites rules for making judgments and carrying out sentences. They were to reflect His character as they dealt with those who committed moral or criminal offenses, and His own representatives, the priests, would hear cases too difficult for a local court to decide.

Justice extended to orphans, widows, and foreigners too, because of God's concern for them. "He defends the cause of the fatherless and the widow, and loves the foreigner residing among you, giving them food and clothing. And you are to love those who are foreigners, for you yourselves were foreigners in Egypt" (Deuteronomy 10:18–19 NIV).

God's character doesn't change. His concern for justice must be ours also. How well are your actions lining up with what He expects?

Heavenly Father, you are righteous, just, and good. Show me how to reflect your goodness and justice in all I do. Amen.

42

True or False

DEUTERONOMY 18

> "It is because the other nations have done these detestable things that the LORD your God will drive them out ahead of you."—Deuteronomy 18:12

Social media bots. Opinion journalism. Radio and TV talk shows. Media bias. Health guidelines. Parenting advice. Is even half of what we see and hear the truth? Some days it seems impossible to know.

But with God, knowing what's true is never the problem. If He says it, we can believe it. If a prophet gave the Israelites a message from the Lord, it would come to pass. If a prediction did not happen, the message wasn't from God.

Sometimes, though, predictions and messages can be true and *not* be from the Lord. God forbade the Israelites to consult or listen to anyone who practiced fortune-telling, sorcery, interpreting omens, witchcraft, casting spells, acting as mediums or psychics, or calling up the spirits of the dead. All these practices dishonored God by acting as substitutes for God. By avoiding them, the Israelites would be protected from the spiritual powers that oppose Him.

What God told the Israelites not to participate in still holds true for us. You might be surprised by the backgrounds and sources of practices that have become accepted among believers in recent years. When you're presented with "new" ways to connect with God, do your own research. Test what you learn against what God says in His Word. He will never, ever deceive you.

> *Father God, I'm so thankful I can trust you to be truthful at all times. Help me be vigilant to avoid looking for truth in dangerous places you have forbidden. Amen.*

43

Choose Life

DEUTERONOMY 27–30

"Today I have given you the choice between life and death, between blessings and curses. . . . Oh, that you would choose life, so that you and your descendants might live!"—Deuteronomy 30:19

God promised the Israelites that keeping His commands would result in good and happy lives in a beautiful, abundant land. Moses spelled out the clear choice ahead for them once again—blessings for obedience, and curses (consequences) for disobedience.

It seems an easy choice to make, right? Yet time and again the Israelites would choose to go their own way, deeper and further into disobedience, until at last God had to pronounce judgment. The nation of Israel fell to the Assyrians and Babylonians. The temple was destroyed. God put the curses into play. His people had chosen.

We can't understand how this could happen. How could the Israelites *not* choose life? But aren't we susceptible to the same mistake? We've been saved by the precious blood grace of Jesus, but how serious are we about pursuing the life He calls us to?

It's worth asking. Christians face persecution in more and more countries around the world, suffering and dying for what they believe. They've made their choice. They're choosing life, but not the good life here on earth. They're choosing life with God *no matter what.*

He's waiting for us to make the same choice. What will that look like for you today?

Dear Lord, when life is good and when life is hard, I want to choose you, I want to choose life. Please give me the courage and conviction to make that choice, over and over again. Amen.

44

Included

DEUTERONOMY 32

"Rejoice with his people, you Gentiles . . . for . . . he will take revenge against his enemies."—Deuteronomy 32:43

Are you into genealogies, or do you know someone who is? My mother loved to connect the dots between generations, countries, and continents. Now DNA kits give us even more insights about the people and places we're part of. We get a little taste, perhaps, of our eternal life with God and His people—not just with those from the nation of Israel God formed in the wilderness of Sinai, but people from everywhere else too—the Gentiles.

Remember the promises God made to Abraham? His family would become a nation that would bless the entire world. How? First by demonstrating what it looked like to live as people who worship the one true God, and second by being the family through which the Savior would come—the Savior of the entire world. The song God gave Moses to teach the Israelites included the Gentiles too. The "foolish Gentiles" (foolish because they had not known God) would come to faith (Deuteronomy 32:21, Romans 3:30), and at God's judgment at the end times, both Jews and Gentiles will rejoice.

Yes, whatever your skin color, nationality, culture, or customs, no matter what story your family genealogy or DNA tells, God's plan has always been for all people—and for you.

Dear God, what a wonderful gift, an amazing plan. You chose a special people with the goal of inviting all. What an experience heaven will be! Amen.

45

Everlasting Arms

DEUTERONOMY 32–34

"The eternal God is your refuge, and underneath are the everlasting arms."—Deuteronomy 33:27 NIV

In a moment of anger and rare pride, Moses had disobeyed God (Numbers 20). The people needed water, and God told Moses He would provide it by making it pour out from a rock. But instead of speaking to the rock in the sight of the people as he was told, Moses spoke harshly to the people and then struck the rock with Aaron's rod.

For not honoring God before the people, Moses would not be allowed to enter the Promised Land. What an incredibly difficult disappointment for Moses this must have been! In His mercy, God did allow Moses to see Canaan from a distance. From the top of Mount Nebo, the Lord showed him the whole land. Then, as God had told him would happen, Moses died, and God himself buried Moses somewhere in the land of Moab (Deuteronomy 34:6).

Near the close of Deuteronomy we read, "There has never been another prophet in Israel like Moses, whom the LORD knew face to face" (Deuteronomy 34:10). Despite the difficulties of his life, Moses remained faithful to the end, warning, blessing, encouraging, and prophesying to the people. After blessing the twelve tribes before his death, Moses also blessed Israel: "The eternal God is your refuge, and underneath are the everlasting arms." Perhaps leaning daily on those everlasting arms was part of the secret of his amazing service.

Heavenly Father, I want to be faithful to the work you've given me to do. In the daily ups and downs, on the mountaintops and in the valleys, let me lean on you, my refuge. Amen.

Encountering GOD'S HEART for YOU in the OLD TESTAMENT

The Books of History

46

Strong and Courageous

JOSHUA 1

"Have I not commanded you? Be strong and courageous. Do not be afraid; do not be discouraged, for the LORD your God will be with you wherever you go."—Joshua 1:9 NIV

Emily Jentes traveled to Guinea to help fight the deadly Ebola outbreak in west Africa. "Whenever I need courage," she said, "I draw from the love, positivity, and support of my husband, family, and friends, as well as the confidence gained from my previous experiences." Once in Guinea, she added, "I was impressed by the strength and the dedication of the local public health and medical communities. It is easy to be brave when you are surrounded by bravery each day."

Four different times as Joshua prepared to lead the Israelites into the Promised Land, God commanded him to be strong and brave, and the basis for his courage was to be God's presence and promises. Joshua also could glean strength from the tribes of Reuben and Gad and the half tribe of Manasseh, already settled on the east side of the Jordan River. They encouraged Joshua with their commitment to help the other tribes cross the Jordan and move west as God had directed.

Large new initiatives and small duties of daily endurance both require strength and courage from God and other believers. How are you experiencing God's presence in your challenges? Who are the people lending you their courage for your task, and who needs you to lend your strength to theirs?

Father God, you are my strength today and every day. Help me be brave, and show me where my strength and courage are needed. Amen.

47

Rahab

JOSHUA 2, 6

"For the LORD your God is the supreme God of the heavens above and the earth below."—Joshua 2:11

Do you worry about your past? Rahab would never be voted "Most Likely to Succeed," but her faith won her a great reward nonetheless.

She was a prostitute in Jericho, an important Canaanite city devoted to idol worship. For years she had heard about the Israelites' escape from slavery in Egypt and their survival in the wilderness. More important, she had heard about the Israelites' God, His mighty power and the miracles He performed to rescue and protect His people. And Rahab had come to believe and trust this God she had heard about.

So when two Israelites came to Jericho to spy out the city, Rahab kept them safe. She hid them from Jericho's king and misled the men he sent to find them. In exchange she asked the spies to keep her and her family safe when the Israelites attacked, and they agreed. She followed their instructions to mark her home with a red cord in the window, and when the fighting began, the Israelites took Rahab and her family to live in safety near their camp.

Eventually, Rahab married Salmon, an Israelite from the tribe of Judah. Matthew 1 records the lineage of Jesus through Joseph of Nazareth, and verse 5 says, "Salmon was the father of Boaz (whose mother was Rahab)." Rahab's history was past, and her faith resulted in a place for her in the lineage of the Savior.

Dear Lord, how good to realize that my past doesn't have to define my future when my faith is firmly in you. Amen.

48

Crossing the Jordan

JOSHUA 3–4

"And as soon as the priests who carry the ark of the LORD—the Lord of all the earth—set foot in the Jordan, its waters flowing downstream will be cut off and stand up in a heap."—Joshua 3:13 NIV

Breaking down an imposing project into smaller tasks leads to achieving the goal—but we still have to take the first step.

In 1406 BC, led by the priests carrying the ark of the covenant, the Israelites stood on the western side of the Jordan River, ready to finally cross into the Promised Land. The water was high; the river had overflowed its banks, but *through* was the only way across. God had told Joshua the water would stop flowing so the Israelites could cross on dry ground—when the priests took their first step into the water.

The priests obeyed. The water in the river heaped up at a town upstream, and the water below that point flowed away. The priests stood in the middle of the dry riverbed until all the people had passed by. Then Joshua chose one man from each of the twelve tribes to bring up a rock from the middle of the riverbed, and he set up the stones on the eastern side of the river as a memorial.

Faith requires action. We may not hear directions directly from God as Joshua and the Israelites did, but we have instructions in His Word. God will always do what He has said He will do when we commit to taking the first step.

Dear God, I want my faith to have feet so I can step out with trust in what you say you will do. Amen.

49

Obey Anyway

JOSHUA 5–6

When the trumpets sounded, the army shouted, and at the sound of the trumpet, when the men gave a loud shout, the wall collapsed; so everyone charged straight in, and they took the city.—Joshua 6:20 NIV

What kind of cook are you? Do you follow recipes exactly, or do you prefer to improvise?

God had commanded the Israelites to push out and destroy the pagan nations living in the Promised Land because of their idol worship and many sins, especially child sacrifice. After the Israelites camped near Jericho, God gave Joshua exact instructions for taking the city, which was surrounded by tall stone walls. Joshua conveyed those instructions to the army and the priests, and we have to wonder what they thought and if they weren't tempted to improvise.

March around the city once a day for six days, with the ark of the covenant leading the way? Keep quiet the whole time, except for the rams' horns blown by the priests? March seven times around on the seventh day, then shout on Joshua's signal and watch the walls fall down? Seriously, God?

Seriously.

The Israelites obeyed, and they saw the results that God had promised. The pagan citadel was destroyed, and not one Israelite died.

Maybe you have found instructions in God's Word to be difficult, unnecessary, or strange: Love your enemies. Pray for those who persecute you. Forgive. Lend. Don't worry. Don't be afraid. Our job is to obey God anyway—and when we do, His instructions work, and the results will be what He promised.

Heavenly Father, help me trust you and your instructions for my life, and help me follow and obey. Amen.

Tricked

JOSHUA 9

They did not consult the LORD.—Joshua 9:14

A life coach can teach us to make decisions wisely—asking questions about the consequences of each option, listing pros and cons, seeking advice, rejecting the fear of failure. But one critical aspect of decision-making isn't on this list, and Joshua and the Israelite leaders made an unwise decision because they failed to use that missing piece of the process.

After the Israelites took the cities of Jericho and Ai, the Gibeonites made a plan to trick the Israelites into making a treaty with them in order to protect themselves. Their ruse worked. Joshua and the leaders believed the Gibeonites' story. They didn't check it out—and they didn't consult the Lord. When they discovered the deception, they couldn't break the treaty without dishonoring God's name. So they allowed the Gibeonites to live within their borders as slaves rather than destroy them as God had commanded. Many years later, King Saul did break the treaty, and eventually seven of his sons were killed as retaliation.

When we try to handle situations on our own, without seeking God's will, it's easy to be deceived. Our poor decisions often bring trouble on ourselves or others, or we may find we have to settle for less than the best. God promises wisdom for difficult situations if we seek it sincerely, however (James 1:5), and we should always look to the Word and do what we already know is right.

Father God, I want to make good decisions that honor you. Help me look to you and seek your will always. Amen.

51

Praying for a Miracle

JOSHUA 10

> There has never been a day like this one before or since, when the LORD answered such a prayer.—Joshua 10:14

Five Amorite kings banded together to attack the Gibeonites, who turned to the Israelites for help. God had promised that the battles for the Promised Land would be His, and now He assured Joshua the Amorites would be defeated. In the sight of all Israel, Joshua prayed for the sun and moon to stand still—for the day to last as long as the battle needed to be fought—and God listened and answered Joshua's bold prayer. "The sun stayed in the middle of the sky, and it did not set as on a normal day" (Joshua 10:13). The Israelites, the Gibeonites, and the defeated Amorites all experienced God's power on display.

God can do anything, and we are free to come to Him with any request. And we are invited, encouraged, and even commanded to pray for God's will to be done. Jesus taught His disciples to pray "May your Kingdom come soon. May your will be done on earth, as it is in heaven" (Matthew 6:10). Joshua made a specific request that lined up with what God had already revealed about His purposes. We may not ever hear directly from God as Joshua did, but we hear from Him in His Word, and He reveals much of His will and purposes there. We have plenty to pray about.

Dear Lord, may I be faithful to pray for your will in every circumstance of my life and for your kingdom to come on earth soon. Amen.

Never Too Old

JOSHUA 13–14

"But if the LORD is with me, I will drive them out of the land, just as the LORD said."—Joshua 14:12

I think the hardest thing about growing old for a woman," said singer and songwriter Amy Grant, "is becoming invisible." When you think about your later years, what do you hope for? Or if you've reached those years already, how do you view them?

Joshua had grown older, but God reminded him there was still work to do to settle the Israelites in the Promised Land. And although Caleb was now eighty-five, he still wanted the land Moses had promised him forty-five years earlier. Still strong, Caleb was willing to take on driving out the tall, warlike people who lived there—the "giants" he had seen when Moses first sent men into Canaan to scout out the land.

We feel invisible as we age only if we believe we are no longer needed. But if we commit ourselves to doing what God has shown us in His Word to do—to love Him and love people—we will *always* be needed. Ask God today to prepare you for your older years—or to inspire you if you're already there—with a firm desire to serve Him in big or small ways as long as you live. We are never, ever invisible to Him.

Dear God, I don't want to fear growing older. Show me the ways I might serve you still, even as I age. Amen.

53

Record Keeping

JOSHUA 15–21

> Not one of all the LORD's good promises to Israel failed; every one was fulfilled.—Joshua 21:45 NIV

When the scrapbooking craze was going strong, one father I know made each of his daughters a beautifully designed scrapbook record of her high school years as a graduation gift. The loving words and photos in the scrapbooks showed the growth of these young women during the four years before they would leave home for college and life as professionals, wives, and mothers.

Throughout the Bible we find passages like these six chapters of the book of Joshua—chapters filled with lists and names of people and places—and it's tempting to skim them or skip them altogether. But for the Israelites they were important historical documents, recording not only their history with one another but also their history with God.

Our histories, individual and collective, matter to us. It's why we write in journals and take thousands of photos of family and friends, and why we read biographies and visit museums. We have a need to remember where we've come from and whom we're part of. Looking back helps us envision how to move forward. Most important, we can see how God has guided and guarded us, rescued and redirected us.

How do you preserve the story of your own personal history? Where along the way do you see evidence of God's care and concern for you?

Heavenly Father, you were guiding my life before I knew it. May my story bring me ever closer to you. Amen.

54

Make the Choice

JOSHUA 24

"As for me and my house, we will serve the Lord."—Joshua 24:15 ESV

No one seems to know how many decisions the average person makes in a day; the estimates range from seventy to thirty-five thousand! Whatever the number is, many of our decisions do not have serious consequences—what to wear, whether to cook dinner or order takeout, how to style our hair, for example. Others—which college to attend, whom to marry, where to work—have much more impact. But the decision that affects us most is whom—or what—we will worship.

Before Joshua renewed God's covenant with the Israelites after they were settled in Canaan, he reviewed their history with God once again. He urged them to choose decisively, not halfheartedly, whom they would serve. He had made his firm decision long ago. He and his family would not worship the gods of Egypt. They would not worship the gods of the pagan peoples all around them. But what would the Israelites decide?

Their decision would be critical for their future. If they were to enjoy the Lord's blessings, the idols among them had to be destroyed. The people needed wholehearted devotion—and so do we.

Developing spiritual maturity is sometimes a "two steps forward, one step back" process. We will always have growing to do and sins to abandon. Everything hinges, however, on how we answer Joshua's challenge: Choose today whom you will serve.

Father God, I want to worship and serve you alone. Forgive my halfhearted waverings, and help me love and obey you with my whole heart today and always. Amen.

55

Dark Days

JUDGES 1–3

After that whole generation had been gathered to their ancestors, another generation grew up who knew neither the LORD nor what he had done for Israel.—Judges 2:10 NIV

The tribes of Israel never completely pushed the Canaanites out of the land as God had commanded, but allowed some to remain in the land and live among them. Soon the Israelites were intermarrying with the Canaanites and worshiping their gods. God allowed them to be attacked and oppressed by surrounding peoples, until finally they cried out to Him for help. Then God raised up leaders called judges for Israel, to rescue them from their enemies.

But despite God's faithfulness to Israel, the nation continued to choose a downward spiral. The book of Judges is a depressing read, documenting the moral rot in Israel after the Promised Land was settled—and all because one generation ignored God's commands. They not only disobeyed Him by worshiping other gods, they failed to teach their children who God is and what He had done for them.

In the Israelites' history we see what happens when faith in God and the reasons for it are not passed down to the next generation. We can learn from the Israelites and avoid repeating their mistakes. The legacy we leave depends on how we live each day. Are you living with obedience and trust in God and His Word as you pray and teach for the next generation?

Dear Lord, I never want to be a stumbling block for my children and grandchildren. Help me leave a legacy of faith to the next generation. Amen.

Deborah and Jael

JUDGES 4–5

"Because of the course you are taking, the honor will not be yours, for the LORD will deliver Sisera into the hands of a woman."—Judges 4:9 NIV

Deborah, a prophetess, served Israel as a judge at the time one of the Canaanite kings had been oppressing Israel for twenty years. Wise and respected, Deborah rendered decisions for the Israelites. It was Deborah who gave Barak the Lord's charge to gather troops and attack, with the promise of victory over Sisera, the enemy's commander, and his troops.

Barak refused to obey—unless Deborah accompanied him into battle. And she did, but not until she gave him the news that because of his hesitation, credit for the victory wouldn't go to him but to a woman. At this point in the story we expect Deborah to be that woman. It wasn't her, however, but a woman named Jael, married to a distant relative of the Israelites. When Sisera appeared outside her tent, she gave him a place to hide, but while he slept, she hammered a tent peg through his temple and he died. Barak discovered that a woman had accomplished what he'd been charged to do.

God routed Israel's oppressors that day as He said He would, and Deborah's victory song praises Him and the brave woman who critically influenced that day.

Dear God, when I'm required to do hard things and to be brave, help me remember that you're the one who leads me and strengthens me. Amen.

57

The Lord Is Peace

JUDGES 6–8

Gideon built an altar to the LORD there and named it Yahweh-Shalom (which means "the LORD is peace").—Judges 6:24

For forty years the land had peace, but the people continued sinning against God, so He handed them over to the Midianites. Once again they cried out to God for help, and God called on Gideon to lead Israel as a judge.

Gideon argued for a while with the angel of the Lord, and then he asked for a sign. When the angel consumed Gideon's offering with fire and disappeared, Gideon realized he had been face-to-face with God himself, and he expected to die. But God reassured him he had no reason to be afraid. At that, Gideon built an altar to honor God and named it *Yahweh-Shalom*, "The LORD Is Peace."

The Hebrew word for peace, *shalom*, is more than a nice way to say hello or good-bye and means much more than the absence of conflict. The Hebrew concept of peace is an inward feeling of wholeness, completeness, and well-being that involves our relationship with our surroundings, with one another, and with God. Gideon realized that to be accepted by God is the source of true peace. God *is* our peace.

So is your life peaceful? Our circumstances might be chaotic, but inwardly we can have peace. Why not seek the source of true peace today?

Heavenly Father, whether my days are long because they are so full or because they aren't full enough, I desire peace. Show me how to seek you, my peace, today. Amen.

58

Strong Samson

JUDGES 13–16

"I have been a Nazirite dedicated to God from my mother's womb. If my head were shaved, my strength would leave me."—Judges 16:17 NIV

The sin-oppression-rescue cycle in Israel continued. When Samson was born, the Philistines had been oppressing Israel for forty years. Although His people lived faithlessly, God remained faithful.

Samson had extraordinary strength, an imposing personality, and a charge to live dedicated to God as a Nazirite (no alcohol, no haircuts, and no contact with dead bodies). But Samson disdained the Nazirite rules throughout his life and lived for himself. His wild ways caused trouble for the Philistines, until Delilah finally learned his secret and betrayed him.

With his hair cut, Samson's strength was gone. God's power had left him. The Philistines captured Samson, gauged out his eyes, and imprisoned him. When the Philistine rulers hosted a festival in the temple of their god to celebrate, the people called for Samson to be brought out to amuse them. Instead, Samson called on God to help him bring the temple down on everyone, knowing he would die too.

Samson could have been a good judge. God had equipped him and was with him, but Samson chose to go his own way. His story is an opportunity for us to evaluate ourselves, because God has equipped us for our tasks too. We are sure to let Him down at times, but what a joy to know He is always faithful, even if we are not.

Father God, help me see more clearly how you have equipped me for your purposes. Thank you for your faithfulness to me always. Amen.

59

The Levite's Concubine

JUDGES 19–21

> In those days Israel had no king; all the people did whatever seemed right in their own eyes.—Judges 21:25

Events in the book of Judges may not be recorded chronologically, but the account of the gang rape and death of an unnamed woman and the civil war that followed seem placed at the end of the book to make a point.

It's a grisly, sordid story, reminiscent of Sodom and Gomorrah, towns of such immorality that God had destroyed them with fire. On a journey with his concubine, a Levite from Ephraim stopped in Gibeah, where an old man from Ephraim invited them to stay with him. That night men from Gibeah came to the old man's house, wanting to have sex with his guest the Levite.

Eventually, to appease them, the Levite pushed his concubine out the door. In the morning, he found her on the doorstep, dead. At home, he cut her body into twelve pieces and sent one piece to each of the twelve tribes as a call to war. The conflict that followed effectively obliterated the tribe of Benjamin and employed kidnapping and more fighting to secure wives for the six hundred men of Benjamin who had survived.

Why was this account placed at the end of Judges? For this reason: we can't escape seeing the moral decline and depravity that occurred when "all the people did whatever seemed right in their own eyes."

Dear Lord, may I always check what seems right to me with what your Word says is right. And hear my prayer for all who choose to go their own way rather than follow you. Amen.

Ruth

THE BOOK OF RUTH

"Wherever you go, I will go; and wherever you lodge, I will lodge; your people shall be my people, and your God, my God."—Ruth 1:16 NKJV

Ruth's beautiful words are often read at weddings. But Ruth spoke these words to her mother-in-law, Naomi, as a childless widow, with no expectation of ever marrying again.

Instead of returning to her father's household after the death of her husband, Naomi's son, Ruth chose to accompany Naomi on her return home to Bethlehem, in Israel. Ruth left everything behind in Moab, including her homeland's pagan gods, to show her love and loyalty for Naomi and, it seems, for Naomi's God.

In Bethlehem, Ruth provided for Naomi and herself by gleaning barley the harvesters left behind in the fields specifically for the poor to gather. Her demeanor and hard work caught the attention of Boaz, owner of the fields and one of Naomi's relatives. As spring turned to summer, Naomi made a bold plan—Ruth would ask Boaz for his protection as his wife.

Naomi's plan succeeded—or was it God's plan? Boaz's father was Salmon, who had married Rahab, from Jericho. Now Boaz married Ruth, also a foreigner, and they had a son, Obed. God had rewarded Ruth's loyalty and devotion, and the family tree leading to the birth of the Savior continued to grow. Obed would have a special grandson, Israel's King David, giving Ruth herself a place in the lineage of Jesus.

Dear God, when I must give up people or places or things, help me remember Ruth, her willingness to sacrifice and follow you, and her rich reward. Amen.

61

Hannah

1 SAMUEL 1

"I am very discouraged, and I was pouring out my heart to the LORD."
—1 Samuel 1:15

Has sorrow ever caused you a good, cleansing cry, the kind that leaves you feeling quiet and calm inside? Prayer poured out from a grieving heart has a similar effect.

We grieve over losses of all kinds, not just death. Hannah, who lived in Israel near the end of the time of the judges, grieved her childlessness. Her husband loved her and treated her kindly, but he had a second wife who taunted Hannah about her childlessness every year when the family worshiped at the tabernacle.

This time, feeling desperate, Hannah escaped to pray. Eli, the priest, encouraged Hannah that God had heard her distress and would grant her request, and Hannah left the tabernacle with a lighter heart.

God did give Hannah a son, Samuel, who became the last judge of Israel, but sometimes the things we grieve over can't be fixed the way we would like. Still, bringing all of ourselves to God—hurts, losses, and sorrows as well as thanks and praises—is precious to Him. Psalm 62:5, 8 says, "Let all that I am wait quietly before God, for my hope is in him. . . . Pour out your heart to him, for God is our refuge." Placing all of ourselves in His hands and waiting patiently for Him to act is the most healing place we can ever be.

Heavenly Father, thank you for caring about all my emotions, and for the relief I find when I'm honest with you about all I experience. Amen.

Listen

1 SAMUEL 3

Then Samuel said, "Speak, for your servant is listening."—1 Samuel 3:10 NIV

Hannah had promised God that if He gave her a son, she would devote the boy to serving Him, and she kept her promise. When Samuel was old enough to be weaned (probably five years old in that culture), she brought him to the tabernacle to live and to serve by assisting Eli the priest. One night, God called Samuel to give him a message for Eli—but it took a while for both Eli and Samuel to understand what was happening. When Samuel heard God call his name the fourth time, he knew what to do. He said, "I'm listening, God," and he paid close attention to what he heard.

You may never hear God calling your name in the middle of the night—but you might be awakened with a prompting to pray for a specific person or circumstance. Whether or not we hear from God like Samuel did, in His Word God is calling us to listen to Him and urging us to pay attention to what He has to say.

As he grew up, Samuel continued to hear from God and to speak to the people. What he said proved true, and Israel recognized him as a prophet and a judge. God's Word to us is always true as well. Are you seeking God's Word to know Him better and understand His will for you? Are you listening?

Father God, I want to listen and understand. Help me take the time I need to hear you clearly in your Word. Amen.

63

All Fall Down

1 SAMUEL 5–6

> But the next morning the same thing happened—Dagon had fallen face down before the Ark of the LORD again.—1 Samuel 5:4

It's been said that watching the antics of a puppy will convince anyone that God has a sense of humor. No puppy? Just read the story of the statue of Dagon, the god of the Philistines.

The Israelites brought the ark of the covenant from the tabernacle into battle with the Philistines, hoping it would give them victory, but God had not commanded this. The Philistines, knowing the power of Israel's God, fought even harder than usual when they heard the Israelites had the ark. They defeated the Israelites badly and captured the ark, which they took into the temple of their god, Dagon, and placed it next to his statue.

In the morning they found the statue of Dagon lying face down in front of the ark. They stood the statue back up, but the next morning it had fallen face down again, and this time its hands and head were broken off and lying in the doorway.

It's a comical story that turns serious. When the ark finally was returned to them, the Israelites continued to mishandle it, with devastating consequences. For the next twenty years the ark was kept in Kiriath-jearim, a city of the Gibeonites, and "during that time all Israel mourned because it seemed the LORD had abandoned them" (1 Samuel 7:2). They had put their trust in a symbol of God's presence rather than in God himself.

Dear Lord, may my trust never be in the latest book, program, practice, or teacher, but always in you. Amen.

Give Us a King

1 SAMUEL 7–8

And the Lord said to Samuel, ". . . They have not rejected you, but they have rejected me."—1 Samuel 8:7 ESV

Twenty-nine million Americans watched the royal wedding of Britain's Prince Harry and Meghan Markle in 2018. Like others around the world, many of us have a fascination with royalty. And so did the Israelites—but not with God, who became their true King when they became His covenant people (Deuteronomy 33:5).

In Samuel's older years he appointed his sons as Israel's leaders, but they were dishonest men. The elders of Israel came to Samuel asking for a king "like all the other nations have" (1 Samuel 8:5), just as Moses had warned. Greatly distressed, Samuel asked God what to do. God answered that He would give the people what they wanted: "They are rejecting me, not you," He said. But first Samuel was to warn the people about what life under a human king would be like.

God led Samuel to anoint Saul as Israel's first king, and Saul reigned for forty years, from 1050 to 1010 BC. Physically, he was handsome and imposing; he would be a skilled military leader. Spiritually, God equipped him to lead the nation. Yet on the day the Israelites gathered to confirm Saul as their king, they found him hiding among the baggage. Not the most auspicious beginning!

Sometimes people say, "Be careful what you pray for." The upcoming years in Israel would be proof of that. The Israelites had rejected the best King and settled for what they said they wanted.

What are you praying for today?

Dear God, help me to always pray according to your will and your Word. Amen.

65

Samuel's Promise

1 SAMUEL 12

"Far be it from me that I should sin against the LORD by ceasing to pray for you, and I will instruct you in the good and the right way."
—1 Samuel 12:23 ESV

How do you respond when someone close to you makes choices that break your heart?

With Saul installed as king, Samuel retired from leading Israel as their judge. He spoke to the gathered people one last time, reminding them of God's care for them since the days of Moses. Although they had rejected God as their king, he said, all would go well for them if they and their new king obeyed God and worshiped Him only going forward. Although it was the dry harvest season, Samuel asked God to send thunder and rain to emphasize what he was saying, and God did. The people realized their sin and felt great fear.

Samuel assured them again that God would never abandon them—and neither would he. He would continue to teach them and pray for them.

Samuel had led the Israelites his whole life, and now he was old. Their desire for a human king broke his heart, and based on the Israelites' history, he had to believe there was trouble ahead. He reminded the Israelites of God's role in their lives but accepted their choice for a human king, and he promised to remain a prayerful resource for them. It's a good model for us when those we love make choices we wish they wouldn't.

Heavenly Father, help me be faithful to pray for your will in the lives of those I love whose choices don't honor you. Amen.

66

But . . . But . . . But . . .

1 SAMUEL 13–15

> "Does the Lord delight in burnt offerings and sacrifices as much as in obeying the Lord? To obey is better than sacrifice."—1 Samuel 15:22 NIV

As we grow spiritually, we find we need to stop making excuses for our own bad choices and for sins we've been reluctant to overcome. King Saul seems to have missed that lesson.

Samuel had told Saul to wait seven days for Samuel to come and offer sacrifices, which only a priest could do. Samuel was late arriving, and Saul's army began drifting away, terrified of the Philistines. So Saul decided to sacrifice the burnt offering himself, placing his authority above God's instructions. When Samuel arrived, Saul had his excuses ready. But because of his foolish behavior, Samuel said, the kingdom would not remain in Saul's family forever.

Later, Samuel gave Saul a command from God to attack and destroy the Amalekites and all their property (a consequence of the Amalekites' attack of Israel in the wilderness). Instead, Saul took the Amalekite king alive, along with the best of the sheep and cattle. When Samuel confronted him, Saul began making excuses once again. The sheep and cattle were for sacrifice, he said.

But obedience is better than sacrifice, Samuel told him. "Rebellion is like the sin of divination, and arrogance like the evil of idolatry. Because you have rejected the word of the Lord, he has rejected you as king" (1 Samuel 15:23 NIV).

Obedience is always better than excuses!

Father God, help me take responsibility for my actions, stop making excuses, and obey you in everything. Amen.

67

The Heart of a King

1 SAMUEL 16–17

"People look at the outward appearance, but the LORD looks at the heart."—1 Samuel 16:7 NIV

In the popular children's-novel-turned-movie *Wonder*, about a boy with severe facial abnormalities, Auggie, the main character, learns and teaches others that it's what is inside that counts.

When God sent Samuel to Bethlehem to anoint one of Jesse's sons as the king who would succeed Saul, Samuel was sure handsome Eliab was God's choice. But God said no, because He doesn't judge by physical appearances; He cares about a person's heart. God had chosen "a man after his own heart" (1 Samuel 13:14) instead—David, who was seventeen, who tended his father's sheep. Jesse hadn't even thought to call David in from the fields before Samuel arrived.

David wouldn't be king for another fifteen years, but he would soon demonstrate his heart for God. He volunteered to fight Goliath, a nine-foot-tall Philistine who was terrorizing the entire Israelite army with threats and taunts. "David said to the Philistine, '. . . I come against you in the name of the LORD Almighty, the God of the armies of Israel, whom you have defied'" (1 Samuel 17:45 NIV).

God chose David because of the condition of his heart. What criteria do you use to evaluate others?

Dear Lord, I want to learn to see others like you do. Give me wisdom to know the changes I must make. Amen.

Waiting

1 SAMUEL 18–24, 26

He said to his men, ". . . I shouldn't attack the LORD's anointed one, for the LORD himself has chosen him."—1 Samuel 24:6

The famous marshmallow test developed at Stanford University evaluated the ability of four- and five-year-olds to delay gratification. They could eat the marshmallow in front of them as soon as the researcher left the room, or if they waited until the researcher returned, they could have two marshmallows. Just a small percentage of the children managed to wait for the greater reward.

Do you find it hard to wait? David waited more than twenty years before he became king over all Israel, and he waited under difficult circumstances.

After he was anointed, David entered King Saul's service, going back and forth between the palace and tending his father's sheep in Bethlehem. He became friends with Saul's son Jonathan; he received a high rank in Saul's army after leading successful military missions. People loved David, and Saul grew jealous and afraid. Realizing that God was with David, Saul viewed David as his enemy and tried to kill him. David had to escape and hide.

Saul chased and hounded David throughout the rest of his reign. Twice, David had an opportunity to kill Saul when Saul was unaware of his presence, but both times he refused to do it because Saul was still God's anointed king. David was willing to wait for the Lord to act.

When our circumstances require waiting, we can trust God's timetable just as David did.

Dear God, you always know best, and your timing is perfect. Help me to trust you as David did when you ask me to wait. Amen.

69

Abigail

1 SAMUEL 25

"Your life is safe in the care of the LORD your God, secure in his treasure pouch!"—1 Samuel 25:29

David and his band of six hundred fighting men had given protection to the shepherds caring for Nabal's flocks and herds, and at sheep-shearing time David sent messengers to ask Nabal for provisions for him and his men. Nabal not only refused but insulted David too. Angered, David planned an attack. But Nabal's wife, Abigail, intervened with wisdom and humility to calm the dangerous situation.

Abigail sent David the provisions he needed and then went to meet him. She asked him to overlook Nabal's foolish behavior and to rethink his plans to carry out vengeance with his own hands. She recognized David as the future king of Israel and reminded him that God was in charge and would deal with David's enemies himself at the right time. David's life, she said, was safely bound up in God's care, but David's enemies were like stones in a sling, destined to be flung away. David praised God for sending Abigail and for her wise words, and he called off the attack on Nabal and his household.

Nabal would never have been awarded husband of the year, and perhaps Abigail's wisdom came from her own dependence on God and her trust that He was taking care of her. Are there difficult circumstances in your life? The wisdom you glean as you lean on God may be just what someone else needs to hear.

Heavenly Father, thank you for Abigail's example and the wisdom she shared with David—and with me. Amen.

70

Desperation

1 SAMUEL 28, 31

Saul then said to his advisers, "Find a woman who is a medium, so I can go and ask her what to do."—1 Samuel 28:7

I opened up our community newspaper to a large headline announcing a weekend expo featuring psychics, mediums, healers, and astrologers. Besides getting personal readings, those who attended could learn how to develop their own psychic powers. Six thousand people were expected.

The problem with this is *not* that psychics and mediums don't have any power. The problem is that they *do* but it isn't power from God. That's why the Bible tells us to stay away from all kinds of occult practices, including calling up the dead, known as spiritism.

Saul had banned mediums from Israel, but Samuel was dead, the Philistines were preparing to attack again, and God was not providing any guidance. So Saul disguised himself and turned to a medium, asking her to bring up Samuel from the dead.

Samuel had only bad news from God for Saul, however. The next day, in fierce fighting with the Philistines, three of Saul's sons died, including Jonathan, and Saul took an archer's arrow. When his armor bearer refused to kill him before the Philistines could capture him, Saul fell on his own sword.

Saul's reign was filled with the turmoil his disregard for God had caused. His death opened the way for David to assume the throne, but first David mourned for Saul and Jonathan with a funeral song (2 Samuel 1:17–27).

Father God, I want to align my actions with your Word always. And hear my prayer for those drawn to dark powers. Amen.

71

Michal

2 SAMUEL 3, 6

Michal the daughter of Saul . . . saw King David leaping and dancing before the LORD, and she despised him in her heart.—2 Samuel 6:16 ESV

Dancing joyfully as the ark of the covenant came into Jerusalem, David was dressed not in royal robes but in the linen clothing worn by the priests and Levites who were transporting the ark. Both his clothing and his behavior dismayed Michal, David's first wife. But why did she react so hatefully? We need to know more of her story.

Saul had given his daughter Michal to David as his wife years before, when David was in Saul's service. Because Michal loved David, she helped him when he escaped Saul's murderous threats. Perhaps as payback for her loyalty to David, Saul gave Michal to another man, Palti, to be his wife. Later, when David was king of Judah, a former supporter of Saul offered to help him gain the support of all Israel. David agreed, but he insisted that Michal be given back to him first, possibly in order to negotiate from a position of strength.

Perhaps Michal, a pawn of the powerful, allowed her pain to prevent her from seeing God's hand. Do you know someone like Michal, whose words and actions are hard to understand? Can you look deeper at that person's story in an effort to understand?

Dear God, give me wisdom and a heart of understanding as I relate to those whose words and actions are uncomfortable and frustrating. Help me love. Amen.

Celebrate Life

2 SAMUEL 6

"He appointed me as the leader of Israel, the people of the LORD, so I celebrate before the LORD."—2 Samuel 6:21

Have you ever thought about your life as a book? Each new life stage is a chapter—student, profession, marriage, motherhood, empty nest, grandparent, senior citizen—each with its own events and opportunities for ministry. Whatever chapter you are currently writing is valuable and worth celebrating.

After Saul's death in 1010 BC, David and his followers moved to Hebron in Judah, and the men of Judah anointed him king over the people of Judah. Saul's supporters made his son Ishbosheth king over the remaining tribes of Israel. Seven and a half years later, David finally became king over a united nation and established his capital in Jerusalem, and then he attempted twice to bring the ark of the covenant to the capital. The first time led to tragedy, but the second effort succeeded because it followed God's instructions for transporting the ark. David led the joyful procession, dancing mightily before the Lord. He recognized that God had called him to lead Israel, and he rejoiced and celebrated this new chapter of his life.

So what chapter of the book of your life are you writing today? What has God called you to? Whatever it is, big or small, public or more private, it is a reason to celebrate!

Dear Lord, sometimes I feel insignificant and not at all useful to your kingdom. Other times I feel overwhelmed by the tasks you've given me. Help me view this life chapter as you see it and help me to rejoice in it. Amen.

73

Praying God's Promises

2 SAMUEL 7

"Confirm forever the word that you have spoken concerning your servant and concerning his house, and do as you have spoken."—2 Samuel 7:25 ESV

David brought peace to Israel by defeating the surrounding enemy nations. With a grateful heart toward God for all He had done for him, David decided the ark of the covenant should have a permanent home in a temple, not a tent. He told his plan to the prophet Nathan, and that night Nathan received a message for David from the Lord.

Rather than David building a house for God, Nathan said, God was going to build a "house" for David—a kingdom that would last forever. God promised David that there would be peace in Israel throughout his reign, that one of David's sons would succeed him and would be the one to build the temple, and that David's family would rule forever (a promise ultimately fulfilled in Jesus).

David received God's message and His promises with joy and thanks. He saw them as coming from God's goodness and not because of anything he had done or deserved. He believed God, and he prayed God would do what He had said.

God's Word to us is filled with promises—about guidance, help, forgiveness, peace, and much more. Thankfully accept God's promises to you and ask Him to do what He has said He will do.

Heavenly Father, how wonderful you are! I am your servant. Do for me and in me what you have promised in your Word. Amen.

74

David and Bathsheba

2 SAMUEL 11–12

> "The sword will never depart from your house, because you despised me and took the wife of Uriah the Hittite to be your own."—2 Samuel 12:10 NIV

Our actions often are attempts to get needs met. What was David's need the spring he stayed in the palace while his army went to war? Scripture doesn't tell us, but it shows us the escalation of David's actions and the devastating results.

We also see God's mercy and plan and the bent of David's heart toward God.

When the prophet Nathan confronted him, David quickly confessed and accepted responsibility for his sin with Bathsheba and the murder of her husband. He also embraced the forgiveness God offered along with the negative consequences of his sin—the death of Bathsheba's child and the family intrigue and distress that would plague him from then on. With faith David looked to the future. "I will go to him, but he will not return to me," he said of the baby who died (2 Samuel 12:23 NIV). He married Bathsheba and they conceived another child, Solomon, who ultimately would succeed David as king.

What need is in your heart today—connection, approval, strength, wisdom, provision? Whatever your need, look to God and His Word to show you how to get it met in positive, godly ways.

Father God, I fail but your Word never does. Show me daily how to receive what I need in beneficial ways that please and honor you. Amen.

75

Absalom

2 SAMUEL 13–20

"O my son Absalom! My son, my son Absalom! If only I had died instead of you—O Absalom, my son, my son!"—2 Samuel 18:33 NIV

David excelled as a warrior and dealt forcefully with his enemies—unless they were part of his own family. He failed to discipline his sons, and God's word that "the sword will never depart from your house" (2 Samuel 12:10 NIV) proved true.

David's oldest son, Amnon, raped his half-sister Tamar. Although angered when he learned of it, David did nothing. David's son Absalom murdered Amnon as revenge, and Absalom fled. When David saw Absalom again, he gave him freedom rather than finding him guilty. Their reconciliation meant little, however, because Absalom began scheming and conspiring to steal the throne away from his father.

When Absalom's supporters proclaimed him king, David again failed to act against his son. Instead, he fled Jerusalem for his life, and a civil war followed. Before Absalom's forces and David's fighting men met, David's troops knew he hoped Absalom would be spared. His great grief on hearing Absalom was dead caused his men to feel rejected and ashamed until David finally went out to congratulate them.

Eventually David did return to Jerusalem as king, but unrest and fighting would continue. Our sins and weaknesses often result in turmoil and problems for those who come after us. Thank God for the Savior who forgives us and will transform our lives if we are willing!

Dear Lord, where my failings have caused harm, forgive me. Help me make amends where I can, and I will trust you with the future. Amen.

76

David's Song of Praise

2 SAMUEL 22

"The LORD lives! Praise to my Rock! May God, the Rock of my salvation, be exalted!"—2 Samuel 22:47

In this song of praise, David recounts God's dealings with him throughout his life and expresses his determination to always praise God because of His goodness. The names and descriptions of God in the song give us insight to David's experience and relationship with God as he went through his challenges and battles: Rock. Savior. Fortress. Shield. Power. Refuge. Yahweh (the LORD). The Most High. Lamp. Strength. The Rock of My Salvation. The Bible is filled with names, titles, and descriptions of God, and each of them tells us something about His character. Learning the names of God in the Bible is a wonderful way to get to know Him better.

This same or similar song also appears later in the Bible, in Psalm 18. My friend Lynn calls it the psalm about "Big Noisy God." It's an apt description because of the verses that describe God's power as He comes to the aid of one who calls on Him for help.

David not only had many physical enemies, but "enemy forces" within himself as well, as we all do. The next time you're in need of rescue, remember David and our powerful God. Ask Him to come to be your rock, your salvation, your shield, your refuge. He will come!

Dear God, you have been my rescuer before, and you will always be there to help me when I call. Thank you for your strong power on my behalf. Amen.

77

Arranged and Secured

2 SAMUEL 23

"He has made an everlasting covenant with me. His agreement is arranged and guaranteed in every detail."—2 Samuel 23:5

Do you have memories of family vacations with everyone's luggage fit together like a puzzle and securely tied down on the roof of the car? That's a perfect image for remembering what David is saying in this recap of the years of his reign as king.

God chose David, a shepherd and the youngest of eight brothers, to be king of Israel—the one whose family line would one day bring the Savior into the world. From his youth, David loved God and sought to honor Him with his life.

His music and lyrics earned David the title "sweet psalmist of Israel," and the Spirit of the Lord indeed still speaks through David's words (2 Samuel 23:1–2).

David understood the value God places on living righteously—doing all things according to His standard and desire. At times David's actions as king were flawed and sinful, but his heart for God always led him to repentance, thankfulness, and praise.

The first chapter of the Gospel of Matthew begins, "This is a record of the ancestors of Jesus the Messiah, a descendant of David" (Matthew 1:1). Although David lived more than a thousand years before Jesus was born, he knew he could trust God's promise that one of David's descendants would reign over God's kingdom forever, because the promise was "arranged and secured in every part" (NIV).

As followers of Jesus, we can trust it too.

Heavenly Father, how you love us! Thank you for sending us a Savior who also is our eternal king. Amen.

At the Threshing Floor

2 SAMUEL 24

And he said to the LORD, "I have sinned greatly by taking this census. Please forgive my guilt, LORD, for doing this foolish thing."—2 Samuel 24:10

Have you ever received good advice but decided to ignore it? How did that turn out?

God had allowed Satan to tempt David to take a census of Israel (1 Chronicles 21:1). David's military commanders knew this was wrong and tried to talk him out of it, but David refused to listen. Why was a census wrong? Primarily because only God could call for a census (Exodus 30:12); Israel belonged to Him, not to David.

After the census was complete, David's conscience began to bother him. He could see the pride that caused him to fall into temptation and ignore godly advice, and he quickly confessed his sin to God. But his sin had a consequence, a plague that killed seventy thousand people.

As the plague ended, David saw an angel at the threshing floor of Araunah, near Jerusalem, with his sword stretched out over Jerusalem. God directed David to build an altar there. David insisted on purchasing the threshing floor first, and after David's death the site became the location of the temple.

God is always ready to forgive! Receiving forgiveness, however, doesn't mean our sins will have no consequences, and often the consequences affect others besides ourselves. All the more reason, then, to be willing to listen to wise advice and follow it.

Father God, thank you for your Word and for those who speak correction into my life. May I listen well. Amen.

79

The Kings of Israel

1 KINGS 1–2

"If your descendants live as they should and follow me faithfully with all their heart and soul, one of them will always sit on the throne of Israel."—1 Kings 2:4

When he was very old, David had one more family battle to face. His son Adonijah attempted to take the throne for himself. Handsome Adonijah, the next oldest after Absalom, had never been disciplined or even challenged by his father (1 Kings 1:6); the effects of David's poor parenting and his sin with Bathsheba continued to play out. Even some of David's officers supported Adonijah.

But the Lord's plan prevailed. In 970 BC, David ordered that Solomon be anointed king immediately. When Adonijah heard this, he sought mercy by running to the altar in the tabernacle. For a time, Solomon spared Adonijah's life, but after David's death, he ordered Adonijah's execution.

Before David died, he instructed Solomon to keep the law of Moses and follow God faithfully so that a descendant of David would sit continually on the throne (1 Kings 2:3–4). The books of 1 and 2 Kings tell us the stories of Israel's good and bad kings—those who followed God and those who did not—and the ultimate results for the Israelite nation. Follow the fingerprints of God's mercy throughout these books as well, thinking about your own life and the mercy He has shown to you.

Dear Lord, help me continue to know you better through your dealings with the kings of Israel and their people. Thank you for your goodness and mercy in my life! Amen.

80

Solomon's Request

1 KINGS 3–4

"Give me an understanding heart so that I can govern your people well and know the difference between right and wrong."—1 Kings 3:9

The Israelites should have demolished all the places of pagan worship throughout their land, known as high places, but instead they used them as their own local worship sites. Solomon tolerated this and even practiced it himself. He went to the high place at Gibeon, where King Saul had moved the tabernacle, to offer a thousand burnt offerings. Despite the location of Solomon's sacrifices, that night God appeared to Solomon in a dream and offered to give him anything he asked for.

Solomon asked for wisdom to govern God's people. His request pleased God, who promised to give him the wisdom he desired along with what he *hadn't* asked for—riches and fame and a long life. God kept His promise. Solomon became known as the wisest man who ever lived. His kingdom prospered, his personal wealth grew, his people lived at peace. And yet . . .

These chapters hint at what was to come. Solomon married a second wife, an Egyptian princess. He established forced labor throughout Israel when work on the temple began. Solomon recognized his father David's deep love for God, but did he desire to love God in the same way *himself*?

It's a question Solomon should have asked, and one we can ask ourselves as well.

Dear God, I don't want to love you as a means to selfish ends. Please show and teach me how to love you because of who you are. Amen.

81

A Temple and a Palace

1 KINGS 5–7

"So I am planning to build a Temple to honor the name of the LORD my God, just as he had instructed my father, David."—1 Kings 5:5

Four years into his reign, Solomon set about to build the temple in Jerusalem. David had spent his last years gathering materials and preparing plans for the temple—plans that 1 Chronicles 28:19 tells us came from God himself. The site of the temple was Mount Moriah, the area where Abraham had come to sacrifice Isaac and where David had seen the angel of the Lord and purchased the threshing floor of Araunah.

Constructed of cut stone and cedar timbers and decorated with carvings, the temple measured ninety feet long, thirty feet wide, and forty-five feet high, with other rooms extending in front and around. The entire interior of the temple was overlaid with pure gold. The temple replaced the tabernacle but served the same functions.

At some point during the seven years it took to build the temple, God reminded Solomon of his need to follow Him closely. But when the temple was complete, Solomon began building his own palace complex, a project that took thirteen years. Despite the scope and beauty of the temple, we might wonder whether Solomon's priorities were what God desired. More important, we need to take time to examine our own priorities. How are you using the time and resources God has given to you?

Heavenly Father, in all the tasks I undertake, help me keep my eyes on you and what you desire for my life. Amen.

82

Glory Fills the Temple

1 KINGS 8

"But will God really live on earth? Why, even the highest heavens cannot contain you. How much less this Temple I have built!"—1 Kings 8:27

Solomon gathered Israel's leaders in 959 BC for a ceremony to dedicate the temple. Priests brought the ark of the covenant from its tent and placed it inside the Most Holy Place, covered by the wings of two gold cherubim. When the ark was in place and the priests came out of the Most Holy Place, the cloud of the Lord's glory filled the temple—the same cloud that led the Israelites out of Egypt and through the wilderness and hovered over the tabernacle.

Once again, God was demonstrating His desire—and working out His plan—to live among His people. And the sense of God's presence and absolute holiness was such that the priests were unable to remain in the temple.

Solomon recognized that the temple could not contain God. His prayer to God at the dedication repeatedly asked God to hear and forgive from His throne in heaven. But the temple signified God's presence just the same, and once a year on the Day of Atonement, the high priest would enter the Most Holy Place to sprinkle the blood of sacrificial animals for his own sins and the sins of the nation.

When do you most sense God's presence with you? How does recognizing His majestic holiness affect your perception of your own sin?

Father God, you are holy, high, and lifted up. And you are with me! Thank you for your presence. Thank you for forgiving my sin through your Son, Jesus. Amen.

83

That All May Know

1 KINGS 8

"In this way, all the people of the earth will come to know and fear you, just as your own people Israel do."—1 Kings 8:43

Solomon addressed the people gathered for the temple dedication and then turned to heartfelt prayer to God. He included a request for the foreigners who would hear of God's name and power and come to Jerusalem to pray at the temple. (People who were not Israelites, later called Gentiles, had access to the temple complex in a courtyard set aside for them.)

Solomon asked that God would hear and answer the foreigners' prayers so they also would know Him as the one true God as the Israelites did. Was Solomon thinking about God's promise to Abraham, "All the families on earth will be blessed through you" (Genesis 12:3)?

Before the temple dedication ended, Solomon blessed the people of Israel and included again a reminder of the purpose for their nation. By how they lived and were governed, Israel was meant to show all the world the goodness and power of God, who is Lord of all.

Christians have a charge to make disciples of all nations, and Jesus said, "Your love for one another will prove to the world that you are my disciples" (John 13:35). We make Jesus known by how we live—in the church and in the world. What opportunities are yours today as a woman, wife, mother, or grandmother?

Dear Lord, you have blessed me to be a blessing to others. Show me how to honor you and obey your Word today so others can know you too. Amen.

84

The Queen of Sheba

1 KINGS 10

When the queen of Sheba heard of Solomon's fame, which brought honor to the name of the LORD, she came to test him with hard questions.—1 Kings 10:1

We don't know her name. We're not sure where she was from, perhaps southern Arabia in what is now Yemen. The queen of Sheba traveled more than a thousand miles to see if all she had heard about Solomon's wisdom and wealth were true. Her visit did not disappoint her; in fact, this woman of royalty, wealth, and intellect found herself overwhelmed by all she saw and heard.

What questions do you think the queen had for Solomon? "When she met with Solomon, she talked with him about everything she had on her mind. Solomon had answers for all her questions; nothing was too hard for the king to explain to her" (1 Kings 10:2–3). Was the queen seeking God? She praised God for making Solomon king and for his wise and prosperous rule, but we have no idea whether she personally came to faith in Israel's God. Jesus, however, praised this "queen of the South" for going to much effort to seek Solomon's wisdom (Matthew 12:42).

What questions might you have asked Solomon? What questions would you ask him today—and are you seeking God for His answers as intently as the queen of Sheba sought out the wisdom of Solomon?

Dear God, I do have questions. Guide my seeking and my study of your Word and plant your answers in my heart. Amen.

85

Turned Away

1 KINGS 11

As Solomon grew old, his wives turned his heart after other gods, and his heart was not fully devoted to the LORD his God.—1 Kings 11:4 NIV

My young grandson recently learned to go down the slide at the toddler playground. It's a skill he's proud of! But slides can be slippery, so he gladly reaches for a hand to hold as he goes down.

Figuratively, King Solomon slid down a slippery slope, but did he even try to hold on?

Solomon had seven hundred wives and three hundred concubines. Many were foreigners who worshiped idols and pagan gods, even though God had commanded the Israelites not to intermarry with foreigners. Eventually Solomon began to worship the gods of his pagan wives and even built special worship locations (high places) for them. Solomon "held fast" to his wives (1 Kings 11:2) and wanted to please them more than he wanted to love and please God.

There were signposts along this slippery slope. Deuteronomy 17 records instructions for Israel's kings. They were to have no foreign wives, they were not to acquire a large number of horses, they were never to send to Egypt to buy horses, and they were not to work to build up silver and gold for themselves. Solomon broke each of these commandments during his reign.

Have you ever found yourself on a slippery slope away from God? Are you there today? Check yourself and reach out for His hand.

Heavenly Father, I want to love and obey you with my whole heart. Keep me from stubborn sins; help me reach to you instead. Amen.

86

Torn

1 KINGS 11–12

"Since this is your attitude and you have not kept my covenant and my decrees, which I commanded you, I will most certainly tear the kingdom away from you."—1 Kings 11:11 NIV

Because of Solomon's attitude and behavior, the kingdom would change hands. God called Jeroboam to be the next king—but over only ten of the twelve tribes. A prophet's cloak torn into twelve pieces illustrated what would happen. Judah (and tiny Benjamin) in the south would remain under Solomon's descendants—for David's sake and the promises God made to him—but Jeroboam would rule the ten northern tribes. Solomon tried to kill Jeroboam, who fled to Egypt and did not return until he heard that Solomon had died.

Solomon's son Rehoboam succeeded him at first, but his actions led the tribes of the north to rebel and call Jeroboam to be their king. Rehoboam prepared to fight, but God sent a prophet to say, "Do not go up to fight against your brothers, the Israelites. Go home, every one of you, for this is my doing" (1 Kings 12:24 NIV).

Does the kingdom torn in two seem a strange plot twist? Much later the apostle Paul wrote, "Oh, the depth of the riches and wisdom and knowledge of God! How unsearchable are his judgments and how inscrutable his ways!" (Romans 11:33 ESV). When life is confusing, hang on and trust the One who loves you and is working out His magnificent plan.

Father God, I can't begin to comprehend your greatness. Help me always lean on you and trust and follow you when I don't understand what's happening. Amen.

87

Follow the Leader

1 KINGS 13–14

Judah did evil in the eyes of the LORD. By the sins they committed they stirred up his jealous anger more than those who were before them had done.—1 Kings 14:22 NIV

After the kingdom split in 930 BC, to keep the northern people from traveling south to the temple in Jerusalem, Jeroboam established a counterfeit worship system for them to follow, with idols, shrines, and priests appointed from among the people (rather than the tribe of Levi). And just as the people of the north followed their king into idol worship and sin, so did the people of Judah. They worshiped at pagan shrines, set up Asherah poles (carvings of the Canaanite fertility goddess), and included male and female prostitutes into their worship rites. "The people imitated the detestable practices of the pagan nations the LORD had driven from the land ahead of the Israelites" (1 Kings 14:24). No wonder God felt jealous anger—His beloved people had abandoned Him once again, and He knew it could not turn out well for them.

Social researchers have demonstrated that we humans frequently go along with opinions or actions of the majority even when we know it's wrong. Still, it's hard for us to understand just how the people of Israel and Judah could turn away from God so quickly and completely. *We* would never do that, right? Wrong!

Let the actions of the people of Israel and Judah after Solomon's death remind you of your own need to cling closely to God and follow Him even when others don't.

Dear Lord, when I'm tempted to follow the culture and the crowd, remind me that I am yours instead. I want to live to please you. Amen.

A Litany of Kings

1 KINGS 15–17

Ahab did more to provoke the LORD, the God of Israel, to anger than all the kings of Israel who were before him.—1 Kings 16:3 ESV

If you like to ride roller coasters, you'll understand the frightening up-and-down, zigzag rule of the kings of Israel and Judah.

In Judah, after Rehoboam's death, his son Abijam reigned for three years. He did not follow God, but his son Asa, who succeeded him and reigned for forty-one years, did.

After Jeroboam, the kings of Israel were Nadab (Jeroboam's son), Baasha (who killed Nadab and all of Jeroboam's descendants), Elah (the son of Baasha), Zimri (who killed Elah and then reigned just seven days before taking his own life by fire), Omri, and Omri's son Ahab. None of these kings followed God; Ahab was the worst. He married Jezebel, the daughter of a pagan king, and together they worked to establish the worship of Baal, a Canaanite god, in Israel.

God sent prophets with warnings to the evil kings of Judah and Israel. The prophet Elijah angered Ahab with his prediction that there would be no rainfall in Israel for several years, until he gave the word. To keep Elijah safe from Ahab, God sent him to live beside a brook east of the Jordan River. There, God sent ravens each morning and evening with bread and meat for Elijah to eat.

Some of us truly enjoy roller coasters, but no one enjoys living in tumult. God is our refuge in times of trouble. Are you desiring to serve Him but faced with opposition? Let your heavenly Father care for you as He did for Elijah.

Dear God, help me look to you for refuge when circumstances press in on me. I know you care and will guide and provide for me in all situations. Amen.

89

The Widow of Zarephath

1 KINGS 17

"Now I know that you are a man of God and that the word of the LORD from your mouth is the truth."—1 Kings 17:24 NIV

The woman Elijah encountered when God sent him to Zarephath was gathering sticks for a fire to cook one last small meal for herself and her son; the drought in Israel also had brought famine to her Phoenician town near Sidon, the heart of Baal worship. But she stopped to give Elijah the drink of water he asked for, and then she used her last oil and flour to bake bread for him instead of for her own needs.

The woman's jars of oil and flour were never empty after that, just as Elijah predicted. She was seeing that God is sovereign and powerful over all lands and that he cares about all people—not only those in Israel. Later, when the woman's son died and Elijah raised him to life again, her faith in Israel's God grew even stronger.

Elijah's life with God greatly impacted this pagan woman. Who are the people in your community like her, who don't yet know God but could meet Him through relationships with believers? Ask God if there's a role for you in making sure they hear His message.

Heavenly Father, forgive me. I've been comfortable worshiping you yet forgetting those who haven't heard the message of your love for them. Show me what you would have me do. Amen.

Showdown

1 KINGS 18

"Answer me, LORD, answer me, so these people will know that you, LORD, are God, and that you are turning their hearts back again."
—1 Kings 18:37 NIV

The drought and famine in Israel continued. Elijah stayed hidden from Ahab, while Ahab's wife, Jezebel, pursued and killed many of God's prophets.

Then God told Elijah to confront Ahab, and that it soon would rain. Elijah challenged Ahab and the 450 prophets of Baal to a contest with the Lord on Mount Carmel, before all the people of Israel. For hours the prophets of Baal danced and wailed and cut themselves, calling on Baal to send fire, but nothing happened. Then Elijah prayed for the people to know God and choose to follow Him once again. "The fire of the LORD fell and burned up the sacrifice, the wood, the stones and the soil, and also licked up the water in the trench" (1 Kings 18:38 NIV).

Baal or God. That was the choice Elijah placed before the people. There was only one correct answer, just as there could be only one possible result in any contest. God is God over *all*. He is always the right choice.

Are you praying for loved ones to make that right choice? Make Elijah's prayer your own: "Answer me, LORD, answer me, so these people will know that you, LORD, are God."

Father God, I don't ever want to turn from your power and love; I want you to always be my choice. And hear my prayer for loved ones who need to know you too. Amen.

91

Overcome

1 KINGS 19

He sat down under a solitary broom tree and prayed that he might die.—1 Kings 19:4

Have you ever experienced such grief, stress, or burnout that you utterly despaired of life? Elijah did too.

After he executed the prophets of Baal and the rain began, Elijah fled to escape Jezebel's threat to kill him. Alone in the wilderness, he confessed to the Lord that he wanted to die; serving as God's prophet in a land turned against God had overwhelmed and depleted him. But God wasn't willing to answer that prayer. Instead, He helped Elijah rebuild his resources with sleep, food, and assurances that he wasn't alone.

God directed Elijah to Mount Sinai and talked with him there. Elijah spoke honestly about his experiences and feelings. He had worked hard. He grieved the way Israel had turned against God. He grieved the prophets Jezebel had killed. Elijah, the only faithful one left, felt isolated and afraid.

God listened, and He answered. He had not abandoned Elijah. A new prophet would come alongside him and then take his place. And there were seven thousand people in Israel who hadn't bowed to Baal, who still worshiped God alone.

Our physical bodies need care, and so do our complex emotions. We are made to be connected to God and other people. When we feel overcome like Elijah did, when emotional issues strike, we need both kinds of connections to move toward healing. And God, if we let Him, will lead the way.

Dear Lord, help me live connected to you, connected to others, and committed to honesty, so I can heal and grow into the woman you created me to be. Amen.

Whisper

1 KINGS 19

"Go out and stand on the mountain in the presence of the LORD, for the LORD is about to pass by."—1 Kings 19:11 NIV

When Elijah moved to the mouth of the cave where he'd spent the night and waited for God to pass by, what do you think he expected to see or hear?

He knew about God's big miracles, like parting the Red Sea. He knew about God's loud appearances, like the time He came down on Mount Sinai in a dark cloud with thunder and lightning to meet with the Israelites. And Elijah had recently seen God send fire down from heaven to consume his sacrifice at the contest with the prophets of Baal. So did Elijah expect God to pass by in some spectacular, noisy way?

Maybe, but it's not what he got. God wasn't in the wind, or the earthquake, or the fire. God came near Elijah in the sound of a gentle whisper.

Some see a lesson here that to hear God speak, *we* must be quiet, undistracted by busyness and noise. But go deeper. What does Elijah's encounter with God tell us *about God*?

Elijah thought his life and his work in Israel had been useless. God wanted Elijah to understand that He had been quietly working in the situation all along and would continue to do so.

When hard times cause us to wonder where God is and what He's doing, the answer is "He's here."

Dear God, how glad I am that you never leave me alone. Help me trust you at all times, in everything. Amen.

93

Learning by Example

1 KINGS 19; 2 KINGS 2

So Elisha returned to his oxen and slaughtered them. . . . Then he went with Elijah as his assistant.—1 Kings 19:21

Did you ever work as an intern or apprentice? The prophet Elisha, chosen by God to be Elijah's successor, prepared for his role by first serving alongside Elijah. Israel's kings and people continued their terrible sins of idol worship and their conflicts with God's prophets.

God planned to take Elijah to heaven in a whirlwind, and Elisha, loyal and devoted, refused to leave Elijah as that day came near. The two men crossed the Jordan River on dry ground after Elijah hit the river with his rolled-up cloak. Then from heaven a chariot of fire drove between them, and a whirlwind carried Elijah into heaven.

Elisha picked up the cloak Elijah had dropped. He rolled it up as Elijah had done, hit the waters of the Jordan with it, and crossed over on dry ground. He had completed his apprenticeship.

Much later, the apostle Paul wrote, "Follow my example, as I follow the example of Christ" (1 Corinthians 11:1 NIV). We all need more mature followers of Jesus to be our examples. Whose example are you watching and learning from, and who is watching and learning from you?

Heavenly Father, thank you for the people you've placed in my life as examples of Christian servants, and help me be a worthy example to someone else. Amen.

94

Best Actor in a Supporting Role

2 KINGS 5

"From now on I will never again offer burnt offerings or sacrifices to any other god except the LORD."—2 Kings 5:17

We can learn a lot about humility and submission to God from Naaman's experience, and it's easy to think Naaman is the main character of this story. But the true headliner in these events is God.

God had allowed the king of Aram (Syria) to win military victories through the leadership of Naaman, the commander of his army.

God had allowed the Arameans to invade Israel and take captives, including a young girl who became a servant of Naaman's wife.

God had placed a prophet in Israel, Elisha, who had already performed miracles and knew that God is the one who can "give life and take it away" (2 Kings 5:7).

God is the one who healed Naaman of his leprosy when he followed Elisha's instructions to dip himself in the Jordan River seven times.

And God is the one Naaman honored when he was healed and worshiped when he returned to his home country.

I do love Naaman's role in this story—his upset pride, the good advice his officers gave him, and his decision to do what Elisha told him to do. In his need, he chose to believe God would help him. He wisely went for best supporting actor and let God have the starring role.

Father God, when situations hurt my pride or when I'm in need, let me remember to turn to you with humility and submission, allowing you to have your way with me. I can trust you! Amen.

95

Lord of Heaven's Armies

2 KINGS 6

> The LORD opened the young man's eyes, and when he looked up, he saw that the hillside around Elisha was filled with horses and chariots of fire.—2 Kings 6:17

Elisha had been deflecting the Arameans' attempts to battle Israel. Whenever they made a plan to surprise the Israelites, Elisha knew it and told the king of Israel in advance. Frustrated, the king of Aram sent his army, with horses and chariots, to capture Elisha. And Elisha's servant, when he awoke and discovered the city surrounded, panicked.

But Elisha wasn't afraid. "There are more on our side than there are of them," he said.

What? Elisha's servant saw no one but the Aramean army.

Then Elisha prayed for his servant to see, and he did—an angel army with horses and chariots of fire, ready to protect and defend Elisha and his servant.

Elisha solved the conflict with another prayer, this time asking for the army sent to capture him to be struck with blindness. Then he led them into Israel's capital city as captives, but insisted they be fed and sent home rather than killed. Elisha could act with confidence because he knew the Lord of Heaven's Armies (in some translations "the Lord of hosts"), the One who rules both earth and the heavenly, unseen realms.

If you had been there, would you have been Elisha or Elisha's servant? Do you have eyes of faith to "see" what is unseen?

Dear Lord, you are mighty. You rule angel armies in heaven and you rule on earth. I know I can trust you; rule in my heart. Amen.

96

Good News Is for Sharing

2 KINGS 7

Then they said to each other, "What we're doing is not right. This is a day of good news and we are keeping it to ourselves."—2 Kings 7:9 NIV

You might have heard the saying "Evangelism is just one beggar telling another beggar where he found bread." Tucked into the accounts of Israel's kings is the story of four beggars who found bread—and much more.

The four were lepers, required to stay away from the city's inhabitants to keep from spreading their disease. A long siege by the Aramean army had left them and all of Samaria's people desperate and starving. Rather than stay at the city gates to die, the lepers decided to go out to the Aramean camp at night and hope for mercy.

Elisha had predicted the siege would end within a day, but no one believed him. He was right, of course. God caused the Arameans to hear the sound of an approaching army, and they ran. The lepers found the camp abandoned—and fully supplied with food and drink, silver and gold, and clothing. After a while they decided it wasn't right to keep the news of what they'd found to themselves, so they went back with a report. When morning came, the people of the city stampeded out to the camp.

We have the privilege of telling others about the wonderful Savior we've found. Do you know someone who's desperately waiting to hear the news?

Dear God, I want to share the good news of Jesus boldly and with love. Help me. May I be sensitive to your leading. Thank you for Jesus and His good news. Amen.

97

Fallen

2 KINGS 8–17

This disaster came upon the people of Israel because they worshiped other gods. They sinned against the Lord their God, who had brought them safely out of Egypt.—2 Kings 17:7

Through His prophets, beginning with Moses, God had warned that abandoning Him for other gods would lead to Israel being cast out of the land He had given them. But Israel's kings ignored the warnings, and the people followed the kings' example. The list of their offenses includes rejecting God's decrees and His covenant with their ancestors, despising His warnings, worshiping idols and false gods, setting up pagan shrines and pillars in all their towns and on the high places, imitating the pagan practices of the surrounding nations, consulting fortune-tellers, practicing sorcery, and even sacrificing their children as burnt offerings (17:9–11, 15–17).

God used the nations of Aram (Syria) and then Assyria to trouble and oppress Israel because of His anger. But He also felt compassion for their plight and sent them relief—until He no longer could. Assyria invaded Israel for the last time in 722 BC, surrounding and conquering the capital, Samaria, deporting and scattering most of the people, and resettling Israel's territory with foreigners from other parts of their empire. The northern kingdom disappeared.

God had warned the Israelites again and again. Their story warns and teaches us about the seriousness of sin.

Heavenly Father, forgive me for the times I've taken your love and my Savior for granted. May I not make excuses for my sins but turn to you in sincere repentance. Amen.

Challenges

2 KINGS 18–19

"This is what the great king of Assyria says: What are you trusting in that makes you so confident?"—2 Kings 18:19

Some of Judah's kings honored God somewhat, and others, like Ahaz, followed the evil example of the kings of Israel (2 Kings 16:3). Then Hezekiah, the son of Ahaz, became king. Hezekiah "did what was pleasing in the LORD's sight, just as his ancestor David had done" (2 Kings 18:3).

In the fourteenth year of Hezekiah's reign, King Sennacherib of Assyria invaded Judah and threatened Jerusalem. Sennacherib sent Hezekiah and the people of Judah a message, inviting them to surrender and taunting their belief that God would rescue them.

Hezekiah did three things: he tore his clothes and put on burlap (signs of distress and mourning), he went into the temple, and he sent a message to the prophet Isaiah. He asked Isaiah if God would intervene against the Assyrian king whose words defied Him, and he asked Isaiah to pray. Then he had to wait.

In 2018 a *GQ* article included the Bible in a list of "21 Books You Don't Have to Read." It called the Bible repetitive, self-contradictory, and even ill-intentioned. Clearly, people still defy the Lord. When you hear challenges to faith and trust in God, how do you react? Can you spot the lies? Who are you trusting, and why?

Father God, my confidence is in you and in your faithfulness, in your Word, and in your love. Grow my discernment as I learn from you in your Word. Amen.

99

Hezekiah's Prayer

2 KINGS 19

After Hezekiah received the letter from the messengers and read it, he went up to the LORD's Temple and spread it out before the LORD. —2 Kings 19:14

The prophet Isaiah told Hezekiah that God would intervene in Sennacherib's plans, and He did. The king of Ethiopia set out to attack Assyria, and Sennacherib and his army left Judah to meet that challenge instead. But Sennacherib wasn't done making threats. He sent Hezekiah a letter to keep the pressure on. "Don't let your God, in whom you trust, deceive you with promises that Jerusalem will not be captured by the king of Assyria. You know perfectly well what the kings of Assyria have done wherever they have gone. They have completely destroyed everyone who stood in their way! Why should you be any different?" (2 Kings 19:10–11).

Hezekiah took the letter into the temple, spread it out before God, and prayed for rescue. First he offered praise for who God is—the creator and ruler of heaven and earth—and then he told God of his need. As he prayed, Hezekiah reminded himself of truth. Yes, the fierce Assyrians had conquered many nations, but those nations worshiped only false gods who could not protect them. Judah's God was the one true God, who would rescue His people for all to see.

Are you in need of God's help? When we pray for His will because of what we know is true about God, He is sure to answer.

Dear Lord, when I am troubled, help me come to you as Hezekiah did, spreading my need before you, offering praises, and confidently relying on the truths of who you are. Amen.

100

Complacency

2 KINGS 20

> Then Hezekiah said to Isaiah, "The word of the Lord that you have spoken is good." For he thought, "Why not, if there will be peace and security in my days?"—2 Kings 20:19 ESV

None of us knows how long we will live, but Hezekiah had more knowledge about that than the rest of us. God had healed him from an otherwise fatal illness and promised him fifteen more years of life.

Hearing that Hezekiah had been sick, the king of Babylon sent messengers with a greeting and a gift. Hezekiah received the envoy as his guests and gave them a tour to show off his wealth—silver, gold, spices and oils, his armory, his palace, and everything in the royal treasuries. After the visit, the prophet Isaiah brought Hezekiah a message about the future: Babylon would carry off everything of value from the palace and the royal treasuries; nothing would be left. Some of Hezekiah's sons would go to Babylon in exile and serve the Babylonian king.

Hezekiah took the sobering prophecy calmly—too calmly. What was coming wouldn't affect him.

But what about the generations yet to come? What about his own children and grandchildren?

We don't know what the days and years ahead will bring, but we always need to be concerned for future generations. Are you praying regularly for your children and grandchildren to be guided and protected by the Lord?

Dear God, you alone know what's coming. I will trust you with each day, and may my children and grandchildren trust you and know your love and protection always. Amen.

101

Good King Josiah

2 KINGS 21–23

> Never before had there been a king like Josiah, who turned to the LORD with all his heart and soul and strength, obeying all the laws of Moses.—2 Kings 23:25

Judah's next king was Hezekiah's son Manasseh, who "did what was evil in the LORD's sight, following the detestable practices of the pagan nations that the LORD had driven from the land" and "murdered many innocent people until Jerusalem was filled from one end to the other with innocent blood" (2 Kings 21:2, 16). His son Amon, who ruled next, was no better. But Amon's son Josiah, who became king at age eight when Amon was assassinated, was a truly good king.

Josiah began repairs to God's temple, and workmen uncovered an old, forgotten scroll—the Book of Law written by Moses. When the scroll was read aloud, Josiah tore his clothes in despair because God's people had so greatly disobeyed the Lord.

Josiah himself read the scroll aloud to a gathering of all the people in Judah, young and old. He led the people in recommitting themselves to God's covenant with them, and he removed all the pagan worship objects and sites throughout the land. Then he called for a Passover celebration to remember and honor God for bringing the Israelites out of Egypt.

Does reading God's Word motivate you to action the way it motivated Josiah? Have you turned to follow God with all your heart and soul and strength as he did?

Heavenly Father, may your Word always be precious to me and be my guide, because of my love for you. Amen.

Destruction and Exile

2 KINGS 23–25

So in the ninth year of Zedekiah's reign, on the tenth day of the tenth month, Nebuchadnezzar king of Babylon marched against Jerusalem with his whole army.—2 Kings 25:1 NIV

Early in their relationship with Him, God gave the Israelites both promises and warnings. But despite God's blessings and the multiple times He showed His erring people mercy, the nation repeatedly chose to ignore Him and disobey His laws. And just as His promises all proved true, so did His warnings. As the northern kingdom of Israel had fallen, so did the southern kingdom of Judah.

Nebuchadnezzer of Babylon besieged Jerusalem, and Judah's King Jehoiachin surrendered. The treasures of the temple were raided and carried away. Most of the people were taken captive to live as exiles in Babylon. Nebuchadnezzar made Jehoachin's uncle, Zedekiah, king in Jerusalem, but Zedekiah eventually rebelled against him.

Nebuchadnezzer began a final siege of Jerusalem. The Babylonians executed Zedekiah's sons and gouged out Zedekiah's eyes. Two years later, in 586 BC, the Babylonian commander Nebuzaradan "burned down the Temple of the LORD, the royal palace, and all the houses of Jerusalem. He destroyed all the important buildings in the city. Then he supervised the entire Babylonian army as they tore down the walls of Jerusalem on every side" (2 Kings 25:9–10).

Such destruction and devastation of God's people seems impossible to comprehend, until we remember that what God says, He means.

Father God, help me listen to you, believing you mean what you say. Give me an understanding heart, willing to obey. Amen.

103

Roots

1 CHRONICLES 1–9

These names all come from ancient records.—1 Chronicles 4:22

Have you explored your family's roots? Do you know who your ancestors were?

In ancient Israel, lineage mattered, and so did record keeping. The author of 1 Chronicles used multiple sources to compile the genealogies that open the book. For the exiles returning after seventy years in Babylon, these ancient records emphasized their relationship with God as His people from the time of Abraham, and even from creation.

The returning exiles greatly needed the reminder. Life in Judah was difficult—Jerusalem's broken walls left the city vulnerable, the temple was gone, and people who had moved into the region during the exile opposed the Jews' return. The books of 1 and 2 Kings explained why God's people had come to such a state; now they needed encouragement that God hadn't abandoned them or His promises to David for a secure and lasting kingdom. The books of 1 and 2 Chronicles provided that perspective. Looking back gave the returning exiles a way to look forward.

When have you needed to hold on to an encouraging outlook? Do you need encouragement today? Review your own story with God to renew your perspective. He is always faithful to His people!

Dear Lord, thank you for your loving faithfulness to all your people, even me. Amen.

Jabez

1 CHRONICLES 1–9

"Oh, that you would bless me and expand my territory!"—1 Chronicles 4:10

Tucked into the genealogies in the opening chapters of 1 Chronicles we find the story of Jabez, with a lesson for each of us about human potential under God's guidance.

The name Jabez sounds like the Hebrew word for *pain*. His mother chose it because his birth had been so physically painful for her, but the name must have caused Jabez emotional pain. He wore the label like a noose around his neck until the day he cried out to God, "Oh, that you would bless me and enlarge my territory! Let your hand be with me, and keep me from harm so that I will be free from pain" (1 Chronicles 4:10 NIV). He'd had enough. He wanted a fruitful life. He didn't want to cause others pain, and he wanted to be free of his own. God heard his prayer and granted his request.

We don't have to be limited by the past or how others see us in the present. We don't have to keep playing the old tapes, listening to the accusing voices—not even our own. What matters is how God sees us today and whether we are seeking to live His way.

Dear God, when I'm mired in regret or letting others' opinions matter more than yours, turn my attention forward again, toward your plan and purpose for my life. Amen.

105

Serving One Another

1 CHRONICLES 11–12

"I could never drink this! It would be like drinking the blood of these men who risked their lives!"—1 Chronicles 11:19 GNT

David had an elite group of fighting men who became known as the Thirty, and the mightiest of those became known as the Three. They weren't interested in making a name for themselves, only in serving David, and he in turn respected and honored them.

Once, while the Philistines occupied Bethlehem, where David had grown up, David began to long for a drink of the good, clear water from the well by the Bethlehem gate. Hearing him say so, the Three broke through the Philistine lines, drew water from the well, and carried it back to David.

But David wouldn't drink it. Instead he poured it out as an offering to God. His men had risked their lives for him, he said, and drinking the water would dishonor what they had done for him.

Families, communities, and churches need such a spirit of honoring and serving one another in love. Do you have relationships that would benefit from a commitment to put others' needs and desires ahead of your own?

Heavenly Father, sometimes I simply want my own way. Forgive me. Show me where I need to concentrate on serving others in love. Amen.

Ask God First

1 CHRONICLES 15

"It was because you, the Levites, did not bring it up the first time that the LORD our God broke out in anger against us. We did not inquire of him about how to do it in the prescribed way."—1 Chronicles 15:13 NIV

Whenever she faced a difficult decision or a situation that puzzled her, my friend Beth followed what she called her three-day rule: don't talk about the problem for three days; just pray and ask God what to do. (This might remind you of Esther's response when the Jews throughout the Persian empire were threatened with annihilation.)

When David wanted to bring the ark of the covenant from Kiriath-jearim to Jerusalem, he would have benefited from following the three-day rule.

God had given Moses specific instructions for how the ark should be transported, and Moses had recorded them in the Book of the Law. David had access to those instructions and would have found them if he had just taken time to think and ask, but in all his preparations for a celebration, it seems that he did not. Three months later, when he prepared again to move the ark, David understood what had gone wrong the first time, and why.

Through God's Word and His Spirit, we have access to godly wisdom and counsel. Do you need those today? Don't forget to ask!

Father God, how grateful I am to be guided by your wisdom and counsel! May I always seek your perspective and instructions for all I face. Amen.

107

Worship the Lord

1 CHRONICLES 16, 22–23

> Ascribe to the Lord the glory due his name; bring an offering and come before him. Worship the Lord in the splendor of his holiness.
> —1 Chronicles 16:29 NIV

Little children worship naturally. Puppies, flowers, sandy beaches, first steps, new skills—every discovery is a reason to praise their Creator with clapping, awe, and squeals of joy.

King David kept that spirit of worship throughout his life and did much to encourage and lead the Israelites to worship God. In Jerusalem David stationed Levites at the tent he set up for the ark of the covenant. At the tabernacle, in Gibeon, he assigned Zadok and other priests to offer daily sacrifices to the Lord as God had commanded, and he appointed musicians to sing songs of praise accompanied by trumpets, cymbals, and other instruments.

God did not allow David to build the temple, but David did make preparations for the day his son Solomon would do so. He purchased land that would become the temple site, and he gathered building materials of gold, silver, iron, bronze, stone, and cedar. He organized the Levites for their service as temple workers, officials and judges, gatekeepers, and musicians. He received the design plans for the temple directly from God himself (1 Chronicles 28:19).

Worship styles and customs may vary from church to church and region to region, and as congregations and individuals, it's worth examining how we worship. But what really matters is *that* we worship God, giving Him glory and telling the nations that He reigns.

Dear Lord, you are worthy! Help me worship you gladly with a thankful heart of praise. Amen.

108

The Ministry of Music

1 CHRONICLES 25

David and the army commanders then appointed men from the families of Asaph, Heman, and Jeduthun to proclaim God's messages to the accompaniment of lyres, harps, and cymbals.—1 Chronicles 25:1

Music is such a mysterious gift. How does it even exist at all? But it does, stirring our hearts and expressing our emotions. Hymnwriter Maltbie D. Babcock, at the beginning of the twentieth century, wrote these words:

> This is my Father's world,
> And to my list'ning ears
> All nature sings, and round me rings
> The music of the spheres.

As David organized the priests and Levites for worship at the tabernacle and the temple, he chose musicians to give thanks, to praise God, and to proclaim God's messages with musical accompaniment.

Do you have a favorite hymn or worship song? The psalms in the Bible were sung as worship. Jesus and His disciples sang a hymn together after their Passover meal on the night He was betrayed. Music styles vary. The songs and hymns of J. S. Bach, Fanny Crosby, and contemporary artists sound and feel quite different. God, I think, enjoys them all, if indeed they proclaim His messages and encourage us to share His Word with a world waiting to hear.

Dear God, thank you for the gift of music and song. Help me choose to sing lyrics aligned with your Word, proclaiming your messages. Amen.

109

Seek Him

1 CHRONICLES 28

"Solomon, my son, learn to know the God of your ancestors intimately. . . . If you seek him, you will find him."—1 Chronicles 28:9

I first began to be serious about getting to know God when I joined a group of women planning to read through the Bible in a year. Our leader, Beth, said as she kicked off the first meeting, "We'll read three chapters a day and meet once a week to discuss what we've read."

And that's what we did—every year for the next ten years. Once we had tasted reading and discussing God's Word in community, we couldn't get enough. Every year brought new knowledge, wisdom, and friendship with God as we got to know Him better.

When King David charged Solomon with building God's temple, he also charged him to know and obey the Lord. Knowing God is more than knowing about God. Knowing God might sound presumptuous, but it is not; it is a gift and a privilege. He *wants* us to know Him.

Seek God and you will find Him. Train your heart and mind to worship and serve Him gladly. And stay in the pages of His Word. Someone has said, "The Bible is the only book whose Author is always present when one reads it."

Heavenly Father, I do want to know you more and more. Thank you for giving us your Word and showing us in its pages who you are and what you do. Help me find you there each day. Amen.

110

Generous

1 CHRONICLES 29

"Everything comes from you, and we have given you only what comes from your hand."—1 Chronicles 29:14 NIV

Have you ever donated to a cause through an online site like GoFundMe or Kickstarter? Before you could do that, someone who was concerned about the situation led the way by setting up the page and getting the word out.

David had gathered and collected a vast amount of building supplies for Solomon to use in the building of the temple. But now, at the end of his reign, he wanted to do more. He donated all his own private treasure of gold and silver, and he challenged all the officials of Israel to follow his example and give offerings to the Lord for the temple as well. They did—tons and tons of gold, silver, bronze, iron, and many precious stones.

David led the assembly in prayer and praise, joyful over the officials' wholehearted giving. Everything that had been done to prepare for the temple, he said, was possible only because everything first had come from God to the people and their king.

Everything we have comes from Him too, and what we do with what He gives us should always be a cause for rejoicing, thankfulness, and praise. Do you need to adjust anything in your use of His gifts today?

Father God, make me generous as you are generous, because I am your child. Thank you for all your gifts and blessings. Amen.

111

Seeking God for the Nation

2 CHRONICLES 3–7

"Then if my people who are called by my name will humble themselves and pray and seek my face and turn from their wicked ways, I will hear from heaven and will forgive their sins and restore their land."—2 Chronicles 7:14

How often do you pray for your country?

After the dedication of the temple, God appeared to Solomon again, promising to hear all the prayers made there, including those made in response to His corrective, attention-getting measures when His people had gone astray. Healing and restoration would come to the nation when the Israelites turned away from sin and turned back to following God again. They were His covenant people—obeying Him brought blessings and prosperity, but turning away from Him led to trouble and distress. As always, God was ready to forgive and restore when His people truly repented.

The nations of the world today don't have the same kind of relationship with God that ancient Israel did, but we can still pray for our country and seek God for our nation. How should we pray? Pray for God to be made known, for the gospel to reach many hearts, for our country's leaders and people to listen to God and turn from sin—these are prayers within the will of God for us, prayers that He will hear and answer.

Dear Lord, who created the nations, help me be faithful in prayer for mine. Amen.

Over All

2 CHRONICLES 10

This turn of events was the will of God, for it fulfilled the LORD's message to Jeroboam son of Nebat through the prophet Ahijah from Shiloh.—2 Chronicles 10:15

While Solomon still reigned, God sent a prophet to tell Jeroboam that he would become king over ten tribes of Israel. Jeroboam fled to Egypt for safety, but after Solomon's death, he returned. Solomon's son Rehoboam was now king, and Jeroboam went to see him along with the leaders of Israel. They asked Rehoboam to lighten the taxes and forced labor that Solomon had imposed on the people. In return, they promised Rehoboam their allegiance.

Rehoboam sought counsel, first from his father's advisors and then from his own—friends he had grown up with. The two groups offered differing advice; Rehoboam chose to listen to his friends. The result? The ten northern tribes of Israel revolted and made Jeroboam their king.

Throughout the Bible we can see that God does use and even direct events for His purposes, although how and why are often hidden from us. We can see, however, that God did provide wisdom for Rehoboam through Solomon's advisors; Rehoboam chose to ignore their advice.

Which generation gave the wise advice isn't the issue. Recognizing God's rule over all His creation and seeking His wisdom for the decisions we make—that's the point. How do you choose your own advice givers? How do you seek God's wisdom?

Dear God, help me gladly seek your wisdom today and every day, trusting in your loving plan for all things, even when I can't fully understand. Amen.

113

Free to Worship

2 CHRONICLES 11

From all the tribes of Israel, those who sincerely wanted to worship the LORD, the God of Israel, followed the Levites to Jerusalem, where they could offer sacrifices to the LORD, the God of their ancestors.—2 Chronicles 11:16

To mobilize Christians to pray for the persecuted church, the Open Doors organization publishes the World Watch List, detailing life in the fifty countries where it's most dangerous to be a Christian.

More than 200 million Christians in those fifty countries experience high levels of persecution, according to the 2018 World Watch List. In some places, shaky governments play up religious nationalism, using the country's majority religion as a unifying prop. Christians then are marginalized and even criminalized.

In ancient Israel, Jeroboam used religious nationalism to unify his kingdom, created by the revolt of the ten northern tribes. But Jeroboam didn't call on an established majority religion. Instead he established his own counterfeit, with pagan shrines, goat and calf idols, and priests appointed from among the people. In his kingdom there would be no reason to go to Jerusalem to sacrifice to God at the temple.

God's priests and Levites and others who wanted to worship the Lord found themselves in the margins. So abandoning their pasturelands and property, they moved south to Judah and Jerusalem. Their freedom to worship God mattered most.

Our freedom to worship God through Christ is a freedom to cherish, and one way to express our gratitude is to pray for our persecuted brothers and sisters around the world.

Heavenly Father, comfort and strengthen persecuted believers everywhere today, and may I be faithful in praying for them. Amen.

114

Bronze for Gold

2 CHRONICLES 12

So King Rehoboam made bronze shields to replace them and assigned these to the commanders of the guard on duty at the entrance to the royal palace.—2 Chronicles 12:10 NIV

When his reign in the southern kingdom was secure, Rehoboam abandoned God's law and led the people to do the same. God allowed King Shishak of Egypt to invade Judah and threaten Jerusalem, but when Rehoboam and the kingdom's leaders repented, God relented—Shishak would not destroy Jerusalem, but the people would become his subjects. The Egyptians ransacked the temple and the palace, taking every treasure, including five hundred gold shields Solomon had made as an ornamental display.

Sometime later, Rehoboam replaced the gold shields with shields of bronze. He kept them in the palace, under guard, bringing them out only when he went to the temple to worship. In the sunlight, they might have glinted a little and, from a distance, seemed to resemble gold.

Trading gold for bronze? Rehoboam wanted to look like he was doing just fine. We do the same thing when we hide hurts behind false smiles and work hard to look as if nothing is wrong.

God is never fooled, of course, but He can help us only when we stop pretending and get real with Him. King David said, "I know, my God, that you examine our hearts and rejoice when you find integrity there" (1 Chronicles 29:17).

Father God, I want to please you with a heart of integrity, willing to always be honest with you. Amen.

115

Finish Well

2 CHRONICLES 14–16

"The eyes of the Lord search the whole earth in order to strengthen those whose hearts are fully committed to him. What a fool you have been!"—2 Chronicles 16:9

Do you have unfinished projects at home, projects that once delighted you but lost their attraction before they were complete?

Like many of the kings before him, Asa began well. He tore down the pagan shrines, sacred pillars, and Asherah poles in Judah. He built and fortified towns throughout the kingdom, and he defeated an Ethiopian attack by calling out for God's help rather than depending on himself. Asa listened to God's prophet and led the people to renew their loyalty to God. He even deposed his grandmother as queen mother because of her idol worship.

But in the thirty-sixth year of his reign, Asa turned to the king of Aram for help against an invasion by the king of Israel. When one of the prophets chastised him, Asa threw the prophet into prison. He also began to oppress some of his own people. A few years later, he developed a serious foot disease and turned only to his physicians, never asking for God's help—and he died.

Asa began well and lived well, but he didn't finish well. We don't know why his heart lost its attraction to following God, but his story reminds us not to let our lives with God end like an unfinished project.

Dear Lord, I want to finish well! May my heart stay fully committed to you and may I always rely on you to strengthen me. Amen.

Compromised

2 CHRONICLES 17–19

> Jehoshaphat enjoyed great riches and high esteem, and he made an alliance with Ahab of Israel by having his son marry Ahab's daughter.—2 Chronicles 18:1

After Asa's death, his son Jehoshaphat became the next king of Judah, and his story echoes his father's.

Jehoshaphat sent out officials with copies of the Book of the Law to teach in all the towns of Judah. He had a strong army, and kings from surrounding nations sent him gifts as tribute. Jehoshaphat also appointed judges for Judah's towns and charged them to make decisions fairly and according to the law of the Lord. During this time, Judah enjoyed great peace.

But Jehoshaphat arranged a marriage between his son and the daughter of Ahab, one of the evil kings of the northern kingdom of Israel. This alliance led Jehoshaphat to visit with Ahab in Israel, where he agreed to join forces with him in battle and listened to the lies of Ahab's prophets (all worshipers of Baal). The military maneuver nearly caused Jehoshaphat his life and brought him a rebuke from God's prophet: "Why should you help the wicked and love those who hate the LORD?" (2 Chronicles 19:2).

Jehoshaphat surely saw his alliance with Ahab by his son's marriage as a small diversion, but it led to big compromise. Is there anything in your life not pleasing to God that you see only as a small diversion from the path of faith? Be careful!

Dear God, point out the small diversions in my life. Lead me away from compromise and back onto your path for me. Amen.

117

The Power of Praise

2 CHRONICLES 20

At the very moment they began to sing and give praise, the LORD caused the armies of Ammon, Moab, and Mount Seir to start fighting among themselves.—2 Chronicles 20:22

As the armies of three nations marched toward Jerusalem, Jehoshaphat responded with faith and wisdom despite his fear. First he pleaded with God for guidance. He ordered the people of Judah to fast, and some of them—men, women, and children—gathered in Jerusalem to seek the Lord's help along with him.

Jehoshaphat prayed before the people, praising God, recounting His promises, and putting complete confidence in Him. God answered immediately, giving a message to one of the men in the crowd: Jehoshaphat was to lead his army out to battle, but they would not have to fight.

In the morning the army set out, and Jehoshaphat appointed men to lead the way, singing praises to God. As they began to sing, God caused the invading armies to begin fighting one another. When Jehoshaphat and the army of Judah reached a lookout point in the desert, all they could see were dead bodies.

Jehoshaphat's complete dependence and trust in God, expressed in prayer and praises, had been rewarded. His plan for facing obstacles and opposition can be ours too. "We have no power to face this vast army that is attacking us. We do not know what to do, but our eyes are on you" (2 Chronicles 20:12 NIV).

Heavenly Father, may I face trouble in my life with the same trust and dependence Jehoshaphat did, praising you all the way! Amen.

Judged

2 CHRONICLES 26

But when he had become powerful, he also became proud, which led to his downfall.—2 Chronicles 26:20

Uzziah became king of Judah when he was just sixteen years old. He sought God and learned how to follow Him from the prophet Zechariah. Uzziah was a builder, a military leader, and a grower, owning fields and vineyards. As long as he depended on God for guidance, God gave him success in all he did. Uzziah's fame spread beyond Judah, and he became extremely powerful.

But one day pride overtook him. He entered the temple and burned incense on the altar there, something only the priests could do. The high priest and eighty other priests went after Uzziah and confronted him. Uzziah responded angrily, and as he raged at them, leprosy broke out suddenly on his forehead. Seeing that, the priests rushed the king out of the temple, and realizing the leprosy was from the Lord, Uzziah didn't fight them. He lived the rest of his life in isolation, alone in his own house.

Only a few times in Scripture is sickness God's judgment; we should not conclude that sickness is a result of sin. People in Jesus' day made that assumption, but when Jesus was asked about a man born blind, He answered that neither the man's sins nor his parents' sins had caused the condition (John 9:1–3). The question we need to ask ourselves is where we might be in danger of letting pride lead us to sin.

Father God, search my heart today and point out anywhere that pride resides. Amen.

119

Tested

2 CHRONICLES 32

God withdrew from Hezekiah in order to test him and to see what was really in his heart.—2 Chronicles 32:31

Hezekiah became king after the death of his father, the wicked King Ahaz. Hezekiah repaired the temple, which Ahaz had shuttered, and he restored temple worship. But like his great-grandfather Uzziah, Hezekiah experienced a problem with pride. God healed Hezekiah of a life-threatening illness, promised him fifteen more years of life, and gave him the miraculous sign of the sundial moving backwards (2 Kings 20). But none of that left Hezekiah filled with thanksgiving and gratitude; instead, the Lord's kindness made him proud.

He did repent, but later when a Babylonian envoy came to Judah to ask about the remarkable events that had occurred, Hezekiah failed God's test of the condition of his heart. Hezekiah welcomed the Babylonians gladly and enjoyed proudly showing them all his personal wealth and the kingdom's temple treasuries. When the envoy had gone, God rebuked Hezekiah through His prophet.

God never leaves us, but have you ever experienced the feeling that He is silent or unresponsive? It could be that God is testing us to show us what's in our hearts, as He did with Hezekiah. God already knows what's there; He doesn't need to be shown, but we often do. He is never truly silent; He is always speaking through His Word. If you feel tested, ask Him to show you your heart.

Dear Lord, thank you for testing my heart to keep me close to you. Thank you for your promise that you are always with me. Amen.

120

Changed

2 CHRONICLES 33

The LORD was moved by his entreaty and listened to his plea; so he brought him back to Jerusalem and to his kingdom.—2 Chronicles 33:13 NIV

Have you heard people say that God could never forgive them because their sins are just too terrible? Have you ever wondered if God really could forgive you?

Hezekiah's son Manasseh became king of Judah when he was just twelve years old. He rejected his father's faith in God and set about undoing Hezekiah's religious reforms. He rivaled and even exceeded the evil of Ahab, king of Israel; he followed Ahab's idolatrous example and also brought astrological worship into Judah. He sacrificed his own children by fire, used witchcraft and sorcery, and consulted mediums and spiritists. He set up pagan altars and an Asherah pole in God's temple, and with the Asherah pole most likely came cult prostitution in the temple as well. Throughout Manasseh's long reign, the people of Judah followed his lead back into idolatry and sin.

No hope for a turnaround, right?

God allowed the Assyrians to capture Manasseh. They put a hook in his nose and took him to Babylon in chains. In Babylon Manasseh humbled himself and turned to God, who saw that his repentance was sincere. God brought Manasseh back to Judah and returned his kingdom. Manasseh's actions to end the idolatrous worship he had promoted earlier proved his turnaround was real.

Manasseh's story shows us clearly that God responds to true repentance. Is true repentance part of your faith story?

Dear God, thank you for your willingness to forgive and restore when we turn to you in complete dependence. Amen.

121

Future Hope

2 CHRONICLES 36

The LORD moved the heart of Cyrus king of Persia to make a proclamation throughout his realm and also to put it in writing.—2 Chronicles 36:22 NIV

Despite the efforts of the good kings of Judah who followed God, the influence of the kings who did evil won out. With compassion, God continued to speak to His people through the prophet Jeremiah, and He began to bring the Babylonians against them. But His warnings were ignored. The last king of Judah was Zedekiah, a puppet king. His reign ended when at last "the wrath of the LORD was aroused against his people and there was no remedy" (2 Chronicles 36:16 NIV). The Babylonians came against Judah; they destroyed Jerusalem and carried those who survived into exile.

The exile lasted seventy years, exactly as the prophet Jeremiah had predicted. During that time, Cyrus of Persia had overtaken the Babylonian empire (exactly as Isaiah had predicted two hundred years earlier). In 538 BC, the first year of Cyrus's reign, God stirred his heart to proclaim that God had appointed him to rebuild the temple in Jerusalem and that the Jews living in any part of the empire were free to return home.

The Jews' future hope remained—God's Word was still true; God was still keeping His promises and working out His plans. The promise of another king from the line of David surely would be kept too. What promises of God are you counting on today?

Heavenly Father, you keep all your promises. May I remember and look forward to the fulfillment of all your promises to me in Christ. Amen.

122

Counted

EZRA 1–2

Now these are the people of the province who came up from the captivity of the exiles.—Ezra 2:1 NIV

Cyrus of Persia issued a proclamation allowing the Jews to return to Judah and to rebuild the temple there. God had commanded this, and Cyrus ordered his own people to assist the rebuilding effort with gifts of silver and gold, goods and livestock, and freewill offerings. Cyrus himself returned all the valuable objects taken from the temple at the time Jerusalem fell. Each dish, pan, bowl, or other article was counted and the number of pieces recorded.

Not all the Jews chose to leave the land of their exile, but those whose hearts had been stirred by God responded. It would have been important to ensure that those returning to Judah had a legal right to return to the ancestral lands. The heads of families, priests and Levites, musicians, gatekeepers, and temple servants who returned were all counted and their names recorded. Each one mattered.

As in other lists and genealogies in the Bible, the names and numbers hold significance. In these opening chapters of the book of Ezra, we can see that God is interested in the large and small details of our lives.

Are there problems you don't pray about because you think they're too small for God to care about? Jesus said He knows the number of hairs on your head and sees each tiny sparrow that falls. You can have confidence He cares about everything that concerns you.

Father God, may I learn to trust your care in the big and small problems—and joys—of my life. Amen.

123

Past and Future Tense

EZRA 3

But many of the older priests and Levites and family heads, who had seen the former temple, wept aloud.—Ezra 3:12 NIV

Before beginning work on the temple, the returned exiles built a new altar within the temple site. Although they feared the people living around them, they began offering the daily sacrifices and sacrifices for the sacred festivals as required by the law of Moses.

Then work on the temple got underway, under the leadership of Zerubbabel. When the foundation had been laid, the people celebrated. Priests and Levites with trumpets and cymbals took their places as King David had prescribed. They sang praises with thanksgiving for God's goodness to Israel, and all the people gave a great shout of praise to God.

Shouts of joy mingled with sounds of weeping, however. Some of the older priests, Levites, and family heads remembered the glory of Solomon's temple, and they wept because of all that had been lost. This new temple could never equal the one the Babylonians had destroyed.

Perhaps like me, you identify with the crying on that day. We all experience losses over time; remembering what's gone from our lives can quickly trigger tears. But just as joy and weeping mingled in the sound of the celebration when the temple foundation was laid, we have reason to look forward whenever we look back. God will never leave us, and He is working out His good plans for our lives.

Dear Lord, you are so good to me! In the losses of my life, I see how you restore and make new. Keep me looking forward, please. Amen.

Rebuilding the Temple

EZRA 4–6

> They completed the Temple as they had been commanded by the God of Israel and by Cyrus, Darius, and Artaxerxes, emperors of Persia.
> —Ezra 6:14 GNT

Enemies of the people of Judah opposed the rebuilding of the temple and tried to stop the work soon after it began.

Outsiders who had been brought into Judah during the exile tried to join the work to sabotage it. They paid bribes to those willing to frighten and discourage the builders. For a period of about fifteen years, the work stopped. (Similar opposition also arose later, during the reigns of the Persian kings Xerxes and Artaxerxes.)

Urged by God's prophets Haggai and Zechariah, the Jews resumed building early in the reign of King Darius of Persia. This time the governor of the region and his associates challenged the work, but a search of the royal records turned up the original decree made by Cyrus. King Darius then gave his full support to the rebuilding. He ordered that the temple be completed, and he reaffirmed all the financial and material resources Cyrus had promised for the project.

The temple was completed early in 515 BC. The following month the people of Judah celebrated by observing Passover with great rejoicing. God had caused the kings of the lands of their captivity to show them favor and help them rebuild His temple. God's purposes can't be stopped—then or now.

Dear God, your purposes always prevail! May I always trust your purposes for my life and follow you through every time of waiting and uncertainty. Amen.

125

Teacher of the Word

EZRA 7

This was because Ezra had determined to study and obey the Law of the Lord and to teach those decrees and regulations to the people of Israel.—Ezra 7:10

Midway through the book that bears his name, Ezra appears. Ezra was a priest from the line of Aaron, Moses' brother, and he was a scribe who copied, studied, and taught God's law. About sixty years after the temple had been completed, Ezra led a second group of exiles back to Judah. He brought with him a letter from King Artaxerxes with specific instructions for the governor and officials of Judah, which was still a province of the Persian empire. They were to allow and support the worship of God in Judah.

Ezra praised God for His favor, which Ezra said God showed to him because of his dedication to knowing, following, and teaching God's instructions. What can we learn from Ezra's choices?

At some point, Ezra made a decision to *study* the law of the Lord. We can't know what God says without giving His Word our attention over time.

Ezra also determined to *obey* God's law. Knowing what the Word says and submitting ourselves to it are not the same thing—but both are needed.

And Ezra made it his goal to *teach* God's instructions to His people. We're not all teachers in a formal sense, but if you have children, grandchildren, friends, or neighbors, you are teaching as you interact with them.

Deciding. Studying. Obeying. Teaching. Where do you need to improve? How can Ezra's approach to God's Word be a help and inspiration to you today?

Heavenly Father, help me faithfully study, obey, and share your precious life-giving, life-changing Word. Amen.

126

Trust His Care

EZRA 8

So we fasted and prayed for God to protect us, and he answered our prayers.—Ezra 8:23 GNT

Ezra had told King Artaxerxes, "Our God's hand of protection is on all who worship him, but his fierce anger rages against those who abandon him" (Ezra 8:22). So he didn't ask the king to provide security for himself and the exiles he was leading back to Judah—he would have felt ashamed to ask for that. But the journey held dangers—especially robbers and people opposed to Judah's rebirth.

Ezra gathered his company and ordered everyone to fast and humble themselves before God. They prayed for safe travel and for God to protect them, their children, and their goods as they traveled. And despite the nine-hundred-mile journey and the vast amount of gold, silver, and bronze they carried, the company arrived safely in Judah after four months. "The gracious hand of our God protected us and saved us from enemies and bandits along the way" (Ezra 8:31).

Soldiers and horsemen for security might have been prudent, but Ezra cared more about God's reputation. He knew God was able to protect the travelers, and he wanted others to know it too. So he decided to simply ask and trust, and God provided.

How easily do you trust God more than you trust your own resources? How often is asking God for help your first thought, rather than relying on yourself? How much do you care about what your actions tell others about our God? We all can learn a lot from Ezra's example!

Father God, may others see in me a testimony to who you are—your power, faithfulness, and love. Amen.

127

Taking Sin Seriously

EZRA 9–10

"LORD, the God of Israel, you are righteous! We are left this day as a remnant. Here we are before you in our guilt, though because of it not one of us can stand in your presence."—Ezra 9:15 NIV

The Jewish leaders confronted Ezra with a situation he had never expected: many of the exiles who had returned earlier—even some of the priests and Levites—had married foreign wives. Intermarriage was leading to the same practices of idol worship that God had judged so severely with the destruction of Jerusalem and the exile in Babylon.

Hearing this news, Ezra mourned. How could such a thing have happened, and what would God do now? Others in the community who felt the same distress gathered with Ezra, and he led them in prayer, confessing the sin of the people as if it were his own.

A short time later, all the exiles gathered in Jerusalem in the rain and Ezra confronted them. They recognized the seriousness of their sin and resolved to separate from their pagan wives, which they did over a three-month period, city by city.

Sometimes taking sin seriously requires difficult action, but true repentance follows through. What hard thing have you done to align yourself with what God desires? What action do you need to take?

Dear Lord, thank you for the forgiveness I have in Jesus, and may my repentance always be true. Amen.

Pray, Plan, Act

NEHEMIAH 1–7

"O Lord, please hear my prayer! . . . Please grant me success today by making the king favorable to me."—Nehemiah 1:11

Before Nehemiah became governor of Judah, he was cupbearer to King Artaxerxes in Persia. Upon learning that Jerusalem was unprotected—the city's walls and gates had yet to be restored—Nehemiah turned immediately to heartfelt prayer with fasting. Four months later, when the king's inquiry gave him an opportunity to present his plan, he was ready.

Artaxerxes approved Nehemiah's request for permission to travel to Jerusalem and for timber for rebuilding. But the army officers and horsemen the king sent with Nehemiah didn't prevent opposition from those living in Judah who disliked the Jews.

Nehemiah mobilized the Jewish leaders to begin rebuilding the wall and all its gates, with family groups and groups of priests and Levites each working on specific sections. When the wall was half its full height, the opposition became intense. Nehemiah prayed, stationed guards, encouraged the workers, and put an emergency plan in place. He foiled a plot intended to intimidate the Jews.

The builders continued working with their weapons strapped on, and they completed the wall in just fifty-two days in 443 BC. For the dedication of the wall, Nehemiah organized two large choirs to praise God from the top of the wall and at the temple (Nehemiah 12:27–43).

Are you a planner or more of a take-it-as-it-comes type? Either way, Nehemiah's prayer-before-action model is one we all can admire, learn from, and follow.

Dear God, prompt me to pray throughout every day as I confront the present and plan for the future. Amen.

129

The Joy of the Lord

NEHEMIAH 8–13

So the people went away to eat and drink at a festive meal, to share gifts of food, and to celebrate with great joy because they had heard God's words and understood them.—Nehemiah 8:12

Soon after the completion of Jerusalem's wall, the people gathered and Ezra read to them from the Book of the Law. Levites throughout the crowd also read to the people and helped them understand what was read.

The people praised God for His Word, and they also wept as they realized they had not obeyed it. But Nehemiah encouraged them: "This is a sacred day before our Lord. Don't be dejected and sad, for the joy of the Lord is your strength!" (Nehemiah 8:10).

The following day, leaders of the community met with Ezra to look at the Book of the Law in more detail. They discovered the instructions Moses had given about the Feast of Shelters to be celebrated that very month each year, and they joyfully obeyed. They read from the law throughout the festival and at the solemn assembly that followed—a time of confession, repentance, and praise.

Hearing God's Word brings both conviction and joy and leads to renewal and change in our lives if we are seeking to understand and obey it. Does this describe how you approach the Bible? Do you need to listen more often, determine to understand, or take action to obey God's Word?

Heavenly Father, your Word holds such blessings—I don't want to miss out! Give me grace to read, study, and obey with a heart that pleases you. Amen.

130

For Such a Time

THE BOOK OF ESTHER

"Who knows if perhaps you were made queen for just such a time as this?"—Esther 4:14

The events of the book of Esther took place in the capital of the Persian empire about thirty years before Nehemiah traveled to Jerusalem. The book never mentions God even once, but He certainly is not absent.

Many of the Jewish exiles had not returned to Judah. Esther's relative Mordecai, who raised her, had advised Esther to keep her heritage hidden, and when King Xerxes chose Esther as his queen, she continued to do so. The king's prime minister, Haman, hated the Jews and especially Mordecai. Haman convinced the king to pass a law giving everyone throughout the empire the right to slaughter their Jewish neighbors on a particular future day. The edict included the Jews in Judah—and of course it included Esther.

Mordecai asked Esther to consider whether God had placed her in her royal position so she could be the one to save her people. Esther fasted for three days, and then she approached the king on his throne without an invitation—which could have resulted in her death—and executed a plan to make her predicament known. The Jewish people were not killed, and they still celebrate Purim as a reminder that God's plans can't be thwarted.

Could it be that God has also gifted you and placed you where your service is needed? You might feel insignificant, but God isn't absent. He's working, and you might be exactly where you need to be, exactly where you belong.

Father God, whether the task is large or small, public or private, help me be and do all that you've planned for me. Amen.

Encountering
GOD'S HEART
for YOU
in the
OLD TESTAMENT

The Books of Poetry and Wisdom

Job's Suffering

JOB 1–2

In all of this, Job did not sin by blaming God.—Job 1:22

The book of Job appears near the middle of the Bible, at the start of the section known as wisdom literature, but Job probably lived near the time of Abraham. His story shows us that from earliest times, human beings have struggled with understanding why bad things happen, and especially why bad things happen to good people.

Job lived a good and prosperous life with great integrity, respecting God and staying away from evil. God allowed Satan to test Job's devotion to Him by taking away his wealth, his children, and his health in a series of catastrophic events. The conversations between God and Satan in the book's opening chapters show us clearly that Satan has no power that God does not allow. Satan's power is limited. Satan is God's enemy, but he is not the opposite of God—they are not equals, one bad and one good.

Of course, Job's wife suffered too. She didn't have the same confidence in God that Job did, and she encouraged her husband to give up, to "curse God and die" (Job 2:9). Job refused to blame God for the calamities he experienced, but that would not keep him from wanting to know why they had occurred—a state of mind and heart we all surely understand.

Dear Lord, I also have questions when tragedies break in on life. Help me learn along with Job the answers you have for me. Amen.

132

Job's Struggle

JOB 3–37

"What miserable comforters you are! . . . If it were me, I would encourage you. I would try to take away your grief."—Job 16:2, 5

Do you know someone who always has an answer for every problem? Job did too.

Three friends came to mourn with Job, and for a week they sat silently, simply offering the support of their presence. But then . . . they started talking. Surely Job had sinned and God was punishing him.

Job insisted on his innocence, but he wanted God to answer his questions: Why had these terrible things happened? Why was he suffering, yet the wicked so often went unpunished?

Job's friends stuck to their theory and accused Job of arrogance. Job tried to reconcile his suffering with what he knew to be true about himself and about God. He gives us amazing glimpses of faith and hope expressed two thousand years before Jesus came: "I know that my Redeemer lives, and he will stand upon the earth at last. And after my body has decayed, yet in my body I will see God!" (Job 19:25–26).

Job's conversations with his friends brought him no comfort. He proclaimed his innocence again and then asked God for answers one more time: "Let the Almighty answer me. Let my accuser write out the charges against me" (Job 31:35). But would he hear from God?

Dear God, let me learn from the example of Job's friends. Show me how to truly comfort others in distress. Amen.

133

God's Answer

JOB 38–42

"Where were you when I laid the foundations of the earth? Tell me, if you know so much."—Job 38:4

God wasn't happy with Job's friends because they misrepresented him (Job 42:7). Job at least had spoken about God accurately. And Job's questions? God never answered them directly—in fact, He had questions for Job that revealed His immeasurable power and wisdom throughout all creation. Job realized the foolishness and futility of his demands for God to explain himself.

But Job received something better than answers from God—the presence of God himself and a deeper, more intimate relationship with Him. "I was talking about things I knew nothing about, things far too wonderful for me," Job said. "I had only heard about you before, but now I have seen you with my own eyes. I take back everything I said, and I sit in dust and ashes to show my repentance" (Job 42:3, 5–6).

God restored Job's health and fortune and blessed him with more children and a long, full life. To move forward is always better than living in the past, but future blessings don't minimize or discount the suffering that preceded them. God never faulted Job for wanting to know why he suffered, only for demanding an explanation. In His wisdom and glory, God himself is the only answer we really need.

Heavenly Father, how I need to learn to trust you! Please help me. Thank you for your presence with me in all my suffering. Amen.

134

Walk This Way

PSALM 1

> Blessed is the man who walks not in the counsel of the wicked, nor stands in the way of sinners, nor sits in the seat of scoffers; but his delight is in the law of the LORD, and on his law he meditates day and night.—Psalm 1:1–2 ESV

I have overseen the demise of numerous houseplants. Yellow leaves, brown leaves, falling leaves, no leaves—I just don't seem to be able to bless my plants with the right combination of whatever it is they need to be happy and grow.

Fortunately, if you and I want to be blessed in life—joyful, contented, fulfilled—the opening psalm of the book of Psalms tells us exactly what we need: thoughts centered on God's Word with great delight.

In the Bible, *meditation* means to fill our minds with God's Word by reading it, studying it, and thinking about it at every opportunity. "The law of the LORD is perfect, reviving the soul; the testimony of the LORD is sure, making wise the simple; the precepts of the LORD are right, rejoicing the heart; the commandment of the LORD is pure, enlightening the eyes" (Psalm 19:7–8 ESV). God's Word, the Bible, has what we need to be fruitful and not wither (Psalm 1:3).

What thoughts fill your days? We have many more opportunities and much more time available to meditate on God's Word than we think we do. Why not take inventory for a few days and see?

Father God, help me evaluate what I think about. Show me how to delight in your Word every day and night so I can walk in your ways. Amen.

Majesty

PSALM 8

O LORD, our Lord, how majestic is your name in all the earth!—Psalm 8:1 ESV

The psalms are poems and songs used in worship in ancient Israel, and all but 34 of the 150 psalms include a notation about musical accompaniment. One of my fondest memories is the morning my daughter's ballet teacher visited our church and danced as the choir sang an anthem based on Psalm 8. In a flowing gown that swirled around her, Janet illuminated the words of the psalm with stunning grace and beauty. The glorious music and dance hushed and humbled every worshiper.

God's creation majesty also humbles us. King David wrote Psalm 8, perhaps reflecting on the long nights he spent outside as a shepherd, with a front-row seat to the glory of the heavens. How could the One who created such a vast display give a thought to human beings?

Yet He does. God gives us glory and honor and a high place in creation, with stewardship and rule over all other creatures on earth. We can only humbly respond as Psalm 8 ends, with repeated praise.

Dear Lord, thank you for the glory and majesty of your creation and my place in it. Help me live as you created me to live. Amen.

136

Don't Be Foolish

PSALM 14

The fool says in his heart, "There is no God."—Psalm 14:1 ESV

When you hear the word *fool*, do you think first of a medieval court jester dressed in a brightly colored diamond-patterned tunic plus tights and a silly hat?

The Bible has a different definition: A fool is someone who lives with no regard for God.

A fool might have decided there is no God or simply decided to ignore the question of His existence. Either way, being a fool is a matter of the heart, and hearts are revealed in a person's actions. Listen carefully to today's musicians, actors, writers, entertainers, journalists, academics, athletes, and politicians. Scoffers—fools—abound.

It's easy to spot foolish behavior in other people but harder to acknowledge it in ourselves. We may not *be* fools, but we can *act* like fools at times. Whenever we choose to disregard and disobey God, we're crossing over into fools' territory. Are you finding yourself there today? Don't become a resident; turn around and get out!

Dear God, so much of the world around me scoffs and disregards you; it hurts my heart to hear and see what they do. Keep me from acting foolishly, and thank you for your forgiveness for the foolish things I have done. Amen.

Forsaken

PSALM 22

My God, my God, why have you forsaken me?—Psalm 22:1 ESV

Some of the psalms are called messianic psalms because they tell about a coming deliverer sent by God. *Messiah* comes from the Hebrew for "anointed one" or "chosen one." (*Christ* is the Greek equivalent.) Moses and the Old Testament prophets wrote of the deliverer God would send to redeem and rescue Israel.

Looking back at the messianic psalms after Jesus' death and resurrection, we see clearly they are about Him. David knew nothing of crucifixion, yet he portrayed Jesus' death on the cross with detailed accuracy. Did David know, as he wrote this psalm about a crisis in his own life, that he also was predicting the agony of Jesus' death and His joyful anticipation of its results? We're not told.

Bearing the sin and guilt of the world on the cross, Jesus felt God had forsaken Him, yet He called out to His Father for help because He knew God's great goodness and love. This psalm tells us that God saw Jesus' suffering and heard His cry. Jesus knew that in the future He would rejoice along with His forever brothers and sisters—all those who accept Him as Savior.

How amazing that words written a thousand years before the crucifixion give us such a poignant, piercing look at what Jesus experienced physically and emotionally—and the fact that He was thinking of you and me.

Heavenly Father, as Jesus looked forward, your Word helps us look back. Thank you for the marvelous gift of Jesus. Amen.

138

Shepherd Song

PSALM 23

The LORD is my shepherd; I shall not want.—Psalm 23:1 ESV

I remember puzzling over this verse as a child. Why would anyone say "I don't want God"? Many years later, I finally caught on. "I shall not want" means "I have everything I need" or "I lack nothing," as more modern translations of this famous psalm by King David now have it.

Throughout Old Testament times, flocks represented wealth. Sheep owners entrusted the care of their flocks to shepherds, who then had complete responsibility for the flock's well-being. Caring for his family's flock, David learned all about sheep.

Sheep can't take care of themselves. Without someone looking after them, they will drink contaminated water, eat pasture grass down to bare nubs, and become prey for wild animals. Sheep are easily agitated, frightened, and distracted. Prone to wander, they're unable to find their way back to the flock if they wander off. Sheep can get into serious trouble quickly.

Does this sound like anyone you know? Do you share any sheep-like traits? I know I do. As a shepherd, David saw to it that his hapless sheep had everything they needed. The rest of Psalm 23 shows us how God as our shepherd provides everything we need.

Are you one of the Lord's sheep? Stay close to the Shepherd.

Father God, my Shepherd, I'm putting my trust in you today, watching for where you lead, following and depending on you. Amen.

Goodness and Mercy

PSALM 23

> Surely goodness and mercy shall follow me all the days of my life: and I will dwell in the house of the LORD for ever.—Psalm 23:6 KJV

Like all former first ladies of the United States, Barbara Bush had a Secret Service detail. The agents chose Tranquility for her code name because of her calm and caring demeanor. She treated them like family, and they loved and respected her. They accompanied her on private and public outings and kept watch outside the Bush home. When Barbara died at age ninety-two, some of the agents had guarded her for decades—and they refused to leave her side until their job was done.

So as her casket lay in St. Martin's Episcopal Church in Houston, Texas, before and after the crowds of mourners came to pay their respects, Secret Service agents stood on each side of her casket in the darkened church. The next day, after the funeral service, two agents rode in the hearse in the family's motorcade from Houston to College Station, Texas, to a private family burial site behind the George H. W. Bush Library. What an image of being followed through life and beyond by loving, watchful, protective care!

David experienced God's loving care daily, and confidently expected it to follow him throughout his life and into a forever future with the Lord. What joy that we can read David's song today with the same confident hope because of Jesus!

Dear Lord, thank you for loving me like a good shepherd, every day and into my forever future with you. Amen.

140

Set Free

PSALM 32

Oh, what joy for those whose disobedience is forgiven, whose sin is put out of sight!—Psalm 32:1

Children sometimes try to hide their misdeeds, thinking all is well if they're not caught. Sadly, adults often act like children and live by a similar plan. King David tried this, but he learned it's a plan that doesn't work.

Undisclosed sin and our sense of guilt create physical as well as emotional distress. So David turned to God and confessed his sin—and God forgave him. He was set free! Not only did David's guilty *feelings* lift, he realized God had put away his guilt. His record was clean.

God is too kind to leave us to self-destruction with no intervention. The distress we feel when we keep sin and guilt hidden is God's "hand of discipline" (Psalm 32:4), prodding us to turn to Him and confess. He is eager to forgive and surround us with victory songs! That's why David encourages the godly to pray to God before judgment comes.

Receiving God's forgiveness should lead to rejoicing. David even invites us to shout for joy. Are you shouting today?

Dear God, today I will shout my praise and thanks for your forgiveness, so willingly extended to me when I confess to you in faith. Amen.

Delight in the Lord

PSALM 37

Delight yourself in the LORD, and he will give you the desires of your heart.—Psalm 37:4 ESV

If you've ever tried to change your eating habits, you know how difficult it can be. If you've never cared much for vegetables, for example, you'll need to give yourself time to learn to love them. But put in the effort, try some new recipes . . . and one day you're likely to find yourself preferring the salad and grilled veggies at a cookout over the hot dogs and the mac and cheese.

In a similar way, when we learn to delight in God and in living our lives as He directs, what we desire in life begins to change. As we gladly seek God and His ways, the desires of our hearts become what God cares about more than what had been important to us previously.

Are you frustrated by the prosperity and well-being of those who choose sinful actions instead of God? Are you even envious of those who do wrong? In this psalm written by an older King David, God says stop. Don't fret. The wicked—those opposed to God—will disappear. The godly—those who choose to delight in God—will experience great blessings. Stay on God's path and trust Him to care for you. Make Him your delight, and your desires will be granted.

Heavenly Father, I have fretted about the wicked and envied them too. Forgive me. Teach me how to delight more and more in you. Amen.

142

Desperate for God

PSALM 42

> Why are you cast down, O my soul, and why are you in turmoil within me? Hope in God; for I shall again praise him, my salvation and my God.—Psalm 42:5–6 ESV

During an exercise class, a friend confided she was feeling depressed. "I think I know why," she said, naming some life challenges. Then she added, "But I've been reminding myself that God still loves me." Like the temple musicians who wrote this psalm, my friend chose to remind herself of God's truth when she felt down.

Deep discouragement and depression are more than simply feeling down, of course. The speaker in the psalm feels overwhelmed with sorrow, isolated, and far from God. "Just have more faith" or "Just pray and read the Bible more" are never the right answer to emotional distress. Sometimes we need someone to listen, sometimes we need medical intervention. Always, we need God.

But what if it feels to us that God cannot be found? Then we must do what the psalmist did—challenge our thinking and remind ourselves of the truth we know. "My soul is cast down within me; therefore I remember you. . . . Deep calls to deep. . . . By day the LORD commands his steadfast love, and at night his song is with me, a prayer to the God of my life" (Psalm 42:6–8 ESV).

Have you been feeling down, discouraged, or depressed? Hope in God and remind yourself of truth. You will praise Him again!

Father God, when I can't feel you with me, still I know you are here. Cause me to remember your truth and keep my hope in you. Amen.

Be Still

PSALM 46

"Be still, and know that I am God. I will be exalted among the nations, I will be exalted in the earth!"—Psalm 46:10 ESV

Hurricanes, volcanoes, blizzards, floods. Terrorism. Mass shootings. War. Immorality and turning away from God. Not the kind of world we mamas and grandmas want our children and grandchildren growing up in. We have reason to fear for them.

But the psalmist says, "God is our refuge and strength, a very present help in trouble. Therefore we will not fear though the earth gives way" (Psalm 46:1–2 ESV). Do you have this kind of fearless confidence in God today? No matter the state of the world, God reigns. He's in control. Nations and kingdoms come and go. He is a safe place for us, a fortress, a help.

And in the end, all the earth will exalt Him. In Psalm 46:10 God speaks to the nations. "Be still" also translates as "Cease striving" (NASB). Another translation puts the verse this way: "'Stop fighting,' he says, 'and know that I am God, supreme among the nations, supreme over the world'" (GNT). This is the One we trust and worship.

With God as our fortress, we can indeed be unafraid in the face of any trouble.

Dear Lord, forgive my fear. Help me put my trust in you and keep it there. Amen.

144

A Clean Heart

PSALM 51

Create in me a clean heart, O God, and renew a right spirit within me.—Psalm 51:10 ESV

Some of the psalms include a notation telling us what event prompted the author to write it. This psalm expresses King David's repentance and desire for God's forgiveness after his sin with Bathsheba and the murder of her husband, Uriah (2 Samuel 11). David understood his sin was rebellion against God, and he felt haunted by what he had done. But David hadn't confessed his sin until God sent the prophet Nathan to confront him.

God's law for Israel, given by Moses, included blood sacrifices to deal with sin, but David realized what God wanted more was the heart of the person making the sacrifice. "The sacrifice you desire is a broken spirit. You will not reject a broken and repentant heart, O God" (Psalm 51:17). David offered God his own contrite heart and asked God to make it new, clean, and right.

God himself made the final blood sacrifice for sin through the death of His Son, Jesus. The sacrifice left for us to offer is the same one David made—a heart truly sorry for sinning against God and a desire to go forward with a new, right spirit.

Dear God, I'm not always aware that my sins are rebellion against you, and I take your forgiveness too lightly. Create in me a clean heart and a right spirit! Amen.

Tears in a Bottle

PSALM 56

> You keep track of all my sorrows. You have collected all my tears in your bottle.—Psalm 56:8

Stop crying, right now!" Confronted with an upset and out-of-control child, haven't we all said it, with great agitation ourselves? But we only upset the child even more.

That's why I passed along a meme I found with ideas for better things to say instead, including, "It's OK to be sad," "I'm here with you," "Tell me about it," "I'll help you work it out," and my favorite, "I'll stay close so you can find me when you're ready."

Then my friend Linda commented, "I think God says the same things to us when we're upset."

She's right. We sometimes think God's too busy with big things to be bothered with what's concerning us, or we're sure that He just doesn't care. But that's not what Scripture says. He sees. He notices. He's aware. He cares! He knows us intimately, and He wants us to call on Him for help.

When we do, David says, our enemies begin their retreat. Our rescue has begun. We remember that God is *for* us, and we can walk hand-in-hand with Him once again.

Rather than telling us to stop crying, God tells us to cry out to Him. What sorrow do you need to take to Him today?

> *Heavenly Father, thank you for your constant love and this reminder of how much you care. May I always bring the concerns that cause my tears to you! You are waiting for me to come. Amen.*

146

All the Nations

PSALM 67

May God be gracious to us and bless us and make his face shine on us—so that your ways may be known on earth, your salvation among all nations.—Psalm 67:1–2 NIV

I walked through the large hall at a missions convention, talking with people waiting to hear a speaker. "Do you know any parents of missionaries?" I asked. "We want to invite them to a special event tomorrow."

Most people looked puzzled. "Parents of missionaries? I don't think so." But then one woman said, "Yes, me!" and her eyes filled with tears.

Moms (and dads!) of missionaries are some of the bravest people I know. They miss having family together for holidays, birthdays, weddings, and funerals. Their grandchildren grow up in faraway places and seldom visit Grandma's house.

These moms often grieve, but not for lack of faith. They grieve the separations, the distances, the fears. But they persevere, put their confidence in God, and build and keep continent-spanning connections. They learn about different cultures. They support and encourage their families on the field. If they have the means to travel, they visit.

They do all these things because they know that just as Israel was a blessing to the world by making God known, so is the church—and that's you and me. Whether we go or send and support, together we have a task to fulfill.

Father God, thank you for those who go to make you known, and thank you for those who send and support. Show me how I can serve. Amen.

147

A Family for the Lonely

PSALM 68

God sets the lonely in families, he leads out the prisoners with singing.—Psalm 68:6 NIV

After a sermon about acting justly toward those who often feel sidelined by others, a friend said quietly, "Not everyone marginalized is poor." We counted several in our church with special needs or mental illness whom others tend to overlook.

In the midst of this psalm about God's power are two verses about His provision for His children—of all ages—who are lonely. Whatever the reason for their loneliness, He sees and He cares, and He powerfully steps in to help—"a father to the fatherless, a defender of widows" (Psalm 68:5 NIV). He also places lonely people in families and groups of friends-like-family. Feeling accepted and connected to safe people is a healing, freeing experience.

The church around the world is a family too—the family of God. Sisters and brothers in Christ fill every local church. So we need to ask ourselves: Who are the lonely ones God has set in our church families, and how are we doing caring for them? Do you know?

Dear Lord, open my eyes to those who are lonely and the ways I might help and care. Amen.

148

Growing Older

PSALM 71

> So even to old age and gray hairs, O God, do not forsake me, until I proclaim your might to another generation, your power to all those to come.—Psalm 71:18 ESV

A century ago, American businessman-turned-poet Samuel Ullman wrote "Years may wrinkle the skin, but to give up enthusiasm wrinkles the soul." Psalm 71 encourages us to never give up our enthusiasm for making God known, especially to the generations behind us.

Aging sometimes shocks us. We don't truly expect to grow old, despite the inevitability. Suddenly, it seems, unwanted changes arrive. And yet . . .

Years spent living with and for God have taught us well. God is our refuge, protector, helper, and hope. We have reason upon reason to praise Him. "I constantly tell others about the wonderful things you do" (Psalm 71:17).

So if you find yourself "suddenly" growing older, pray with the psalmist to hang on to your enthusiasm for the Lord and continue serving Him. And if you are young, decide to live each day with God so that in years to come you can say, "My life is an example to many, because you have been my strength and protection. That is why I can never stop praising you" (Psalm 71:7–8).

Dear God, make me a sweet example to the next generation of living with faith in you, today and every day, even as I grow older. Amen.

Bitter

PSALM 73

Then I realized my heart was bitter, and I was all torn up inside.—Psalm 73:21

I'm sure you've asked yourself why it is that people who do evil so often seem to prosper. The author of Psalm 73, named Asaph, wondered too.

Asaph, from the tribe of Levi, sang in the choirs celebrating the return of the ark of the covenant to Jerusalem and later at the dedication of the temple. King David appointed him to serve as a choir director. Asaph loved God and set his heart to follow and obey Him, but anger and frustration over the easy lives and the influence of the wicked almost caused him to slip away. What good was it to lead a life of moral purity, he asked—but only secretly.

Asaph tried to figure out why the wicked prosper, but no answers came. Then at the temple he finally understood the destiny of those who ignore God, and at the same time he realized what his envy and bitterness were doing to him. Asaph confessed his sin to God, and this psalm records the joy that followed: "Yet I still belong to you; you hold my right hand. You guide me with your counsel, leading me to a glorious destiny" (Psalm 73:23–24).

God guides and counsels you as well. Trust God to deal with those who reject Him, and trust Him to take care of you.

Heavenly Father, I am following you, yet I experience trouble. Sometimes I do envy those who reject you but have seemingly carefree lives. Forgive me. Keep me focused on your goodness to me today. Amen.

150

Generation to Generation

PSALM 78

> We will not hide these truths from our children; we will tell the next generation about the glorious deeds of the LORD, about his power and his mighty wonders.—Psalm 78:4

Remember the time that . . ."

"When you were little . . ."

"When Mommy was your age . . ."

Children love hearing stories, especially family stories and stories that include them. Even adult children enjoy reminiscing about family adventures when they were growing up. But there's no better story to tell children of any age than the story of God's relationship with His people and His plan for the whole world.

Psalm 78 recounts the history of God's early dealings with Israel. He brought the people out of Egypt and cared for them in the wilderness with many miracles, but they rebelled. Later, in the Promised Land, they continued their disobedience throughout the time of the judges, until the Philistines captured the ark of the covenant and many Israelite lives were lost. Yet God had not abandoned His people. He sent David, a good and upright king, to rule and shepherd them.

The generation that hadn't experienced these things needed to hear these truths. They needed to know God's law and learn from their ancestors not to be disobedient. Hearing about God's power, wonders, and care should lead each generation to give their hearts to God.

Our children and grandchildren need to hear this story too—and the continuation of the story with the Good News of Jesus. Do the children in your life know the story and their place in it?

Father God, my children and grandchildren need you. Help me find ways to tell them your story today. Amen.

Pilgrimage

PSALM 84

Blessed are those whose strength is in you, whose hearts are set on pilgrimage.—Psalm 84:5 NIV

My friend Lena recently made a three-week road trip from Kentucky to the West Coast and back again. One reason for the trip was to search for her great-uncle's homestead in the desert of northern New Mexico. She climbed to the top of Moro Rock, hugged the trees of Yosemite, painted a view of Half Dome, stood on the Pacific shore at Carmel, visited relatives she'd never met, and drove through canyons and over mountains before returning home. She echoed the thoughts of her friend Tammy, who traveled with her and said, "I feel like more of an American now."

Three times each year God's people traveled from their homes to Jerusalem to worship God at the temple and celebrate the three great festivals—Passover, Harvest, and Shelters. To make the trip by foot or wagon required stamina, determination, and great desire to experience the presence of God in His holy courts. A pilgrimage to Jerusalem rewarded these travelers with a renewed and growing sense of their place as the people of God.

"A single day in your courts is better than a thousand anywhere else!" (Psalm 84:10). Do you desire God's presence and look forward to heaven? Our daily choices are *our* pilgrimage, making us stronger and more sure of our destination, and the reward waiting for us is great.

Dear Lord, give me strength for my pilgrimage today and every day; show me how to keep my focus and desire on you. Amen.

152

Make It Count

PSALM 90

Teach us to number our days, that we may gain a heart of wisdom.—Psalm 90:12 NIV

This psalm is a prayer of Moses, making it the oldest of the psalms. Moses was eighty when God called him at the burning bush to lead His people out of Egypt, and he served God another forty years before he died.

Despite his exceptionally long life, Moses realized the brevity of our human existence compared to the unchanging, eternal nature of God. And because life is so short, we need to "number our days," to understand we are here for just a short while and to make each day count. That means acknowledging our relationship to God as our Creator, being sustained by His love, and learning to live for Him.

The psalm ends with a request for God to "establish the work of our hands" (Psalm 90:17). He may care more about the time we spend talking with a co-worker, listening to the heart of our spouse, or tending a sick child than the hours we labor to acquire more and better material possessions. What is the work of your hands today?

Dear God, I have wasted too much time on things that won't matter in eternity. Teach me how to make my days count and establish the work of my hands. Amen.

Let God

PSALM 94

O God who avenges, shine forth. Rise up, Judge of the earth; pay back to the proud what they deserve.—Psalm 94:1–2 NIV

When our oldest daughter was five, my husband and I told her it would be okay to punch back at the young neighborhood bully who wouldn't stop pestering her. She did, and he ran out of the backyard crying and never bothered her again. Not long after this, a co-worker told how she was handling a similar situation. She and her first-grade twin sons were praying for the classmate who was daily giving the twins a lot of trouble.

Ouch! Even though "paying people back" sometimes works, it's never right. There's a better way. Psalms like this one look to God to take action against the wicked rather than us taking on this task ourselves. At the time God decides, those who reject God and His ways will face accountability and punishment.

Are you struggling with wanting to pay someone back for hurting you or others? Like the psalmist, tell God how you feel, then leave the outcome up to Him.

Heavenly Father, sometimes I want to be judge, jury, and prison warden when I'm faced with those who do evil. Forgive me and help me leave all vengeance up to you. Amen.

154

Praise His Name

PSALM 100

Enter his gates with thanksgiving and his courts with praise; give thanks to him and praise his name.—Psalm 100:4 NIV

Negative attitudes have a way of creeping up on all of us at times. Good advice for turning them around is keeping a gratitude journal—a list of the things you're thankful for each day. When we put our focus on the positive aspects of our lives, the impact of the negatives begins to shrink.

Psalm 100 can be viewed as a prescription for keeping a gratitude journal about God—for learning to thank Him and praise Him for who He is and what He does. Coming before God to worship with thanksgiving and praise is easy when we're keenly aware of His nature.

Some of the things the psalms encourage us to thank God for are

- His creation,
- His provision and care,
- His compassion,
- His salvation,
- His guidance, and
- His power.

What else can you add to this list? Why not start your own gratitude journal about God today and use it often to praise and worship Him?

Father God, you are good, and you are good to me. Help me to worship you for who you are. You are worthy! Amen.

Resting in God

PSALM 116

Let my soul be at rest again, for the LORD has been good to me.—Psalm 116:7

A nine-year-old losing her fight with leukemia, a ninety-six-year-old entering hospice—just two of the heartaches friends have posted about on social media recently. Each time, the families expressed deep faith and confidence in God despite their distress and sorrow. They walk closely with Him daily in all of life and faced trouble and death with continued trust that outweighed their anxiety. They chose to rest in Him.

Life's hardships and challenges unnerve us, making us anxious. We have to remind ourselves to trust God, to rest in Him once again. He is good and will continue to be good to us. And He cares deeply. He "bends down to listen" as we pray (Psalm 116:2). He watches over our loved ones as they make their passage from earthly life to life with Him, and He will be with us when we make that same journey. "Precious [and of great consequence] in the sight of the LORD is the death of His godly ones [so He watches over them]" (Psalm 116:15 AMP).

Dear Lord, help me choose again and again to rest in you, because you have been good to me. Amen.

156

Sweeter Than Honey

PSALM 119

May all who fear you find in me a cause for joy, for I have put my hope in your word.—Psalm 119:74

The longest psalm in the Bible, Psalm 119, is a Hebrew acrostic poem. There are twenty-two stanzas, one for each letter in the Hebrew alphabet, and within each stanza the verses all begin with that letter. The format aided memorization, which underscores the theme of the psalm—the inestimable worth of knowing and following God's Word.

Although we may not know Hebrew, we can find images throughout the psalm to help us remember its message, such as the heart as a storehouse for the Word (Psalm 119:11) and the Word as a path toward happiness and delight (Psalm 119:35). The psalmist also describes God's Word as

- a taste sweeter than honey (Psalm 119:103),
- a lamp and a light (Psalm 119:105),
- a delightful treasure (Psalm 119:111),
- a source of hope (Psalm 119:114), and
- truth that stands (Psalm 119:160).

The psalmist also mourns that people often ignore God's Word: "My tears pour down like a river, because people do not obey your law" (Psalm 119:136 GNT). Decide today not to be one of those the psalmist cried over. Instead, let Psalm 119:74 describe your life: "May all who fear you find in me a cause for joy, for I have put my hope in your word."

Dear God, may I bring joy to those who love you because I love and obey your wonderful Word. Amen.

Pleasing Coach

157

PSALM 119

> I have hidden your word in my heart, that I might not sin against you.—Psalm 119:11

My friend Lynn tells a story about one of her sons that perfectly illustrates what it means to honor God and the instructions in His Word.

In high school, Cason played basketball for a legendary, winning coach who had rules and expectations for his players. One strict rule was no showing off, which meant no slam dunks during pregame warmups. And although players could choose to slam dunk during games, their coach preferred that they not.

Lynn says she often watched games with tears in her eyes because a player would sail toward the basket perfectly positioned to dunk but pull back at the last minute, letting the ball fall in without doing the slam. She says she felt as if the boys were saying, "See, Coach, I could've dunked it. But out of respect for your preference, I didn't." And how wonderful it would be, she says, if we chose to honor God the same way, to love and respect Him and choose to say proudly, "The Lord wants this" and "The Lord doesn't want that."

When we sin, we hurt ourselves and others, but even more, we dishonor God. How much better if we can say with joy, "I will pursue your commands" and "How I love them!" (Psalm 119:32, 47) because we revere and want to please our own legendary, winning Coach.

Heavenly Father, help me pay attention to your commands and run hard to obey them because I love you. Amen.

158

Enter His Presence

PSALMS 120–134

I was glad when they said to me, "Let us go to the house of the LORD!"
—Psalm 122:1 ESV

How do you prepare for worship with other believers?

Psalms 120–134 share the same notation at the start: "A song of ascents" or "A song for pilgrims ascending to Jerusalem" (NLT). Travelers on their way to worship at the temple sang these psalms together as they approached Jerusalem. They recalled God's blessings—His help, forgiveness, material provisions, rescue, peace, and unity, and the gift of family life. They acknowledged and lamented sin and eagerly anticipated their shared worship experience.

So how do *you* get ready for worship? Are you a planner—laying out clothes, breakfast, and Bibles the night before? Or do you roll out of bed and head for the door? Can you gladly say "Let's go!" with King David, the author of Psalm 122, even with children to get ready as well as yourself? (Maybe a song together in the car would be a good idea!) There's no right or wrong here—as long as we set aside some moments to prepare our hearts to give God our best praise and to receive what He has for us that day.

Father God, too often I've come to worship with my heart and mind filled with thoughts of so many things other than you. Forgive me, and help me cultivate a glad, prepared heart ready to praise you instead. Amen.

Never Apart

PSALM 139

O LORD, you have examined my heart and know everything about me.—Psalm 139:1

When parents work outside the home, summers require creativity, especially planning for the children. One year while I attended a conference in Colorado and my husband worked his job in Ohio, our teenager traveled to Mexico on a work project with her youth group while our middle-grader spent the week with her grandparents in Washington state. We were in four different time zones, and I felt disoriented whenever I thought about that.

It wasn't a problem, of course, for God. He always knows exactly where we are and what we're doing. Each of us. All the time. Everyone in the world. And He is present wherever we go. Anywhere. No matter how far, how high, or how deep. Darkness? Not a problem. Day and night are the same to Him. I have to say with the psalmist, "Such knowledge is too wonderful for me, too great for me to understand!" (Psalm 139:6).

Human beings desire to be known; women especially value intimacy. God knows everything about every person, what we think, what we're going to say, what we're going to do. He has known us since before we were born, forming us and watching as we developed in the womb. His knowing is constant; when we sleep and when we're awake, we're still in His care.

Such power and such love for us—why do we so often act as if we are on our own?

Dear Lord, you are mighty and you rule over all, yet you think of me and know me! Show me how to follow you on the path of life. Amen.

160

Honest Prayers

PSALM 142

I cry out to the Lord; I plead for the Lord's mercy. I pour out my complaints before him and tell him all my troubles.—Psalm 142:1–2

My friend Cheryl, a licensed clinical counselor, often says, "People just like to be together." That's why the groups she leads always include plenty of time for people to talk and share with one another. The conversations need to move beyond superficialities so true connections can develop. We humans can feel lonely in a group or in a relationship if honest thoughts and emotions are never shared.

In a similar way, we can feel lonely in our relationship with God if we're not willing to speak honestly to Him. The psalmists expressed deep emotions to God, without fear or embarrassment, setting an example we can follow—even those of us with more reserved personalities.

This psalm by David describes his feelings as he hid in a cave while on the run from King Saul, who wanted to kill him. Expressing our feelings of distress, grief, and isolation to God in a lament like this psalm releases the grip those emotions have on us. We feel connected to God again and can begin looking forward to how He will resolve our situation.

When you are overwhelmed by trouble, let God know how you feel. He listens carefully, and He will help you.

Dear God, thank you for listening to my sorrows as well as my praises. May I always turn to you in every troubled time. Amen.

Hallelujah!

PSALM 150

Praise the Lord! Praise God in his sanctuary; praise him in his mighty heaven! Praise him for his mighty works; praise his unequaled greatness!—Psalm 150:1–2

Given a choice of rhythm instruments, young children often reach for the cymbals, happy for the opportunity to make lots of noise by clanging them together again and again. I think God might smile as they do.

Psalms 146–150, the final five in the book of Psalms, begin and end with "Praise the Lord!" or in Hebrew, *Hallelujah!* It's a big, noisy word, a word to be shouted rather than whispered.

These psalms call for loud, joyful celebration by all ages and all creation for everything God is and does. They encourage worshipers to remember God's goodness and power and respond to Him with musical instruments (loud, crashing cymbals included!), with dancing, and with singing—as a group and individually.

Worship styles vary within cultures, of course. But we roar our approval at sporting events, political rallies, and concerts, so why not make some noise at times to praise our awesome God?

Hallelujah! Hallelujah!

Heavenly Father, you are worthy! Help me remember your greatness every day and offer you my praise. Amen.

162

How to Do Life

PROVERBS 1

These are the proverbs of Solomon, David's son, king of Israel. Their purpose is to teach people wisdom and discipline, to help them understand the insights of the wise.—Proverbs 1:1–2

Anything you want to learn, someone's probably written a book to tell you how to do it. A search on Amazon for books with "how to" in the title turned up more than eighty thousand results.

But the book of Proverbs is the ultimate how-to book. If you want to know how to be successful in life, Proverbs will show you the way.

A proverb is a short saying that describes an observable truth. King Solomon, known for his great wisdom, wrote most of the sayings in the book of Proverbs and collected and compiled the others. Proverbs aren't *promises* from God, but they express what God says we can expect to happen based on the choices we make, and for that reason they are a trustworthy guide.

Remember that in the Bible a fool is someone with no regard for God. The book of Proverbs clearly contrasts the life of the fool with the life of the wise. So resolve never to act like a fool, and seek instead to be wise. "To acquire wisdom is to love yourself; people who cherish understanding will prosper" (Proverbs 19:8).

Father God, I want to live wisely and well. Help me acquire the wisdom I need from your wonderful Word. Amen.

Guard Your Heart

PROVERBS 4

Above all else, guard your heart, for everything you do flows from it.—Proverbs 4:23 NIV

On a hill overlooking Washington, DC, in Arlington National Cemetery, stands the Tomb of the Unknown Soldier. Twenty-four hours a day, 365 days a year, in all weather, men and women from the elite 3rd U.S. Infantry Regiment guard the tomb, walking at a cadence of ninety steps per minute. Changing of the guard occurs every thirty minutes in the summer and every hour in the winter.

The sentinels, all volunteers, qualify for the honor by completing a two-week trial phase and then a training phase. They memorize pages of cemetery history and the grave locations of nearly three hundred veterans. They learn to perform the guard-change ceremony and keep their uniforms and weapons immaculate. They also must pass tests on every aspect of their responsibilities.

Guarding the Tomb of the Unknown Soldier requires diligence, discipline, and high motivation as well as training. Keeping watch over our hearts in order to live our lives according to God's instructions requires the same. How well are you guarding your heart today?

Dear Lord, may your wise instructions be a guard for my heart so my life will stay on the course you have for me. Amen.

164

Fear the Lord

PROVERBS 9

> Fear of the LORD is the foundation of wisdom. Knowledge of the Holy One results in good judgment.—Proverbs 9:10

Just like Psalms, the book of Proverbs focuses often on the source of wisdom—our fear of God, which means our respect for Him. And how do we learn to respect God? By getting to know Him well. How can we *not* respect and reverence God when we understand His power and His love?

Our respect for God, our healthy fear, leads us to want to live in ways that please Him. We want to hear and do what He says, and that's the starting point of true wisdom. When we know God, we can make good decisions about all aspects of our lives.

Healthy fear leads us to good choices. Mountain climbers and deep-sea divers respect the environments they explore; they know the mountains and the oceans well, including the dangers. This knowledge and understanding allows them to pursue their climbs and dives safely.

Probably you, like me, have made some unwise decisions and choices throughout your life. I'm so thankful our forgiving God continues to invite us to know Him, respect Him, and learn to be wise!

Dear God, help me live with respect for you today and every day. May I grow in wisdom daily because of my love and respect for you. Thank you for loving and teaching me. Amen.

Words, Words, Words

PROVERBS 16

From a wise mind comes wise speech.—Proverbs 16:23

Proverbs has a lot to say about the words we speak, and for good reason. Perhaps as a child you repeated the little rhyme "Sticks and stones may break my bones, but words can never hurt me." It's just not true. Words *can* hurt, a lot. So the book of Proverbs has wise advice for us about how to use our words in positive ways.

For example, *don't talk too much*. "If you talk a lot, you are sure to sin. If you are wise, you will keep quiet" (Proverbs 10:19 ICB). "A truly wise person uses few words; a person with understanding is even-tempered" (Proverbs 17:27). "Even fools are thought wise when they keep silent; with their mouths shut, they seem intelligent" (Proverbs 17:28). (That one always makes me laugh!)

Speak kind, gracious words that build others up. "There is one whose rash words are like sword thrusts, but the tongue of the wise brings healing" (Proverbs 12:18 ESV). "Kind words are like honey—sweet to the soul and healthy for the body" (Proverbs 16:24). "The wise are known for their understanding, and pleasant words are persuasive" (Proverbs 16:21).

Think before you speak. "There is more hope for a fool than for someone who speaks without thinking" (Proverbs 29:20). "Be careful what you say and protect your life. A careless talker destroys himself" (Proverbs 13:3 GNT).

"Wise words are more valuable than much gold and many rubies" (Proverbs 20:15). What value are you placing on the words you say?

Heavenly Father, may the words I speak be thoughtful, kind, careful, and wise. Guard the words I say! Amen.

166

The Woman We Love to Hate

PROVERBS 31

"A woman who fears the LORD is to be praised."—Proverbs 31:30 ESV

She's the woman we all love to hate, and she used to really bug me. The woman Proverbs 31 praises so highly—she's just too perfect. She meets everyone's needs with a smile and looks great doing it. And she gets up early, well before sunrise, and gets right to work. Ugh.

Through the years, I've tried to follow her example. I had my couponing-and-three-store-menu-planning phase, my make-crafts-and-sell-them phase, and I've even had more than one let's-get-up-before-the-sun-and-get-this-day-going phase. But eventually I learned I was trying to copy this much-maligned woman's *activities* rather than her *character*.

What the Proverbs 31 woman actually models for us is a godly life. She's a wife and mother, a homemaker and an entrepreneur, but she could just as easily be a college student, a single mom, a grandmother. She's faithful, diligent, industrious, generous, compassionate, kind, and wise—all virtues the book of Proverbs advises women *and* men to develop. Why? Because they honor God and make life work.

When we fear (respect and honor) the Lord, we begin to understand the world and ourselves as His, which is true knowledge. Taking what we know to be true and applying it correctly is living with godly wisdom. That's what the book of Proverbs is all about, and that's what the Proverbs 31 woman is good at.

Turns out there's no reason to dislike her after all!

Father God, thank you for including this portrait of a godly woman in your Word. Help me emulate her character and live your way. Amen.

167

Finding Contentment

THE BOOK OF ECCLESIASTES

> After all this, there is only one thing to say: Have reverence for God, and obey his commands, because this is all that we were created for.—Ecclesiastes 12:13 GNT

Remember King Solomon, the wisest man who ever lived? Because he asked God for wisdom rather than wealth or fame, God gladly granted his request and gave him wealth, fame, and a long life too. Solomon ruled well for many years, but eventually the influence of his many foreign wives led him away from God. He established shrines where his wives could worship their pagan gods, and he even joined them in their idol worship.

Solomon lived what many would call the good life, fueled by his extraordinary power and wealth. With his wisdom and curiosity, he observed his own life and the human condition on earth and tried to discern its meaning. The book of Ecclesiastes is part memoir, part investigative report, and part teaching.

Solomon concluded that life apart from God is meaningless, and he points us to life with God as the way to contentment. "It is good for people to eat, drink, and enjoy their work under the sun during the short life God has given them. . . . To enjoy your work and accept your lot in life—this is indeed a gift from God" (Ecclesiastes 5:18–19).

God wants us to reverence Him, obey Him, and find contentment with Him. Are you content today?

Dear Lord, you give good gifts! Thank you for my life. Help me follow you always and find contentment in my life with you. Amen.

168

Celebrate Love

THE BOOK OF SONG OF SOLOMON

> Many waters cannot quench love, neither can floods drown it.—Song of Solomon 8:7 ESV

The Song of Solomon might be the least-read book of the Bible in contemporary times, but it has a message current times greatly need: Human sexuality was designed by God to joyfully express love between a man and a woman joined in marriage.

The book is a poem that tells a story about the love, courtship, and marriage between King Solomon and a young country woman called the Shulamite, which reflects the region of Galilee that was her home. The story can be difficult for modern readers to follow; the character's speeches and events don't necessarily follow a chronological order, and a chorus often interrupts them or is addressed by them.

As the story develops, both the king and the Shulamite describe their passion and longing for each other. Their descriptions either surprise us with explicit frankness or make us laugh—who today wants her teeth described as a flock of newly shorn and washed sheep, with none of them missing?

But besides its celebration of married sexual love—and its argument to maintain sexual purity until marriage—the book also emphasizes the dedication, commitment, and loyalty married love requires. Each of us, whether married or single, widowed or divorced, can give thanks for God's creation of male and female and His plan for the bonds of love.

Dear God, your gifts to us are good! Thank you for love, for sex, for marriage. Help me understand and experience them according to your plan. Amen.

Encountering GOD'S HEART for YOU in the OLD TESTAMENT

The Books of Prophecy

Holy One of Israel

ISAIAH 1–6

And they were calling to one another: "Holy, holy, holy is the LORD Almighty; the whole earth is full of his glory."—Isaiah 6:3 NIV

Isaiah's call to serve God as a prophet to the southern kingdom of Judah came in a vision in the last year of King Uzziah's reign, 740 BC. (Isaiah also prophesied under three more kings of Judah: Jotham, Ahaz, and Hezekiah.) Chapter 6 of Isaiah records the vision: Isaiah saw God on His throne in heaven, worshiped by mighty angels called seraphim. Isaiah's own sinfulness compared to the holiness of God overwhelmed him; from then on he often referred to God as the Holy One of Israel.

In his vision Isaiah received forgiveness from God and a message for Judah comprised of both judgment—because God's people continued turning away from Him—and future restoration, including the return to Jerusalem under Cyrus and the coming of the future Messiah. The New Testament quotes Isaiah dozens of times, and Jesus himself read aloud from the book of Isaiah when, in the synagogue of Nazareth, He announced His mission on earth (Luke 4:16–21).

The people of Israel and Judah reaped devastating consequences because they repeatedly broke their covenant with the Holy One of Israel; His perfection and power stopped meaning anything to them. What implications does the holiness of God hold for you today?

Heavenly Father, you are holy, high, and lifted up—perfect and good in all your ways. Help me honor you for your holiness with obedience, today and every day. Amen.

170

A Light in the Darkness

ISAIAH 7–9

The people who walk in darkness will see a great light. For those who live in a land of deep darkness, a light will shine.—Isaiah 9:2

God sent Isaiah to tell King Ahaz not to fear the kings of Syria and Israel who were threatening Judah, and to ask God for a sign to confirm God's promise the invasion wouldn't happen. Faithless Ahaz refused, pretending to want to avoid testing the Lord. So instead, Isaiah gave Ahaz a sign from God: a virgin would bear a son and call him Immanuel (which means "God with us"; the early Christian church quickly recognized this as a prophecy of Jesus). In addition, Isaiah said, the kingdoms of Syria and Israel that Ahaz feared so much would soon be deserted.

Israel and Judah would be invaded by the Assyrians, Isaiah predicted, and the northern kingdom would suffer the most (Israel's capital, Samaria, fell to Assyria in 722 BC; the people of the north were captured and scattered). The darkness experienced by the north wouldn't last forever, however. In the future that same land would see a great light—the coming of a child born to govern from David's throne forever. "He will be called: Wonderful Counselor, Mighty God, Everlasting Father, Prince of Peace" (Isaiah 9:6)—a clear prophecy of Jesus, the Light of the world (John 8:12).

Bringing light into darkness is a trademark of our merciful God. Where do you need His light to shine in your life today?

Father God, shine your light of love into my life and help me bring that light to others. Amen.

The Branch

ISAIAH 11–12

A shoot will come up from the stump of Jesse; from his roots a Branch will bear fruit.—Isaiah 11:1 NIV

Good gardeners know the importance of pruning the plants in their care. Cutting away dead or overgrown parts shapes a tree or bush and increases fruitfulness and growth. Too much cutting and chopping can destroy a plant, however.

When God destroyed Jerusalem at the hand of the Babylonians, Judah was like the stump of a tree cut down so far it could not grow again—but Isaiah said it would! From the stump that David's royal line had become, a new Branch would grow, a powerful new ruler full of God's Spirit whose reign would be peaceful and just—another prophecy of Jesus the Messiah.

In chapters 13–23, Isaiah pronounces God's messages of judgment on the godless nations surrounding His people. But the nations of the world would not be without hope, because God's plan involves the whole world. The Branch from David's family, the heir to David's throne, would be "a banner of salvation to all the world," Isaiah said, and "the nations will rally to him" (Isaiah 11:10).

Isaiah saw that at the end of time, God will gather His people from all corners of the earth and live among them, as He planned. Jesus, the righteous Branch, has opened the kingdom of God to all who trust in Him.

Dear Lord, thank you for your Son, Jesus, the Branch, and His righteous rule in the lives of your people. Amen.

172

Sheltered

ISAIAH 25–26

> You are a refuge from the storm and a shelter from the heat.—Isaiah 25:4

I've never experienced the need to go to a shelter in an emergency, but I can imagine the relief I would feel to have a shelter to go to with my family after a fire, a flood, or a tornado. In these chapters, Isaiah talks about the joy—the shelter—of salvation when a day of destruction comes upon the earth. Waiting will be over, death will end, and tears will be wiped away. The people of God will be safe with Him forever and will celebrate with Him. Peace—perfect peace—will overflow. In Hebrew, "perfect peace" (Isaiah 26:3) is *shalom shalom*. The repetition indicates intensity.

Can we experience this shelter and perfect peace even now? Yes, because God is our refuge and shelter, and we find His perfect peace by keeping our eyes and thoughts centered on Him, trusting Him completely. "You keep him in perfect peace whose mind is stayed on you, because he trusts in you" (Isaiah 26:3 ESV).

In the midst of any trouble or trauma, let God be your shelter and your peace. Choose—over and over again—to trust Him. Fix your mind on Him and ask Him for His perfect peace.

> *Dear God, you are the one I need—my refuge, shelter, and peace in every storm of life and daily trouble. Help me keep my focus on you at all times. Amen.*

The Word Stands Forever

ISAIAH 40

"The grass withers and the flowers fade, but the word of our God stands forever."—Isaiah 40:8

In four historical chapters (36–39) in the middle of his book, Isaiah recounts the Assyrian threats to Judah, King Hezekiah's response, and God's intervention to spare Jerusalem. But chapter 39 ends with Isaiah's prediction to Hezekiah that in the future Judah *would* fall—not to Assyria but to Babylon.

Beginning with chapter 40, Isaiah's tone and message shift to a focus on God's promises of comfort, restoration, and hope for His people. And unlike our short human lives, what God says stands unchanging, forever.

God has guarded and preserved His written Word to us, the Bible. Josh McDowell wrote in *Evidence That Demands a Verdict*, "The Bible, compared with other ancient writings, has more manuscript evidence than any ten pieces of classical literature combined." The Dead Sea Scrolls, for example, were more than eight hundred years older than any other manuscripts when they were discovered in the 1940s. Comparing them to more recent manuscripts shows how carefully and accurately the texts have been transmitted.

Throughout history the Bible has been blamed, banned, and burned, but no efforts to erase it have ever succeeded. None ever will. As you read the Bible, God's Word, give thanks and drink it in deeply. God has spoken, His Word stands, and He is speaking to you today.

Heavenly Father, thank you for your Word, rich and strong, standing forever. May I listen and give thanks to you always. Amen.

174

No Comparison

ISAIAH 40

> "To whom will you compare me? Who is my equal?" asks the Holy One.—Isaiah 40:25

Do you often find yourself comparing yourself to other women? Wishing you were as thin, fit, attractive, rich, or happy as ________ (fill in the name of your friend, co-worker, sister, or favorite celebrity)? It's a common experience, but it's never a good idea. Social media makes the comparison game easier and more tempting than it's ever been, but researchers warn about the consequences.

We're deluged daily with opportunities to judge ourselves and our lives against the lives of others. We might feel arrogantly satisfied that we're better than the women whose posts we're viewing, or we might feel despondent and depressed because "she has it so much better than I do." Our mental health is endangered either way. Besides, there's really only One we need to compare ourselves to, and He's already told us that He loves us and died to set us free.

God himself has no need to play the comparison game, Isaiah tells us. There's simply no one His equal—not even close. God's people had flirted with and fallen for the "gods" of the pagan peoples around them, with devastating consequences. Now Isaiah proclaimed God's message of comfort: He was coming to restore His people. They needed to recognize who He is, however—the wise, just, powerful, strong Creator, sustainer, and ruler of all that is. The idols they had worshiped in the past could never compare.

Are there any idols in our lives? We need to let them go. Nothing, no one compares to the Lord our God.

Heavenly Father, may I always see you as your Word proclaims—unlike any other. May I turn from any idols in my life and live for you alone. Amen.

On Eagles' Wings

ISAIAH 40

> The Lord is the everlasting God, the Creator of all the earth. He never grows weak or weary. . . . Those who trust in the Lord will find new strength.—Isaiah 40:28, 31

Ernestine Shepherd first began working out when she was fifty-six. She stopped going to the gym when her sister, Velvet, suffered a brain aneurysm and died. But Ernestine resumed training as a way to combat the depression and panic attacks she experienced after Velvet's death. In 2010, Guinness World Records named Ernestine, at age seventy-four, the world's oldest performing female bodybuilder.

Most of us will never hold a bodybuilding title, but Isaiah says we can still find new strength every day—the kind of strength that allows us to make our way through life without giving in to the challenges and obstacles we face. This is inner strength of the spirit, strength God gives us when we trust and hope in Him.

When an eagle senses a coming storm, it flies to a high perch and waits. Then, spreading its wings to catch the wind, the eagle soars above the storm. The new strength of those who wait for God and trust Him is like the strength of the eagle lifted above the storm until it passes. God's strength is unlimited. Are you letting Him carry you today?

Father God, may I always turn to you first for help and strength. I need your strong presence! Please carry me today. Amen.

176

The Lord's Chosen Servant

ISAIAH 42, 49–50, 52–53

> We all, like sheep, have gone astray, each of us has turned to our own way; and the LORD has laid on him the iniquity of us all.—Isaiah 53:6 NIV

While Judah still feared the Assyrian threat, Isaiah prophesied that Judah would fall to Babylon. Isaiah also foresaw the return of the exiles to Jerusalem more than 150 years before it happened, and even named Cyrus as the ruler who would allow them to go home. Still more amazing, more than seven hundred years before Jesus was born, Isaiah proclaimed a Servant would come to deliver God's people by giving His life as a sacrifice for sin.

Isaiah 42, 49–50, and 52–53 contain four "Servant Songs," describing a Servant who would

- set captives free,
- restore Israel to God,
- be a light to the Gentiles,
- obey God perfectly, and
- give His life to make it possible for many to be counted righteous.

"By his wounds we are healed" (Isaiah 53:5 NIV). Isaiah 53 describes details of the Servant's suffering and death as He carried the sins of the whole world on the cross. But Isaiah also anticipated the resurrection! The Servant would die without descendants (Isaiah 53:8), yet "when his life is made an offering for sin, he will have many descendants" (Isaiah 53:10) and "when he sees all that is accomplished by his anguish, he will be satisfied" (Isaiah 53:11).

Isn't it wonderful to know that, as followers of Jesus today, we are counted among the descendants who satisfy and give the Servant joy?

Dear Lord, thank you for your Word, unfolding your plan. Thank you for Jesus, setting me free. Help me live for Him daily, bringing Him joy. Amen.

Promises Ahead

ISAIAH 61–66

For since the world began, no ear has heard and no eye has seen a God like you, who works for those who wait for him!—Isaiah 64:4

I'm not good at waiting. Stuck in traffic on the highway is one of my least favorite places to be. Find an alternate route—I've got to keep moving!

As Isaiah finishes up his book of prophecy, Jerusalem hasn't yet fallen. The people of Judah are continuing to sin—worshiping idols, oppressing the poor, believing that God doesn't really see or care what they're doing. The judgment Isaiah warns about is a hundred years off; beyond that are the return from exile and God's promises of comfort and restoration.

Isaiah longed for revival for God's people, but they weren't ready. Isaiah would have to wait. He knew, however, that God is a miracle-working God who does indeed work for those who love Him. Even if it is in the background, unseen, God is working and will act when the right time comes.

The judgment, exile, and return of God's people to Judah lies behind us, but the promise of salvation and a new life with God in a kingdom ruled by Christ forever lies ahead. In the meantime, God's Spirit lives with His followers, and God is working for those who love Him. Until it's time for Jesus to return, we will wait.

Dear God, your great promises fill my soul! Help me to wait on you and trust you to act in all circumstances when the time is right. Amen.

178

Plow the Hard Ground

JEREMIAH 1–6

> This is what the LORD says to the people of Judah and to Jerusalem: "Break up your unplowed ground and do not sow among thorns."—Jeremiah 4:3 NIV

God chose Jeremiah as a prophet before he was born and called him to prophesy when he was still a young man. Jeremiah began his work about sixty years after Isaiah. His messages to Judah span more than forty years, beginning in 626 BC and ending sometime after the destruction of Jerusalem in 586 BC.

Jeremiah is known as the weeping prophet. His warnings of God's impending judgment weighed on his heart, and so did the people's reaction of utter disregard. They had rejected God, and they rejected Jeremiah too. Jeremiah struggled at times with what God required of him, but he remained faithful to God and committed to the people God had called him to serve.

Through Jeremiah, God gave the people of Judah another chance to repent; otherwise their destruction was inevitable. But repentance had to be sincere. Human hearts can be like fallow ground—plowed and planted in the past but uncultivated and hardened over time. Weeds can grow there, but nothing useful. Judah was hard, fallow ground. When God advised them, "Stop at the crossroads and look around. Ask for the old, godly way, and walk in it," they replied, "No, that's not the road we want!" (Jeremiah 6:16).

How is the ground of your heart today, and what road are you traveling?

Heavenly Father, you are so ready to forgive when repentance is real. Help me plow up the hard ground of my heart and walk with you. Amen.

The Potter's Hand

JEREMIAH 18

"O Israel, can I not do to you as this potter has done to his clay? As the clay is in the potter's hand, so are you in my hand."—Jeremiah 18:6

God directed Jeremiah to use images and signs to communicate His messages—a linen loincloth, a shattered jar, a wooden ox yoke, and more. Chapter 18 relates the message God gave Jeremiah after a visit to the potter's shop.

Jeremiah found the potter at his wheel, creating a jar. But the jar didn't turn out the way the potter hoped, so he smashed the clay back into a lump and began again. God told Jeremiah that, like the potter, He has the right and the ability to build up or tear down His clay. Judah and Jerusalem were in danger of being smashed just as the potter had crushed the wet clay on his wheel, if they did not repent.

Jeremiah gave the people God's warning, but they weren't interested in changing their ways, and they didn't fear the promised disaster. They were no longer interested in being molded into something useful and good.

Earlier God had told Jeremiah, "The heart is deceitful above all things and beyond cure. Who can understand it?" (Jeremiah 17:9 NIV). God, the Potter, searches the hearts of people—His clay—and He understands our motives and actions. Why would we not want to be molded and made into something beautiful by the Master Potter?

Father God, you are the Potter and I am the clay. Help me co-operate with you; mold me into a new creation by your hand. Amen.

180

False Messengers

JEREMIAH 23

> "I have not sent these prophets, yet they run around claiming to speak for me. I have given them no message, yet they go on prophesying."—Jeremiah 23:21

Like Isaiah's prophecies, Jeremiah's messages included the promise of a future ruler sent by God. "I will raise up a righteous descendant from King David's line. . . . And this will be his name: The Lord Is Our Righteousness" (Jeremiah 23:5–6). God declares us righteous when we place our faith in Jesus, His Son, who was a descendant of David through both Mary and His earthly father, Joseph.

God's prophets always spoke the truth; their messages could be believed. But false prophets, not from God, also were speaking, telling people the things they wanted to hear. God condemned the false prophets and warned people to listen to Jeremiah instead. "Let my true messengers faithfully proclaim my every word. There is a difference between straw and grain!" (Jeremiah 23:28).

A bank teller learns to spot counterfeit bills by becoming familiar with the characteristics of genuine currency. Knowing the difference between what God has and hasn't said requires spending time in His Word, the Bible, and having hearts that want to hear Him and obey.

Decide to tune out false messages about God and listen instead to His true words!

Dear Lord, thank you for the prophets' true messages, and for the promise of Jesus, our righteousness. Guide me to listen always to your truth and not the false messages in the world. Amen.

God's Anger

JEREMIAH 25

"I have begun to punish Jerusalem, the city that bears my name. Now should I let you go unpunished?"—Jeremiah 25:29

Perhaps you've been involved with an organization or ministry seeking to set wrongs right. Maybe you thought about lending your support for a long while, becoming more aware of harmful situations over time, until one day your anger and frustration overflowed. You had to act.

In a small way, this scenario illustrates God's anger, or what we sometimes call the wrath of God. As Creator and Sovereign Ruler, God sets the standards. Having made a covenant with the Israelites, He expected His people to obey, but again and again they abandoned Him, despite His warnings and pleadings throughout their history. Their hearts grew hard; repentance ceased to be an option. God had no choice but to act. He is loving *and* just, and His anger is His just response to unrepentant, willful sin.

Not only did Israel and Judah experience God's wrath, but so will all the nations of the world. God told Jeremiah to say, "His cry of judgment will reach the ends of the earth, for the LORD will bring his case against all the nations" (Jeremiah 25:31). All the prophets and Jesus himself declared this.

It is right for a holy and just God to be angry about sin. It's amazing that in His love He also chose to send His Son to take it away from us.

Dear God, you act toward us with judgment and with mercy. Thank you for Jesus, who bore your anger as sin in my place. Amen.

182

Hope and a Future

JEREMIAH 29

"For I know the plans I have for you," declares the LORD, "plans to prosper you and not to harm you, plans to give you hope and a future."—Jeremiah 29:11 NIV

Jeremiah wrote a good news/bad news letter to the Jewish exiles in Babylon. The bad news was the length of their captivity—seventy years, just as had been prophesied. The good news was that God hadn't abandoned His people and would bring them back to Judah. He had good plans for them. They could prosper in Babylon and live with a sense of hope for the future, even though, because of their age, many of the exiles would never see their homeland again.

How could the exiles prosper in Babylon? By following the instructions God gave them in Jeremiah's letter. They were to build homes, plant and harvest food, marry and have many children and grandchildren. And, perhaps most important, Jeremiah told the exiles, "Work for the peace and prosperity of the city. . . . Pray to the LORD for it, for its welfare will determine your welfare" (Jeremiah 29:7).

God wanted the exiles to be a blessing to their Babylonian neighbors, even in the dark time of their own captivity. They could live without fear or despair, confident in His good plans. We can do the same.

Heavenly Father, thank you for your good plans and for my future hope because of Jesus. Hear my prayers for my community, and show me how to bless my neighbors. Amen.

A New Covenant

JEREMIAH 31

"This is the covenant I will make with the people of Israel after that time," declares the LORD. "I will put my law in their minds and write it on their hearts. I will be their God, and they will be my people."—Jeremiah 31:33 NIV

Despite the destruction of Jerusalem and the exile, God promised hope and restoration. The people would return to Judah and flourish there. Jerusalem would be rebuilt. Even more reassuring, however, was the promise of a new covenant.

God had given instructions written on stone tablets when He made the covenant with the Israelites at Mount Sinai. In the future, His instructions would lie deep within each person, written on the heart, and sins would be forgiven. With His promise of a new covenant, God showed His people He was not rejecting them.

Jesus brought us that new covenant, open not only to the Jews but to all people. At the Last Supper, on the night He was betrayed, Jesus said, "This cup is the new covenant in my blood, which is poured out for you" (Luke 22:20 NIV). And Jeremiah's prophecy speaks to a time even beyond Jesus' ministry, a time when everyone on earth will know God.

God's words of reassurance through Jeremiah and the new covenant through Jesus are for us as well. Are you living under God's new covenant, with His instructions written deep in your heart?

Father God, thank you for your mercy, extended to all through your Son, Jesus. Show me how to live daily as one of your new-covenant people. Amen.

184

The Weeping Prophet

JEREMIAH 42–44

"We will not listen to your messages from the LORD! . . . We will do whatever we want."—Jeremiah 44:16–17

Jeremiah suffered greatly. He faced scorn and personal danger as he warned of Judah's coming destruction and when he advised surrender to the Babylonians. He was falsely accused of deserting to the Babylonians during the siege of Jerusalem. Again and again Jeremiah witnessed complete contempt for God among His people.

Jeremiah was placed in stocks outside the temple, imprisoned in King Zedekiah's palace, and later held in a dungeon. Some of the king's officials lowered him into an empty cistern in the prison yard, and he would have died there but for a court official from Ethiopia who received permission from the king to rescue him.

Jeremiah remained a prisoner in the palace until the day Jerusalem was captured. Nebuzaradan, captain of the Babylonian guard, found him bound in chains among the captives being taken to Babylon and released him. When the governor installed by the Babylonians was murdered, the small number of Jews left in Judah asked Jeremiah whether to stay or go to Egypt. God directed Jeremiah to tell them not to go to Egypt, but they ignored his message and forced him to go with them. In Egypt they continued worshiping idols, and Jeremiah kept up his warnings.

Jeremiah wept often, but he was faithful all his life. Whatever hardships are ours, we can be faithful too.

Dear Lord, we are not called to an easy life. When I face circumstances I don't want, help me to trust you and be faithful. Amen.

185

Truth for Sleepless Nights

JEREMIAH 46-52

"Tell the whole world, and keep nothing back. Raise a signal flag to tell everyone that Babylon will fall! Her images and idols will be shattered."—Jeremiah 50:2

Awake in the middle of the night for several hours, I thought about Jeremiah and the messages for the nations that come at the end of his book. God truly does reign over all the earth, even when the world seems out of control based on what we see.

At different times God gave Jeremiah messages for the foreign nations whose stories intertwined with events in Judah. All faced war and some faced ruin because of their idol worship and their disregard for God and for His people. And although God allowed Babylon to destroy Jerusalem and take His people into exile, Babylon also would be destroyed in the future.

Within Jeremiah's messages to the nations, God also communicated hope to His people: "I will bring you home again from distant lands, and your children will return from their exile. . . . I will completely destroy the nations to which I have exiled you, but I will not completely destroy you. I will discipline you, but with justice" (Jeremiah 46:27–28).

How mysterious it is that God oversees the rise and fall of nations to accomplish His purposes! "For who is like me, and who can challenge me? What ruler can oppose my will?" (Jeremiah 50:44). On sleepless nights, this is a truth we can rest in.

Dear God, because you are good and you rule the nations for your purposes, I will trust in you. Amen.

186

Mourning with Hope

THE BOOK OF LAMENTATIONS

I will never forget this awful time, as I grieve over my loss. Yet I still dare to hope.—Lamentations 3:20–21

When losses make your heart hurt, how do you deal with the pain? That's the question the exiles in Babylon faced after the fall of Jerusalem. This book of five short poems, or laments, shows us how the author found an answer in mourning before God—mourning with hope.

Jeremiah, who may have traveled to Babylon from Egypt, is the likely author. Writing about the destruction of Jerusalem and the exile from different perspectives—as the city, as an observer, and as himself—he gives us an example of pouring out to God the details of what has happened to us and our feelings of pain and despair. Sometimes we can do nothing to change a situation, sometimes we need to name and accept our own part in causing our suffering, and always we need to call on God for His help in total trust.

Of the five laments, the third focuses on hope and is three times as long as the other four poems, perhaps for emphasis. Remembering who God is gave Jeremiah hope. "The faithful love of the Lord never ends! His mercies never cease. Great is his faithfulness; his mercies begin afresh each morning" (Lamentations 3:22–23). When sorrow comes, remember to lament with hope.

Heavenly Father, you listen attentively when I mourn before you and you offer me comfort, direction, and hope. I am thankful. Amen.

The Watchman

EZEKIEL 1–4

"I have appointed you as a watchman for Israel."—Ezekiel 3:17

Ezekiel, a priest, arrived in Babylon in 597 BC with the second wave of Jewish exiles. Five years later, God called him to prophesy to the Jews in Babylon. Ezekiel was a contemporary of Jeremiah, who was prophesying in Judah, and of Daniel, who arrived in Babylon ahead of him as part of the first deportation about 605 BC.

Ezekiel's prophecies contain dramatic imagery, such as the living beings and God's glory in chapter 1. He used dramatic actions, such as lying on his side near a model of the siege of Jerusalem, to illustrate what was coming. He warned of the fall of Jerusalem until it happened and then fell silent for the next thirteen years. (Throughout his book, Ezekiel addresses Israel, but Judah is meant; Judah was all that was left of Israel.)

As a watchman, Ezekiel was charged to proclaim God's messages whether the exiles listened or not—and God told him they would not. God also told Ezekiel how to stay strong as a watchman to Israel, and it is good advice for us as we seek to share God's love and redemption plan: "Let all my words sink deep into your own heart first. Listen to them carefully for yourself. Then go to your people in exile and say to them, 'This is what the Sovereign LORD says!'" (Ezekiel 3:10–11).

Father God, may I take seriously your admonition to listen and reflect on your Word and put it into practice myself as I seek to share your love and forgiveness. Amen.

188

Hearts of Stone, Hearts of Flesh

EZEKIEL 8–11

"I will give them an undivided heart . . . ; I will remove from them their heart of stone and give them a heart of flesh."—Ezekiel 11:19 NIV

The Spirit transported Ezekiel in a vision to the temple in Jerusalem, where Ezekiel saw again the glory of God as he had in his earlier vision. He saw the extent of the idolatry and corruption taking place throughout the temple, culminating with those bowing down to worship the sun instead of God, and then he watched as God's glory left the temple.

God gave Ezekiel a message of judgment for Israel's leaders, who had been deceiving the people about the seriousness of their situation. The people left in Jerusalem felt self-satisfied; they expected to stay in their land forever despite God's warnings of coming judgment. They also did not expect the exiles to return, but God told Ezekiel to assure the exiles they *would* go home. When that happened, God said, He would give them undivided hearts, devoted to Him and willing to obey and follow Him. The new life we have through Jesus fulfills this prophecy.

Ezekiel watched as God's glory moved again, this time leaving the city altogether. Then the Spirit took Ezekiel back to Babylon, and he shared his vision with the exiles.

What is the condition of your heart today? What are you devoted to? Is your heart undivided?

Dear Lord, even as you require justice for sin, you promise hope and new life. May I use the new heart you've given me to obey you and make you known. Amen.

Repent and Live

EZEKIEL 18

"Do you think I enjoy seeing evil people die?" asks the Sovereign Lord. "No, I would rather see them repent and live."—Ezekiel 18:23 GNT

Popular among the exiles was the belief that they were being unfairly judged by God for the sins of previous generations. The proverb "The parents have eaten sour grapes, but their children's mouths pucker at the taste" expressed their feelings perfectly: God should have punished their ancestors and should not be punishing them.

But just because the proverb was popular didn't make it true, and God gave Ezekiel a message to counter the exiles' assumption and their arrogance. Every person is His to judge, He said, and all people are individually responsible for their own actions. God's desire for every one of the exiles was that they would turn to Him and live.

That is His desire for us too. "Repent, and turn from your sins. Don't let them destroy you! Put all your rebellion behind you, and find yourselves a new heart and a new spirit" (Ezekiel 18:30–31). A proverb of our time is "God has no grandchildren." That proverb is true. Each of us must make our own choice to turn to God, become His child, and receive His gift of salvation.

Dear God, thank you for your inestimable concern and love for every person, and for me. Thank you for your incredible gift of salvation through your Son, Jesus. Amen.

190

Stand in the Gap

EZEKIEL 22

> "I looked for someone among them who would build up the wall and stand before me in the gap on behalf of the land so I would not have to destroy it, but I found no one."—Ezekiel 22:30 NIV

Do you ever wonder if your prayers for your church, your community, or your nation matter? Ezekiel would say that they do.

In a message to Ezekiel about Israel's leaders, God listed the leaders' many sins. Rulers, priests, and false prophets extorted and lied, committed murder, disregarded God's clear teachings, and enabled the people to do the same. "Even common people oppress the poor, rob the needy, and deprive foreigners of justice" (Ezekiel 22:29). If the right living of God's people was like a wall guarding the land, that wall had broken down, and God couldn't find anyone among Israel's leaders to stand in the gap, to rebuild the wall and keep it standing. The land would be destroyed.

One way to stand in the gap for people we love is to let our lives be an example. Another is to pray, asking God to intervene in their lives and circumstances. Think of your prayers as a defense of God's territory and never doubt their impact—God looked for just one person to stand in the gap for Israel.

Heavenly Father, show me how to stand in the gap for people and situations around me. Help me be faithful and trusting as I stand. Amen.

The King of Tyre

EZEKIEL 26–28

> "You were blameless in all you did from the day you were created until the day evil was found in you."—Ezekiel 28:15

Where does evil come from? How did it begin? Nearly everyone has asked these questions. And though the Bible doesn't answer them directly, one of Ezekiel's prophecies gives us a glimpse of the spiritual power behind the evil in the world.

God gave Ezekiel messages of judgment for Tyre, a prosperous Phoenician trading city on the Mediterranean coast where Baal was worshiped, and for Tyre's king. The city's businesses dealt dishonestly; the people had rejoiced when Jerusalem fell. Tyre's prideful king regarded himself as a god. After a message addressed to the king as the prince of Tyre, Ezekiel received another message, a funeral song, for the king of Tyre.

In that message, the king of Tyre is Satan, the angel who attempted to take God's place in heaven (Isaiah 14:13–14). Satan became God's enemy and our enemy, doing all he can to ruin and obscure the image of God in every person.

Satan's sin was pride. "Your heart was filled with pride because of all your beauty. Your wisdom was corrupted by your love of splendor" (Ezekiel 28:17). But just as destruction came to Tyre and its king, Satan and all evil spiritual powers will ultimately be vanquished and destroyed.

Father God, every good gift in my life comes from you! Please keep me thankful, humble, and free of pride. Amen.

192

The Good Shepherd

EZEKIEL 34

"This is what the Sovereign LORD says: I myself will search for my sheep and look after them."—Ezekiel 34:11 NIV

I love animals and get upset whenever a story of animal abuse comes to my attention. I just don't understand it. Our animals depend on us.

Ezekiel's message from God to Israel's leaders compared them to shepherds, bad shepherds who looked after themselves and left their flock—God's people—to starve, wander, and be killed. God promised that those leaders would face His justice, and He promised that He himself would be a good shepherd for His people. He would find, restore, care for, and ultimately judge every one of His flock.

In addition, God would make a covenant of peace with His people, breaking their chains of slavery and sending them showers of blessings. Once again they would know Him as Yahweh ("I AM"), the Lord, the God who always has been and who is always present with His people—something God declares fifty times throughout Ezekiel's prophecies.

God promised another Shepherd too, one who would come from the line of David and tend all of the people of God. Ezekiel didn't know His name, but we do. Jesus said, "I am the good shepherd; I know my own sheep, and they know me, just as my Father knows me and I know the Father. So I sacrifice my life for the sheep" (John 10:14–15).

Dear Lord, I am so happy and thankful to be one of the sheep of your flock. Your care for me has shown me who you are! Thank you for Jesus, your Son, the good Shepherd. Amen.

A New Spirit

EZEKIEL 36

"And I will put my Spirit in you so that you will follow my decrees and be careful to obey my regulations."—Ezekiel 36:27

In an earlier prophecy, God had promised through Ezekiel to give His people new hearts—tender hearts of flesh rather than stone, hearts that would desire to follow and obey Him. But how would He do that? Ezekiel had only a clue before, but now the plan became more clear. God's own Spirit would come to live in His people! Their sins would be washed clean; their lands and their lives would be renewed and blessed.

God also revealed the reason He would do this—not because anyone deserved it but for the reputation of His name. "I am bringing you back, but not because you deserve it. I am doing it to protect my holy name, on which you brought shame while you were scattered among the nations" (Ezekiel 36:22). Because of who He is, God could not allow His people to continually be disgraced as exiles. Instead, He would display His power and holiness through them as He forgave them, washed them clean, and brought them home again.

Sound familiar? After Jesus' resurrection, on the Day of Pentecost, God sent the Holy Spirit to live within all who would believe and follow the Savior, empowering us to live for Him.

Not because we deserve it, but because of who He is.

Dear God, how glad I am to be forgiven and to live each day with your Spirit to guide me! Amen.

194

Dry Bones

EZEKIEL 37

He said to me, "Son of man, can these bones live?" And I answered, "O Lord God, you know."—Ezekiel 37:3 ESV

In exile, the people of Israel felt like old, dry bones. Surely there was no hope for them or for their nation.

But God looked on their situation differently. He told Ezekiel in a vision to speak to a valley filled with dry bones, calling them to listen to Him and promising them new life. When Ezekiel delivered the message, the bones came together, creating skeletons. After muscles and skin formed over the skeletons, God breathed life into the bodies, and they stood up, looking like a vast army. God would renew His people and bring them back to their homeland, where they would live and prosper.

Do you live in a community or nation that needs to be renewed today? Do you need renewal yourself—have your hopes and dreams withered, and do you feel like dry bones? Spiritual renewal begins with listening to God, just as the dry bones in Ezekiel's vision did. God makes His Spirit available to us when we believe in His Son, Jesus. And with the Spirit in our hearts, we can live again.

Heavenly Father, you are so good to me. When I am feeling like dry bones, restore me, renew me, lead me. Show me how to live again. Amen.

The Lord Is There

EZEKIEL 38–48

"And the name of the city from that time on will be: THE LORD IS THERE."—Ezekiel 48:35 NIV

Ezekiel's final prophecies extend beyond the restoration of Israel after the exile and beyond our current time. Israel's enemies are defeated, God's Spirit is poured out, and a new temple is built. The sacrifices resume, God's glory returns to the temple, and a prince in the line of David rules. Ezekiel saw a river of healing flowing from the temple and new, larger allotments of land for each of Israel's twelve tribes. Gentiles have a place in this restored kingdom, gates in the city walls are named after the twelve tribes, and the city has a new name—The Lord Is There—because God has fulfilled His plan to once again live among His people.

Perhaps the details in the prophecies will be literally fulfilled; perhaps they are figurative. The exiles who heard Ezekiel describe what God showed him would have understood his language as picturing God living with His people in a perfect relationship. However and whenever that day comes, it is God's promise. Are you looking forward to that day? How does your future hope affect your life today?

Father God, how wonderful that you desire a home among your people! I can look forward to a forever life with you in a perfect place, in perfect love. Amen.

196

Determined

DANIEL 1

But Daniel resolved not to defile himself with the royal food and wine, and he asked the chief official for permission not to defile himself this way.—Daniel 1:8 NIV

The first captives taken to Babylon included young men like Daniel from Judah's noble class. When King Nebuchadnezzar ordered that the most exemplary of the young captives train for three years to enter his royal service, Daniel was among those chosen. They received new Babylonian names, studied the language, literature, and customs of the culture, and were assigned daily portions of the royal food and wine.

The Babylonian menu, however, included foods that God had declared ritually unclean for the Jews. Daniel wouldn't eat them; instead, he tactfully proposed a test. He and three friends would eat only vegetables and drink only water for ten days. At the end of the test, Daniel and his friends looked so healthy, they were no longer required to eat the royal food.

When the king talked with all the trainees at the end of three years, he was most impressed with Daniel and his friends, and they were selected to begin to serve the king. Daniel remained in royal service throughout his long life. He served with excellence, but he never gave up his faith or his identity as a worshiper of God. He was tested as a young man by exile and efforts to change his loyalty, but Daniel's determination to follow God regardless of circumstances set the course for his whole life. Let Daniel be your example today and every day.

Dear Lord, may I be as determined as Daniel to follow you in every way, every day, all my life. Amen.

In the Fire

DANIEL 2–3

"If we are thrown into the blazing furnace, the God we serve is able to deliver us from it, and he will deliver us from Your Majesty's hand. But even if he does not, we want you to know, Your Majesty, that we will not serve your gods or worship the image of gold you have set up."—Daniel 3:17–18

Daniel's friends seem to have learned well from his example. Nebuchadnezzar had a strange dream and demanded that his wise men tell him the dream as well as what it meant. God revealed the dream and its meaning to Daniel: three strong kingdoms would succeed Babylon one after the other, but during the third, God would establish a kingdom that would never be destroyed.

Grateful to God, Nebuchadnezzar appointed Daniel ruler over the province and made him chief of all his wise men. But the king's grateful response to God didn't last. He built a huge golden statue of himself and ordered everyone at the dedication to bow down to it. Daniel's three friends—now known as Shadrach, Meschach, and Abednego—refused, and soon they were thrown into a fiery furnace as Nebuchadnezzar watched.

Suddenly the king jumped up—there were four men, not three, walking around unharmed in the fire. Immediately the king called for Daniel's friends to come out. And they did, completely untouched by the flames. Like Daniel, they had decided to do what was right no matter what and to trust God's purpose and plan.

Dear God, I want to be like Daniel's three friends, completely committed to you. Help me and strengthen me to live as they did. Amen.

198

Faithful

DANIEL 6

> "My God sent his angel, and he shut the mouths of the lions. They have not hurt me, because I was found innocent in his sight."—Daniel 6:22 NIV

Throughout his life, Daniel faithfully served every king he worked under. Daniel 6 records an event that occurred late in Daniel's life. Persia had overtaken Babylon, and King Darius made plans to set Daniel over all his other high-level administrators. Jealous of Daniel, two officials sought a way to remove him. They convinced the king to make a law that no one could pray to anyone but him for thirty days.

Daniel continued to pray toward Jerusalem from a window in his room three times a day, and spies brought Daniel's infraction to the king's attention. The punishment? A den of hungry lions.

Darius realized his mistake, but kings were not allowed to change their edicts, so Daniel was thrown to the lions. In the morning, Darius rushed to the lions' den and called, "Daniel . . . was your God, whom you serve so faithfully, able to rescue you from the lions?" (Daniel 6:20). Yes, oh yes! Daniel emerged without a scratch. God had honored Daniel and proved himself to Darius.

In a culture that opposed him, Daniel served well and stood firm, honoring God and trusting Him all his life. The next time you feel pressured and coerced by culture, remember Daniel. Don't bend. Stand strong.

Heavenly Father, thank you for Daniel's example. Help me stand for you even when all around me others are trying to knock me down. I want to be faithful. Amen.

199

Prophetic Visions

DANIEL 7-12

"At that time your people—everyone whose name is found written in the book—will be delivered. . . . Those who are wise will shine like the brightness of the heavens, and those who lead many to righteousness, like the stars for ever and ever."—Daniel 12:1, 3 NIV

The final chapters of Daniel's book contain prophetic visions given to Daniel at different times throughout his life. In these prophecies full of symbolic imagery, Daniel saw representations of the kingdoms that would rise and fall after Babylon. He also saw Jesus, "someone like a son of man coming with the clouds of heaven" (Daniel 7:13), given authority to rule the world. The angel Gabriel came to Daniel twice to explain and expand these visions. Gabriel said the Anointed One would be killed, "appearing to have accomplished nothing" (Daniel 9:26), and that Jerusalem and the temple would be destroyed.

Daniel's final vision came during the third year of the reign of King Cyrus. In this vision, a messenger came to Daniel to explain "times of war and great hardship" (Daniel 10:1) with insight into the spirit realm and the end times of history—including the promise of resurrection.

Daniel desired to understand more, and we do too. But the messenger's instruction to Daniel was "Go your way" (Daniel 12:13). The future is safe with God, and we are safe with Him today.

Father God, you tell us everything we need to know. Thank you for your promises, and thank you that I can trust you to do everything you say, now and forever. Amen.

200

The Ones I Love

THE BOOK OF HOSEA

"My people have made up their minds to turn away from me. The prophets call them to turn to me. But none of them honors me at all."—Hosea 11:7 ICB

Hosea was the last prophet to the northern kingdom of Israel. God told Hosea to marry a prostitute, and He used Hosea's marriage to Gomer and her adultery as a living picture of His relationship with Israel. The names of Gomer's three children illustrated the state of that relationship: *Jezreel* for "God scatters," *Lo-ruhamah* for "Not loved"—meaning not forgiven—and *Lo-ammi* for "Not my people."

Gomer left Hosea and returned to prostitution, but God told Hosea to go and redeem her, bring her home, and love her again. The couple remained abstinent, showing the long time Israel would go without a king, sacrifices, or priests before returning to the Lord.

God charged Israel with adultery and prostitution because of the people's continual sin and idol worship. But always, He promised restoration after judgment. The names of Gomer's children would change and have new meanings. *Jezreel* would mean "God plants" because God would bring His people back and plant them in their land again. The men and women of Israel would be known as *Ammi* for "My people" and *Ruhamah* for "The ones I love."

God's love for all His people never wavers!

Dear Lord, thank you for your faithful love and promises, extended now in Jesus, Your Son, to me! Amen.

Now Is the Time

HOSEA 6, 10

Oh, that we might know the LORD! Let us press on to know him. He will respond to us as surely as the arrival of dawn or the coming of rains in early spring.—Hosea 6:3

Hosea wrote about what should have been the people's response to God's warnings and discipline—a cry of repentance and returning to God's care. Sadly, the people of the northern kingdom chose a different response and suffered the consequences. But it didn't have to be that way.

Good gardeners know they have to choose good seed as well as loosen the soil before they plant in it. Planting seasons matter too. Through the prophets, God had said, "Plant the good seeds of righteousness, and you will harvest a crop of love. Plow up the hard ground of your hearts, for now is the time to seek the LORD" (Hosea 10:12).

Without knowing God, we easily make choices that destroy our lives (Hosea 4:6). But God invites and encourages us to follow and obey Him instead to experience a life of love. Where our hearts are hard, we need to do some cultivating work and seek His presence and His help. The right time to do this is now, today and every day. And God will surely respond!

Dear God, I want to press on, continuing to know you! Help me plow up the hard ground of my heart, seeking you daily. Amen.

202

The Day of the Lord

THE BOOK OF JOEL

> The sun will become dark, and the moon will turn blood red before that great and terrible day of the LORD arrives.—Joel 2:31

We know little about Joel—not when he prophesied or even where. His message followed a devastating invasion by four kinds of locusts, one after the other, that destroyed all the field crops, vineyards, and orchards. Joel warned that a day of judgment was coming that would be as ruinous to God's people unless they repented and turned to Him sincerely. "Return to the LORD your God, for he is merciful and compassionate, slow to get angry and filled with unfailing love. He is eager to relent and not punish" (Joel 2:13).

Looking even further out, Joel saw the day when God's Spirit would be poured out and available to all people. After the resurrection, when the apostle Peter spoke to the crowd in Jerusalem who were hearing the gospel proclaimed in their own languages, he said, "This is what was spoken by the prophet Joel" (Acts 2:16 NIV), and he quoted Joel 3:28–32.

That same prophecy also looks ahead to the day of final judgment of the whole world, which Scripture often calls the day of the Lord. But on that day, all who belong to God will be safe with Him as their refuge and fortress.

Do you sometimes feel deep regret over sins and missteps in the past? God promised Israel He would restore what they had lost to the locusts. He promises to restore us too, today and forever!

Heavenly Father, I'm handing over my regrets! Help me to leave them with you. Thank you for forgiveness and the promise, every day, of new life! Amen.

Roar

THE BOOK OF AMOS

The lion has roared—who will not fear? The Sovereign LORD has spoken—who can but prophesy?—Amos 3:8 NIV

Have you ever felt out of place, unwelcome, because of your faith in God? Amos was most unwelcome when he arrived in the northern kingdom of Israel. God had called him from his home in Judah, where he was a shepherd, and sent him to Israel with a message no one in Israel wanted to hear.

From 760–750 BC (also the first ten years of Hosea's ministry), Amos challenged Israel's superficial religion and their corruption, pretension, and complacency. He called them out especially for their treatment of the poor. But justice would come, Amos warned.

Amos pictured God as a roaring lion and wondered why the people hearing Him were unafraid. Israel believed that because they were God's people, judgment was for other nations. They were shocked and disbelieving to hear God's prophet say that both Israel and Judah would be destroyed. But because they knew Him, God said, their actions had to be dealt with. "From among all the families on the earth, I have been intimate with you alone. That is why I must punish you for all your sins" (Amos 3:2).

As followers of Jesus, we also know God. We may feel as out of place and unpopular as Amos did at times. But we've heard the lion roar, and we have to ask ourselves, Are we living as He asks us to?

Father God, I want to live in ways that please you. Am I doing that? Show me how I can walk more closely in your paths. Amen.

204

Reaping What We Sow

THE BOOK OF OBADIAH

"The day is near when I, the LORD, will judge all godless nations! As you have done to Israel, so it will be done to you. All your evil deeds will fall back on your own heads."—Obadiah 1:15

Obadiah likely was a contemporary of Jeremiah. His short prophecy, just twenty-one verses, focuses on the nation of Edom, whose people were the descendants of Esau, Jacob's older brother.

When Judah fell to Babylon, the Edomites rejoiced and even took advantage of their relatives' distress. They seized property, killed those they saw trying to escape, and captured others to turn over to the Babylonians. God let the people of Judah know that what had happened to them would one day happen to Edom as well.

And what happened to Edom would one day be the experience of all godless nations, God said through Obadiah. All the nations that disregard and disobey God will be judged, reaping what they sowed.

And what about you and me, followers of Jesus? Praise God, He sent His Son to pay the penalty for our sins. Because of His death and resurrection, we won't reap the eternal consequences of sin but the forever consequences of His love.

Dear Lord, both just and good, help me treat all people fairly and well, especially those related to me through faith in Jesus. Thank you for your love and forgiveness that take away all fear of judgment. Amen.

Mercy for All

THE BOOK OF JONAH

"Nineveh has more than 120,000 people living in spiritual darkness, not to mention all the animals. Shouldn't I feel sorry for such a great city?"—Jonah 4:11

Jonah, a contemporary of Amos, lived in an area of Israel near the border with Assyria during the reign of Jeroboam II (793–753 BC). The Assyrians, who would capture the capital city of Samaria in 722 BC, were already threatening. They were a pagan people known for their cruelty, and Jonah wasn't happy with God's command to go to the Assyrian capital of Nineveh to warn the people to repent. Jonah decided to go in the opposite direction; he bought passage on a ship sailing far away, and soon found himself in the belly of a great fish. He prayed, repentant, and when the fish spit him out on dry land and God told him again, "Go to Nineveh," this time he went.

When the king and people of Nineveh listened to Jonah's warning from the Lord, they also repented. Seeing this, God relented from the destruction He had warned about. Jonah should have been glad, but instead he became angry, and God chastised him. God, who is unchanging, sometimes changes His plans so that His actions remain true to His nature. Jonah needed to understand that God's mercy is available to all.

Are there unsaved people you dislike? How will you feel if they turn to Jesus? Do you need to learn and apply what God was teaching Jonah?

Dear God, I confess it's hard at times for me to care about people who oppose you and do evil. Forgive me. Help me extend your loving mercy to all. Amen.

206

Insignificant

MICAH 1–5

"But you, Bethlehem Ephrathah, though you are little among the thousands of Judah, yet out of you shall come forth to Me the One to be Ruler in Israel, whose goings forth are from of old, from everlasting."—Micah 5:2 NKJV

God often chooses the insignificant to do something extremely significant.

Micah prophesied in Judah from 735–686 BC, during the reigns of kings Jotham, Ahaz, and Hezekiah. He was a contemporary of Isaiah, and like Isaiah he warned of the judgment coming to both Israel and Judah because of the idol worship, oppression, and corruption among God's people. Also like Isaiah, Micah saw wonderful hope for the future. He prophesied about a day when the Lord's teaching would go out from Jerusalem to the entire world.

Micah's book of prophecy in the Bible contains seven chapters; the book of Isaiah has sixty-six. Length is the primary reason the prophets are called either major prophets or minor prophets. Did Micah ever feel insignificant, overshadowed by Isaiah? We don't know. I hope not, because Micah is the prophet who foretold Jesus' birthplace—tiny, seemingly insignificant Bethlehem, in the district of Ephrathah in Judah.

Though only a small village, Bethlehem experienced notable happenings. Jacob's wife Rachel was buried there, Ruth met and married Boaz there, and Samuel anointed King David there. But most significant of all would be the birth Micah prophesied, the coming of the Savior, Jesus.

Heavenly Father, thank you for sometimes choosing the small to do great things! Help me remember the only thing that matters is staying faithful to you. Amen.

Do What Is Good

MICAH 6

"No, O people, the LORD has told you what is good, and this is what he requires of you: to do what is right, to love mercy, and to walk humbly with your God."—Micah 6:8

Throughout Micah's prophecies, God presents His case against Israel, including their continued ritual worship of Him even while they refused to give up their idol worship and other sinful practices. Hearing the charges, the people responded rhetorically. What did God want from them? More sacrifices and offerings? Their firstborn children as offerings?

"No, no, no," Micah said. They already knew what God wanted from them; He had told them over and over: Do what is right. Love mercy. Walk humbly with Him.

The people of Judah didn't like this list, and plenty of people today don't like it either. For followers of Jesus, though, it's a good list to live by. Let the Spirit lead you daily and strengthen you to make right choices. Extend God's mercy by sharing the gospel. Don't be proud—your faith in Jesus is what saves you, not anything you have done.

Check yourself often against this simple list. How are you doing according to Micah's list today?

Father God, thank you for this reminder to follow you closely and with humility. I want to please you! Amen.

208

Refuge

THE BOOK OF NAHUM

The LORD is good, a strong refuge when trouble comes. He is close to those who trust in him.—Nahum 1:7

Nahum, who lived in Judah, received a vision from God about Nineveh, the Assyrian capital, sometime after 663 BC and before 612 BC, when the city was completely destroyed by Babylon—exactly as Nahum had prophesied.

Nineveh's repentance after Jonah brought God's warning didn't last. As the Assyrian empire expanded, so did its reputation for cruelty. When Israel's capital city, Samaria, fell to the Assyrians, the people of Israel were captured and scattered. Now God was letting Assyria know that His judgment would overtake them as well.

Nahum's message also brought comfort for God's people—their oppressor would fall. "The LORD is slow to get angry, but his power is great, and he never lets the guilty go unpunished" (Nahum 1:3). God also is good, Nahum reminded those who listened to him. He's a strong refuge, a place of safety, when trouble comes. The people of Judah could still experience God's goodness if they would turn to Him and trust in Him.

Evil has an end date. Until then, let God be your strong refuge. Find safety there and trust Him today.

Dear Lord, you are my refuge when trouble comes! Thank you for all you are—both loving and just. Amen.

Even Though

THE BOOK OF HABAKKUK

Even though the fig trees have no blossoms, and there are no grapes on the vines . . . yet I will rejoice in the LORD! I will be joyful in the God of my salvation!—Habakkuk 3:17–18

Do you ever look around or listen to the news and think that things just can't get worse? That's how Habakkuk felt as the people of Judah grew more and more sinful and corrupt. "Wherever I look, I see destruction and violence. . . . The wicked far outnumber the righteous, so that justice has become perverted" (Habakkuk 1:3–4). Habakkuk wanted to know when God was going to do something about it, so he asked. But the answer shocked him and caused more questions. His short prophetic book records his questions and God's answers.

God never chastised Habakkuk for his questions. He told Habakkuk He was raising up Babylon to destroy Judah, and in the future Babylon—and all proud, godless nations—would be judged. All the earth would one day be filled with God's glory. Habakkuk realized that God was still on the side of His chosen people, and he himself sided with God, calling on God to remember mercy.

Even though he feared the Babylonian invasion that would come and even though devastation would surround him, Habakkuk chose to put his trust in God. He would wait patiently for God to work, and depend on Him to lead and guide.

Dear God, in times that feel uncertain and distressing, help me trust you the way Habakkuk did. You are my strength. Amen.

210

When God Sings

THE BOOK OF ZEPHANIAH

"The Lord your God is in your midst, a mighty one who will save; he will rejoice over you with gladness; he will quiet you by his love; he will exult over you with loud singing."—Zephaniah 3:17 ESV

Watching your children or grandchildren play sports or perform on-stage, you're sure to make your presence known because of how proud you are! But have you ever thought of God reacting in a similar way because He's pleased with you?

Zephaniah prophesied in Judah during the reign of good King Josiah. Josiah's much-needed religious reforms postponed the destruction God warned about through the prophets, but the nation's sins were too great to avoid punishment forever.

Zephaniah said that humble people could still repent and be protected, however, and after God's judgment of the nations would come a glorious time of renewal and restoration. God himself would live among His people, and His love would quiet all their fears. What a reason for people to rejoice—but Zephaniah's surprising message is that God will be the one rejoicing! He will gladly exult over His people with loud songs like a triumphant, mighty warrior.

So when you have resisted a temptation, stepped out to take on a task God has asked of you, or simply need encouragement from your Father, remember Zephaniah's words—and think of God rejoicing over you.

Heavenly Father, thank you for saving me and all who turn to you with faith in your Son, Jesus. Thank you for wanting me to be yours. Amen.

Put God First

THE BOOK OF HAGGAI

The LORD Almighty said to Haggai, "These people say that this is not the right time to rebuild the Temple."—Haggai 1:2 GNT

How do you decide how to spend your time, where to put your resources, attention, and energy?

After the exiles returned to Judah from Babylon, they began to rebuild the temple but stopped when harassment and opposition from non-Jewish local residents became too discouraging. Instead, they focused on building fine homes for themselves while the temple lay in ruins. But life back in Judah wasn't what they'd hoped for. Where was the abundance God had promised?

Enter Haggai. He prophesied to the exiles for just four months, but that was long enough to get the exiles back to rebuilding the temple. Their problem, Haggai said, was their focus. They'd been making excuses. But God couldn't bless them the way He wanted to as long as they were prioritizing themselves over Him.

How often we tend to focus on what matters to us more than on what God says matters to Him! Haggai encouraged the exiles to turn that around, put God first, and be blessed. Let his message encourage you to do the same today.

Father God, I confess I don't always give you my best. I don't always seek what you say matters. Help me get my priorities right, ordered according to your Word. Amen.

212

By My Spirit

ZECHARIAH 1–6

> Then he said to me, "This is the word of the LORD to Zerubbabel: Not by might, nor by power, but by my Spirit, says the LORD of hosts."—Zechariah 4:6 ESV

Do you read the assembly instructions that come with products you buy? Which helps you more—the diagrams or the written directions? Most of us need the illustrations to understand more quickly how to put the item together. "One picture is worth a thousand words" is often true!

Zechariah, both a priest and a prophet, was born in exile and came to live in Judah with the returning exiles. God gave Zechariah messages for the exiles to encourage them as they resettled the land and began new lives. In visions, God used images as symbols for Zechariah to communicate with His people.

Many of the images in Zechariah's visions would have been familiar to people at that time and easily understood; for example, horns represented power, eyes represented God's ability to see everything, and oil represented God's Spirit. With the image of a golden lampstand holding a bowl of oil surrounded by seven lamps, God sent a clear message to Zerubbabel, governor of Judah, who was in charge of rebuilding the temple. Although only a small beginning had been made, the work on the temple would be completed—but by the power of God's Spirit rather than any human strength.

That's a truth to remember in all our endeavors too.

Dear Lord, you delight in small beginnings. Help me move forward today by following your directions and depending on you. Amen.

King and Priest

ZECHARIAH 9–14

"On that day a fountain will be opened for the dynasty of David and for the people of Jerusalem, a fountain to cleanse them from all their sins and impurity."—Zechariah 13:1

In the first half of Zechariah's book, the high priest in Zechariah's vision symbolized the Branch, the ruler who would be both king and priest (Zechariah 3:8, 6:12–13). The second half of Zechariah's messages came after the temple had been rebuilt and included more prophecies about the Branch—the Messiah, Jesus, the Son of God:

- He would ride into Jerusalem on a donkey's colt (Zechariah 9:9).
- He would be betrayed for just thirty pieces of silver (Zechariah 11:12–13).
- His body would be pierced (Zechariah 12:10).
- His followers would be scattered (Zechariah 13:7).

Zechariah looked ahead to the time a healing, cleansing fountain would open (Zechariah 13:1), the day God would "remove the sins of this land in a single day" (Zechariah 3:9), and to a future day when God will be king over all the earth (Zechariah 14:9). God cannot lie, and the prophecies He gives all come true. We can trust Him!

Dear God, how you encourage us with your Word! Give me understanding, and help me communicate your hope to others. Amen.

214

Wearying God

MALACHI 1–3

You have wearied the LORD with your words. "How have we wearied him?" you ask. By saying, "All who do evil are good in the eyes of the LORD, and he is pleased with them" or "Where is the God of justice?"—Malachi 2:17 NIV

Malachi prophesied in Judah eighty or ninety years after the temple was rebuilt and shortly after Nehemiah came to Jerusalem to rebuild the city walls. God sent Malachi to challenge His people to remain faithful even when it seemed He was slow about keeping His promises.

Malachi called out the priests and the people for breaking the covenant God had made with their ancestors. God had seen what they were doing that revealed the true condition of their hearts: offering diseased and disabled animals as sacrifices, neglecting to teach His law, divorcing their wives, worshiping idols, neglecting justice, neglecting to tithe, and calling evil good. Despite all this, the people still thought God was in the wrong, and they accused God of not loving them and not accepting their worship.

God not only sees what we do, He hears what we say. Some of the people took Malachi's challenges seriously. "Then those who feared the LORD spoke with each other, and the LORD listened to what they said" (Malachi 3:16). May our actions match our words, and may both reflect hearts fully devoted to loving and following God.

Heavenly Father, I confess I am sometimes careless with my words, and I don't always honor you fully. Forgive me and help me, for I do love you, and I want to serve and please you. Amen.

Messengers

MALACHI 3–4

"Look! I am sending my messenger, and he will prepare the way before me. Then . . . the messenger of the covenant, whom you look for so eagerly, is surely coming," says the LORD of Heaven's Armies.—Malachi 3:1

Malachi's book of prophecy closes the Old Testament. God wouldn't speak again for another four hundred years, but He left the promise of two future messengers, one who would be sent to prepare the way for the other.

The first messenger would be like the prophet Elijah in the power of his message (Malachi 4:5). Jesus and the Gospel writers show us that this messenger was John the Baptist, sent to prepare God's people to respond to Jesus when He began His ministry.

The second messenger was the Lord himself—Jesus, the Son of God, fully God and fully human. Malachi warned his listeners that, although they were eager to have God living among them as He promised, His presence would be a refining fire, burning away the dross in His people to reveal pure silver and gold and making it possible for them to worship Him again.

Malachi closed his book with a reminder that a day of judgment will come. When that future day arrives, however, those who love and fear God will experience freedom rather than judgment. Jesus, the messenger of the covenant, was coming to make things right again.

Father God, thank you for your plan to save us and for the Old Testament record that shows us your love in preparing to send your Son, Jesus. Amen.

Encountering GOD'S HEART for YOU in the NEW TESTAMENT

The Gospels

One Message

MATTHEW 1

All this took place to fulfill what the Lord had said through the prophet: "The virgin will conceive and give birth to a son, and they will call him Immanuel" (which means "God with us").—Matthew 1:22–23 NIV

Four books we call Gospels open the New Testament, but there's just one gospel message: Jesus is the Messiah (or *Christ*, in Greek)—the Anointed One—and the Son of God. Each Gospel author had a specific purpose for writing and an intended audience.

Matthew (also known as Levi) was a Jewish tax collector who became a disciple when Jesus called him (Matthew 9:9). Matthew wrote to a Jewish readership to convey that the Messiah whom God had promised through the prophets had come. To make this point, Matthew frequently quotes the prophets (especially Isaiah), as he does in chapter 1 while recounting Jesus' birth to Mary, a virgin.

The genealogy that opens Matthew's Gospel traces Jesus' legal lineage from Abraham through David to Joseph, the husband of Mary, Jesus' mother. Arranged in three blocks of fourteen generations each, Matthew's genealogy makes omissions his Jewish readers would have understood. However, they would not have expected the presence of four names in the list—Tamar, Rahab, Ruth, and Bathsheba ("the widow of Uriah")—four women, two of them foreigners. Their mention in Jesus' lineage signals the fact that Jesus came not only for the Jewish people—He came for all.

Heavenly Father, thank you for the Gospels and the singular gospel message they convey—Jesus is the Savior who came for all who believe. Amen.

217

Worship Him

MATTHEW 2

"Where is he who has been born king of the Jews? For we saw his star when it rose and have come to worship him."—Matthew 2:2 ESV

Who were the wise men, and how did they know the new star they saw was a sign a new king had been born?

In the ancient world, wise men (also called magi) were scholars interested in astrology, often called on to interpret dreams and signs. Babylon and Persia lay east of Judea, as the lands of Israel were called. Perhaps as a result of the Jewish exile, the Jewish scriptures spread and were studied by these wise men from the east. They could have read this prophecy by Balaam: "I see him, but not now; I behold him, but not near. A star will come out of Jacob; a scepter will rise out of Israel" (Numbers 24:17 NIV).

Somehow they knew. Somehow they were watching. And somehow they desired to see this newborn king, to worship Him! God surely guided them to the house in Bethlehem where they found the child with His mother. They gave Him gifts of gold, frankincense, and myrrh—gifts that could finance a hurried trip and stay in Egypt to keep the child safe from the angry, apprehensive King Herod. Then, through a dream, God guided them home by a different route.

Wise men, those magi. They heard about a powerful king sent from God, they watched for Him, and they sought Him out. May you and I be wise like them.

Dear Lord, how you work things together according to your plan! May I always seek and worship Jesus. Amen.

Baptism

MATTHEW 3

Then Jesus went from Galilee to the Jordan River to be baptized by John.—Matthew 3:13

Someone has said that integrity is doing the right thing even if no one is watching. Jesus showed us the importance of doing the right thing because it pleases God.

God sent John the Baptist to call the Jewish people to stop sinning and to be baptized as a sign of their repentance. John was the voice calling in the wilderness prophesied by Isaiah who would prepare people to be ready to receive Jesus. But why did Jesus come to John to be baptized, since He had never sinned? One reason is this: "to fulfill all righteousness" (Matthew 3:15 NIV).

Jesus showed God's approval of John's message and baptism by coming to be baptized himself. Though He had no need to repent, He showed the crowds—and us—that repentance is the right state of heart and pleases God. Christian communities may differ over the method and purpose of baptism, but Jesus has shown us it's the right thing to do.

At Jesus' baptism, He identified with the sinners He came to save. As He came up out of the water, the Holy Spirit descended on Him in the form of a dove, and God spoke from heaven of His pleasure with His Son. Jesus was doing what God had sent Him to do.

Dear God, how could I ever please you as Jesus did, sinner that I am? Only by receiving the righteousness of Jesus through faith in Him who never sinned and always did what is right. Amen.

219

Tested

MATTHEW 4

"Be gone, Satan! For it is written, 'You shall worship the Lord your God and him only shall you serve.'"—Matthew 4:10 ESV

After Jesus' baptism, the Spirit led Jesus into the wilderness, where He fasted forty days and forty nights. Satan came to tempt Him—first to use His power as God's Son to satisfy His hunger, then to manipulate God to action, and then to rule the world by worshiping Satan instead of going to the cross. Jesus resisted each temptation, countering Satan's challenges with "It is written" followed by truth from Scripture, God's Word. What a powerful demonstration to us of *our* great need to know God's Word and use it when we are tempted!

Satan knows God's Word too and is happy to twist it to confuse us—all the more reason for us to know what God says. When we know the truth, we can discern Satan's lies and deceptions.

Jesus identified himself with human sinfulness by being baptized, and in the wilderness He identified himself with human temptations—"the lust of the flesh, the lust of the eyes, and the pride of life" (1 John 2:16 NIV). Fully human as we are, yet without sin—that's our Savior, Jesus.

Lord Jesus, help me live for you, resisting the temptations that come, secure in your love and your Word. Amen.

Blessed

MATTHEW 5

"Blessed are the poor in spirit, for theirs is the kingdom of heaven."—Matthew 5:3 NIV

When someone dies, we talk about heaven. But Jesus talked about heaven in the context of living. He taught often about the kingdom of heaven—the rule of God in people's hearts.

Matthew opens his account of Jesus' Sermon on the Mount with teaching we call the Beatitudes. They sum up the traits and attitudes of those who live with trust in God, depending on Him because they recognize their own spiritual lack. Humility, mercy, purity, peacemaking, desiring justice, seeking righteousness, mourning the sin in the world and their own lives—people who live with these attitudes and actions, Jesus says, are blessed.

Blessed sometimes is said to mean "happy," but the meaning is more broad—"spiritually prosperous, happy, to be admired" (AMP). When we live with the kingdom attitudes listed in the Beatitudes, we can anticipate amazing rewards. Does it seem unreasonable that persecution because you follow Jesus will bring blessing? Jesus says it is not only reasonable but certain—and a cause for great gladness.

Are you living as a citizen of the kingdom of heaven? You will be blessed.

Lord Jesus, help me see my spiritual need and find relief in you. Rule in my heart! Amen.

221

Kingdom Living

MATTHEW 5

> "You have heard that it was said, 'Love your neighbor and hate your enemy.' But I tell you, love your enemies and pray for those who persecute you."—Matthew 5:43–44 NIV

Pray for my enemies? I'd rather not. I don't want harm to come to them; I just want to get away and forget about them.

How do you handle the people who oppose you?

The law God gave Moses for Israel includes the command "Love your neighbor as yourself" (Leviticus 19:18). By the time of Jesus, Jewish religious leaders had added "and hate your enemy." Jesus corrected things with the reminder that from God's perspective, all people are our neighbors, even our enemies. To do good to them and pray for them is to imitate God, who sends rain and sunshine on those who love Him and on those who don't. We need to love perfectly, as God does. How is that possible?

Throughout the Sermon on the Mount, Jesus presents a kingdom where God rules in people's hearts. The Jewish religious leaders thought that with their extreme rule keeping, they were perfectly righteous, but Jesus said that to enter the kingdom of heaven we need a righteousness greater than that of the rule keepers (Matthew 5:20). How is that possible?

Rule keeping can't make you perfect. Let Jesus, the only One who ever lived a perfect life, give you *His* righteousness instead.

> *Heavenly Father, may Jesus' righteousness and power rule in my life. Amen.*

How to Pray

MATTHEW 6

"This, then, is how you should pray."—Matthew 6:9 NIV

We needed to pray for our co-worker, and Rob didn't hesitate. Eyes open, head unbowed, he began. It wasn't for show; he wasn't praying to impress us. We could all see and hear how comfortable he was talking to our Father. I've never forgotten it. Clearly, Rob had spent much time alone with God, praying as Jesus taught His followers—simply, directly, humbly, and with great trust.

The Jewish religious leaders loved to be seen praying long, flowery prayers, with their presumed spiritual superiority on view for everyone to see. But Jesus said that being seen was all the reward they would receive. Impressing other people isn't the purpose of prayer, and we can't impress God either. He already knows what we need.

Spend time alone with God, praying as Jesus taught—asking for His name to be honored and His will to be done. Ask for what you need each day, and ask Him to guide you out of temptation's way. With a heart of forgiveness toward others, bring your desire for God to forgive you. Pray with other believers too, but when you do, remember that you're praying to an audience of One.

Dear Lord, I want to talk to you, heart to heart, and I'm so happy that I can. May my prayers always be pleasing to you as I pray as Jesus taught us. Amen.

223

What Do You Treasure?

MATTHEW 6

"Store up for yourselves treasures in heaven. . . . For where your treasure is, there your heart will be also."—Matthew 6:20–21 NIV

Are you a collector? Do you own art or jewelry you plan to pass on to younger members of your family? Trendwatchers tell us that many young modern families aren't interested in inheriting the possessions the older generation has valued. They place importance on newer styles and trends.

So what *do* you treasure? More valuable than any possession you could ever own are the treasures you store up in heaven.

It's all about focus. Keep your mind focused on what God says is important, and your heart will follow. Money decisions will simplify. It's impossible, Jesus said, to serve both God and money. Only one or the other can rule in your heart.

And as a bonus, when you're banking treasures in heaven and your first focus is seeking His kingdom and His righteousness, there's no need to worry. Jesus assures us that our heavenly Father will provide everything we need (Matthew 6:33). You are of great value—a treasure—to Him.

Dear God, I don't want my possessions to rule my heart. Help me to start banking my treasures in heaven with you. Amen.

Specks and Logs

MATTHEW 7

"How can you say to your brother, 'Let me take the speck out of your eye,' when all the time there is a plank in your own eye?"—Matthew 7:4 NIV

My husband, who worked as a probation officer, enjoys watching *Judge Judy* on TV. Judge Judy asks pertinent questions, listens carefully to the answers, and quickly sizes up the situation and the people involved. She decides who's telling the truth and who's lying, who's guilty and who's not.

That's her job, passing judgment. But it's never ours, according to Jesus.

We can judge—in the sense of evaluation—but condemning others means we will be judged with that same harsh measure. Instead, our attitude toward others should be mercy because God has been merciful to us.

Jesus sometimes used humor to make a point. Why would we try to correct someone's speck-sized error when we're walking around with a log-sized sin in our own life? It's ludicrous—and makes me wonder if that's how God sees our hypocrisy when we act that way.

Are there others you've been judging for specks in their eyes? Maybe it would be a good idea to find a mirror, see the log, and adjust your mindset to mercy.

Lord Jesus, sometimes I do judge others, writing them off, thinking I am a better person. I forget the mercy you show to me. Forgive me and help me to judge rightly—with mercy. Amen.

225

Build Wisely

MATTHEW 7

> "Therefore everyone who hears these words of mine and puts them into practice is like a wise man who built his house on the rock."—Matthew 7:24 NIV

In Shanghai, China, stands the world's second-tallest skyscraper, the Shanghai Tower, with 128 floors. It hosts offices, shops, a hotel, and the world's highest observation deck, on the 118th floor. Most amazing about the tower, though, is its unique twisting, spiral design.

Before anything so complex and tall could be built above ground in Shanghai's soft soil, a super strong foundation had to be built below. Nearly a thousand steel beams extend three hundred feet down, and concrete forms a wall twenty feet thick.

Jesus contrasted two builders to emphasize our need for a solid foundation for our lives. What makes our foundation strong? Hearing Jesus' words and putting them into practice. Find the narrow way and follow it. Don't listen to the false teachers and false disciples; be discerning.

The crowds who heard Jesus' Sermon on the Mount recognized that He taught them with authority, not as their teachers of the law. Let Jesus be your authority. Then build your life with Him as your foundation, and no matter what storms may come, you will stand.

Lord Jesus, I want to build wisely. I want to stand firm every day I live. Help me hear you and do what you say. Thank you for your loving direction for my life. Amen.

What Kind of Man?

MATTHEW 8–9

The disciples were amazed. "Who is this man?" they asked. "Even the winds and waves obey him!"—Matthew 8:27

As rescuers planned and worked for days to free eleven young soccer players and their coach from a flooded cave in Thailand, they feared that monsoon rains would foil their efforts. Christians at the church attended by one of the boys prayed throughout the rescue effort, as did Christians around the world. Though some rain fell during the mission, pumps kept up until the very end.

Jesus slept soundly as wind and waves threatened the disciples' boat at night on the Sea of Galilee. When the terrified disciples woke Him and the wind and waves obeyed His order to settle down, the disciples' terror turned to both awe and confusion. Who *was* this teacher they were following? What kind of man could command the elements like that?

Only the Son of God.

In the region of Galilee, as Isaiah had prophesied, the people living in darkness saw a great Light. Jesus ministered throughout their region with power. He healed diseases and deformities. He commanded the weather. He cast out demons. He forgave sins and raised the dead.

Jesus often called himself the Son of Man, a title of the Messiah prophesied by Daniel. Fully God, and fully human, He was "given authority, glory and sovereign power" (Daniel 7:14 NIV).

What kind of man is this? This is Jesus.

Heavenly Father, how wonderful it would have been to see and hear Jesus on earth! Thank you that I can know Him now through your Word and His presence in my heart. Amen.

227

Harvest Workers

MATTHEW 9–10

> "The harvest is plentiful but the workers are few. Ask the Lord of the harvest, therefore, to send out workers into his harvest field."—Matthew 9:37–38 NIV

I never expected to be a POM—parent of a missionary. But suddenly, it seemed, my oldest daughter and her husband were serving God in another country. Jesus' call for harvest workers took on new importance. Six and half years later, my daughter and her husband, along with their firstborn, returned to the states to live, but they continue to work in God's harvest field in a variety of ways.

And so can you and I. Some of us send, and some of us go, but all of us can be harvest workers right where we are.

As He went from place to place, teaching, proclaiming the good news of the kingdom, and healing, Jesus felt compassion for the crowds "because they were harassed and helpless, like sheep without a shepherd" (Matthew 10:36 NIV). Take a look around your neighborhood, your school, your workplace, the shopping mall—don't the people you see also fit Jesus' description?

The harvest is still plentiful. People still wait for someone to bring the good news of a God who cares and a Savior who rescues. Don't be shy—tell them! You don't have to be a missionary in a foreign country to be a harvest worker. And perhaps you'll be the answer to someone's prayer for more workers in God's harvest field.

Lord Jesus, help me see the people around me as you see them, and help me offer them your message of salvation and hope! Amen.

Rest

MATTHEW 11

"Come to me, all who labor and are heavy laden, and I will give you rest."—Matthew 11:28 ESV

What's the most tired you've ever been? Are you tired today? Is your fatigue due to lack of sleep, illness, physical exertion, emotional stress?

Or are you worn out from trying to do the impossible—to earn your way into heaven?

The religious leaders of the Jews interpreted God's law by adding hundreds of additional requirements, a heavy burden. No one could follow all the rules no matter how hard they tried. (Of course, the religious leaders thought they did a pretty good job of it.) What hope of pleasing God did anyone have?

"Come to *me*," Jesus said. "Take my yoke upon you and learn from me, for I am gentle and humble in heart, and you will find rest for your souls" (Matthew 11:29 NIV). To be yoked is to be connected side by side, like two oxen pulling a plow. Jesus' image here means we can go through our lives as His disciples, side by side with Him. Learning His ways. Not worrying. Letting Him lead. (It's *His* yoke, remember?)

Even more, being yoked to Jesus sets us free from trying to be good enough for God. Being yoked to Jesus means living with faith that He's already done the work and paid the price. We can rest in the safety of knowing we belong to Him.

Lord Jesus, you lived a perfect life and then gladly died for sinners. Thank you for doing for me what I could never do for myself. Amen.

229

Parables of the Kingdom

MATTHEW 13

He told them many things in parables.—Matthew 13:3 NIV

Most of us love a good story, and Jesus was a master storyteller. Not everyone who listened to Him heard His stories—called parables—exactly the same, however.

Jesus told parables to illustrate His points in memorable ways. Those with spiritually sensitive, seeking hearts could hear the parables and understand the teaching. But for those who weren't seeking God, who perhaps came to hear Jesus because He was a novelty, for them the parables *hid* spiritual truths. They simply heard Jesus tell stories. Isaiah prophesied that some who heard Jesus' parables would miss the truths they contain (Isaiah 6:9–10).

The parables aren't allegories; every detail in a parable doesn't have another meaning. Instead each parable generally teaches one or two spiritual truths, most often about God's kingdom on earth during the present age, before Jesus returns. (Matthew uses the term *the kingdom of heaven* instead of *the kingdom of God* because he was writing to the Jews, who avoided saying God's name aloud.)

We can learn so much from Jesus by listening to His stories with seeking, sensitive hearts. Is that how you are listening to Jesus' parables today?

Lord Jesus, I want to listen to you and learn from you. Help me hear your parables with a teachable, seeking heart. Amen.

230

Son of God

MATTHEW 14, 16

> Simon Peter answered, "You are the Messiah, the Son of the living God."—Matthew 16:16 NIV

Have you ever been in the presence of someone famous or powerful? How did you respond? I once sat across the airplane aisle from Yo-Yo Ma and his cello, and on another trip, as I entered an airport restroom, I encountered Maya Angelou preparing to leave. Both times I played it cool, trying to act as if I encountered celebrities every day.

But when the disciples saw Jesus walking toward them on the choppy water of the windy Sea of Galilee just before sunrise, Peter had a different response. If this was truly Jesus and not a ghost, Peter wanted to be right where Jesus was, doing what He was doing.

Jesus said, "Come."

So Peter climbed out of the boat and walked on the water toward Jesus—until fear took over. Then he began to sink, and Jesus reached out to save him, asking gently, "Why did you doubt?" (Matthew 14:31 NIV).

Back in the boat, as the wind died down, the disciples worshiped Jesus. They were beginning to understand who He was. Soon Peter would confidently answer Jesus' question "Who do you say I am?" with "You are the Messiah, the Son of the living God" (Matthew 16:16).

We never need to hang back from Jesus. He was sent to save us and give us life; He encourages us to come and not doubt, no matter our circumstances. Do you need to walk confidently closer toward Jesus today?

Lord Jesus, I need to hear your encouragement today! May I walk through every circumstance with my eyes on you. Amen.

231

Tangled

MATTHEW 16–17, 20

"If any of you wants to be my follower, you must give up your own way, take up your cross, and follow me."—Matthew 16:24

The disciples didn't like what they were hearing. Why was Jesus talking about suffering and dying? He was the Messiah, God's Son, sent to save His people. How could He rescue anyone if He were dead? They didn't understand, and they seem to have completely missed that He also told them He would be raised from the dead. Peter even challenged Jesus—"Never, Lord! Not going to happen!"

But Jesus rebuked Peter. Insisting on our own way works against God's purposes. Looking at the world from only a human point of view, we will miss what God is doing. Have you ever held a beautiful piece of tapestry? On the underside, it's only a tangle of threads.

Our desires often conflict with God's will. To be Jesus' disciple, His student, to live life His way, we have to put His desires ahead of our own. This isn't a call to a spartan existence; Jesus isn't talking about treating ourselves roughly. He's not asking us to deny ourselves *something*. He's telling us we can't insist on our way *and* follow Him at the same time.

Think again of a beautiful tapestry and the tangle of threads that create it. Give your life over to Jesus and let Him design the tapestry of you. You can trust Him!

Lord Jesus, you gave yourself up for me and all who believe. Help me take up my own cross, letting you be Lord over all my desires. Amen.

Seventy Times Seven

MATTHEW 18

"Shouldn't you have had mercy on your fellow servant just as I had on you?"—Matthew 18:33 NIV

Actions leave evidence. The number on the scale says whether you've been sticking to your new healthy eating habits. The mess on the kitchen floor means the dog has gotten into the trash again. The chocolate smeared across your grandchild's face? That's evidence he found the cookie jar.

And your ability to forgive others from your heart is evidence you know you've been greatly forgiven.

The Jewish rabbis (teachers) promoted forgiving an offender three times. Peter thought seven times was much more generous than that. But Jesus removed these artificial limits. Seventy-seven times or seven times seventy—the idea is the same. You don't keep count.

In Jesus' parable, a master forgave his servant's huge, unpayable debt, yet the servant refused to forgive the debt of a fellow servant who owed him a small amount. We are all like that first servant—with a debt for sin we could never pay completely erased by the blood of Jesus. Given such extravagant freedom, how can we not forgive others who hurt us in big or little ways?

Forgiveness won't always lead to reconciliation or restored trust. Sometimes it shouldn't. But always, our willingness to forgive others is evidence of our own forgiven hearts.

Dear Lord, you have forgiven me of so much! Help me be forgiving of others in return. Amen.

233

Statements

MATTHEW 21

When the chief priests and the Pharisees heard Jesus' parables, they knew he was talking about them.—Matthew 21:45 NIV

I recently looked at an eyeshadow collection called Statement, with deep, bold colors. The fashion industry often entices us to show others who we are by how we look. Be free! Be bold! Make a statement!

Jesus rode into Jerusalem on a donkey colt as the prophet Isaiah had predicted the Messiah would do. He was making a statement the Jewish leaders couldn't miss—He was the one sent by God to be king. He had been making this statement in big and small ways all along, but the leaders didn't want to hear it. Their desire to be rid of Him intensified.

Jesus had harsh words for them. Refusing to accept Him and repent, they were like the son of the vineyard owner who said he would go to work for his father but didn't. They were like the tenant farmers who tried to take over the enterprise by killing off the owner's servants and then his own son.

The chief priests and Pharisees knew Jesus was talking about them as He told these parables. They understood His reference to the cornerstone—himself—and the consequences to those who would try to thwart God's plan. But they were stubborn and unmoved and continued to look for a way to arrest Jesus. They were making a statement of their own.

Dear God, may the statement of my life be repentance and thankfulness because of the love and mercy Jesus offers! Amen.

Be Ready

MATTHEW 24–25

"Therefore keep watch, because you do not know on what day your Lord will come."—Matthew 24:42 NIV

I've never liked being late to appointments and events. Wherever I'm headed, I want to be ready.

When Jesus told His disciples the temple would one day be a pile of rubble, they wanted to know when. His answer mixed details of the coming Roman conquest of Jerusalem with descriptions of His return to earth—the second coming. No one but God the Father knows when that will be, Jesus said. The important thing is to be ready and to remain faithful while we wait, serving others with the abilities and resources God gives us. Faithfulness, watchfulness, service—these make us ready to meet our Lord.

So how are you doing with that?

Elisabeth Elliot, author and missionary, said, "The life of faith is lived one day at a time, and it has to be lived—not always looked forward to as though the 'real' living were around the next corner. It is today for which we are responsible. God still owns tomorrow."

Be responsible for your today, every day. An ICU nurse told me how she managed to keep training her five children spiritually even after her long, busy shifts. "Sometimes I'm too tired to pray with each one separately at bedtime," she said. "So I let them all tuck me in, and they pray for me!"

Lord Jesus, I want to be ready and watching for you on that wonderful day you come back for all who are yours. Show me how I can be responsible for every day. Amen.

235

Opening the Way

MATTHEW 26–27

> At that moment the curtain of the temple was torn in two from top to bottom.—Matthew 27:51 NIV

Betrayal, a last meal, agonizing prayer, false arrest and a sham trial, desertion, denial, mocking—the painful events leading up to Jesus' death on the cross went unseen by most of the people in Jerusalem. But crucifixions were public events. As Jesus hung on the cross, His behavior and the surrounding atmosphere were visible to all.

Mocking and insults continued, from the chief priests, teachers, and elders as well as from two criminals crucified at the same time. Jesus did not respond to their remarks. He refused wine laced with pain-numbing gall. Darkness fell at noon. Then at the moment Jesus died, at around three in the afternoon, rocks split as an earthquake shook the land. (Matthew even tells us that tombs opened and bodies of holy people were raised to life!) Seeing all that happened, the terrified Roman centurion and others guarding the crucifixion site exclaimed that surely Jesus was the Son of God (Matthew 27:54).

But in the temple, yet another unseen event marked the significance of the cross. Only the high priest could approach God's presence in the Most Holy Place, and only once a year, to make atonement for the sins of the people. As Jesus died, the heavy curtain in front of the Most Holy Place ripped in two—from top to bottom. Jesus' death had opened the way to God for all who would believe.

The terrible day still seemed shrouded, but Sunday was coming.

Lord Jesus, I struggle to fully appreciate what you suffered for me, but I am thankful. Amen.

Risen

MATTHEW 28

"He is not here; he has risen, just as he said. Come and see the place where he lay."—Matthew 28:6 NIV

I grew up during the era of Saturday morning cartoons. Popeye, Mighty Mouse, Bugs Bunny, Wile E. Coyote, Road Runner, and so many others got into impossible-to-survive scrapes week after week. But episode after episode, the characters bounced right back. No one ever died. Cartoons are for children, and children don't have a clear understanding of the finality of death.

Adults do, of course. But do we sometimes think like children when we consider Jesus' death and resurrection? We have only known Him risen. We forget how astounding and wonderful it is that He is *alive*.

Matthew says that early Sunday morning two women "went to look at the tomb" (Matthew 28:1 NIV). Mourning, still trying to process that Jesus had died, they were abruptly confronted with the news—from the lips of an angel—that Jesus was alive. And as they ran to tell the disciples, feeling "afraid yet filled with joy" (Matthew 28:8 NIV), suddenly, there He was.

Jesus. Was. Alive. Can you *imagine*?!

Before He returned to heaven, Jesus told the disciples, "Go and make disciples of all nations" (Matthew 28:19 NIV). Do you sometimes wonder what your role is in Jesus' command? Try starting here. Share the news and the undeniable wonder that Jesus, who died on the cross, is oh-so-very alive!

Lord Jesus, what joy! Death couldn't hold you, the sinless, perfect sacrifice for sin. Thank you, thank you, for being my Savior. Help me lead others to know you too. Amen.

237

Divine Authority

MARK 1

"What is this? A new teaching with authority! He commands even the unclean spirits, and they obey him."—Mark 1:27 ESV

Mark was a cousin of Barnabas, who later traveled with the apostle Paul on some of his missionary journeys. Mark wrote his fast-moving Gospel to communicate to a primarily Gentile audience that Jesus' actions proved His deity and His authority. It's believed that Mark wrote from Rome and that the apostle Peter was his primary source for this account of Jesus' life.

Gospel, or "good news," comes from the Greek *euangelion*, which Roman messengers used to shout to gather a crowd before delivering a dispatch from the emperor. Jesus began His preaching ministry by proclaiming God's good news—"The kingdom of God has come near. Repent and believe the good news!" (Mark 1:15 NIV). Mark begins his Gospel by declaring that what he's about to present is "the good news about Jesus the Messiah, the Son of God" (Mark 1:1 NIV).

In Capernaum, the people at the synagogue heard Jesus' authority as He taught. Then they saw that authority demonstrated when Jesus ordered an evil spirit to be quiet and to leave a man. For Mark, Jesus' actions and His many miracles proved His authority to speak as He did and validated His claim to be the Son of God.

How have Jesus' miracles and authority impacted your life? How have you responded to the good news of Jesus, the Son of God?

Lord Jesus, Son of God, may I bow before your divine authority now and every day. Help me see you, hear you, and follow you. Amen.

238

Lord of the Sabbath

MARK 2–3

> And he said to them, "The Sabbath was made for man, not man for the Sabbath. So the Son of Man is lord even of the Sabbath."—Mark 2:27–28 ESV

When do you gather with other believers to worship? How do you typically spend your time on Sundays?

For the people of Israel, the Sabbath served as a reminder of their covenant relationship with God. The Creator had blessed the seventh day and set it apart after He completed His work of creation. Through Moses, God commanded the Israelites to treat the Sabbath as a holy day of rest, but by the first century, the Sabbath had become a burden rather than refreshment. The religious leaders had added restriction upon restriction to God's simple command to rest and honor Him.

So Jesus clashed with the Jewish leaders over the Sabbath. They viewed themselves as Sabbath authorities, but Jesus was the true Lord of the Sabbath. As God, He had created the Sabbath, and He had the right and the authority to determine its purpose. He could even abolish it or re-create it. After the resurrection, the first day of the week became the church's usual day of worship.

We do need rest. For many, taking a sabbath means taking a break, setting aside time for quiet interaction with God and for other activities that refresh us. It's worth considering how the concept of sabbath might enrich your life. Why not ask the Lord of the Sabbath to guide you?

Lord Jesus, show me how to honor you with times of rest, reflection, and service apart from my usual busy week. Amen.

239

Family Circles

MARK 3

"Here are my mother and my brothers! Whoever does God's will is my brother and sister and mother."—Mark 3:34–35 NIV

Jesus attracted a crowd wherever He went. Sometimes so many people pressed in on Him, with so many needs, He couldn't even find time to eat.

Jesus' family set out to find Him and bring Him home, thinking He must be out of His mind. But the religious leaders were having deeper, more destructive thoughts about Jesus. They accused Him of being controlled by Satan and getting His power to cast out demons from Satan himself. Jesus warned that they were dangerously close to the hardness of heart and rejection of God that would keep them from ever desiring God's forgiveness.

Jesus' family did catch up with Him, surrounded by a crowd. I'm sure Jesus welcomed them kindly and gladly, but His first response probably wasn't what anyone expected to hear. Jesus spoke of a bigger family than those related to Him by blood. He said His family is formed by those who do God's will. As wives, moms, and grandmas, we struggle with this sometimes.

But God created the family. We can love and care for our families yet keep Him first, praying for His family circle to grow.

Lord Jesus, thank you for my place in your family because of my faith and trust in you. Help me care for those I love yet keep you first in my heart. Amen.

The Sower

MARK 4

"Others, like seed sown on good soil, hear the word, accept it, and produce a crop—some thirty, some sixty, some a hundred times what was sown."—Mark 4:20 NIV

If you have ever planted a garden, you know the importance of good soil. But have you ever thought of human hearts as potential garden plots?

In Jesus' parable of the sower, seed represents the Word of God. As the seed is sown, it falls on four kinds of soil—representing the hearts of four kinds of people—with four different results.

The seed bounces off the hard soil of a footpath—a hardened heart. It sprouts but withers in the thin soil covering rocky ground—a heart without strength for facing trials. The seed grows but is soon choked out in the soil full of thorns (or weeds)—a heart that allows other desires to take priority over God. But in the rich, good soil—an open, accepting heart—the seed of God's Word sprouts, takes root, becomes a strong plant, and produces a crop of good things.

It's wise for us to consider what kind of soil we are. Don't worry—hearts can change!

Even in good soil, not all plants produce the same amount of fruit, and all who receive the Word into receptive hearts don't produce same-sized results either. We don't need to compete with others or compare our crop of goodness to theirs. We just need to let God's Word keep growing and blooming in our hearts and lives.

Lord Jesus, may my heart always be good soil so your Word can grow there and produce a good crop. Amen.

241

What God Has Done

MARK 5

"Go home to your own people and tell them how much the Lord has done for you, and how he has had mercy on you."—Mark 5:19 NIV

During the terrible Carr fire that devasted Redding, California, in 2018, a pastor in Redding asked friends on social media who had experienced other fires to send him messages of hope to share with his congregation. Personal stories engage us, sustain us, encourage us, and give us hope that we also can experience God's love and mercy.

Perhaps that's why Jesus refused the request of the Gerasene man He had delivered from demon possession.

The grateful man begged to join the disciples and follow Jesus, but Jesus said, "Go home. Tell people about God's mercy. Tell them all that God has done for you." The man then traveled throughout the whole region, telling his story. Those who heard this completely changed man proclaim what Jesus had done for him were amazed. What a wonderful introduction to Jesus the people in this Gentile region received!

What has Jesus done for you? How has He shown you mercy? How have you been changed? Your life stories can bring Jesus close to those who haven't met Him and encourage fellow believers to persevere. Sometimes we have to be discreet about the details, but always we can testify to the results—our stronger faith and changed lives. So what are you waiting for? Go and tell!

Lord Jesus, you have done so much for me! Help me share my stories with the people who need to hear. Amen.

Multiplication

MARK 6

But he answered, "You give them something to eat."—Mark 6:37 NIV

The disciples felt shock and dismay when Jesus instructed them to feed the huge crowd of hungry people. How could they possibly provide enough food for everyone?

"What have you got to work with?" Jesus asked. The disciples investigated. They had five small loaves of bread and two dried fish.

Jesus took the bread and fish and blessed it. Then He divided it into pieces—enough for the disciples to serve to more than five thousand people! Everyone ate until they were satisfied, and the disciples gathered twelve baskets of leftovers. What an amazing demonstration of Jesus' power, and what a lesson about using what we have to meet needs around us! Five little loaves and two fish for a crowd? Impossible. But not when the loaves and fish were offered to Jesus.

Australian James Harrison began donating blood and plasma when he turned eighteen. In 2018, at age eighty-one, Harrison made his final blood donation—number 1,173! Since 1967, a rare antibody in Harrison's blood had been used to create an injection to save the lives of unborn Rh-positive babies whose mothers were Rh-negative. The Red Cross in Australia estimates that Harrison's blood donations saved the lives of 2.4 million babies.

What need is tugging on your heart? What do you have to work with? Offer that to Jesus and see what wonderful things He will do!

Lord Jesus, multiply my efforts as I offer you myself and my resources. Amen.

243

Hypocrisy

MARK 7

"You have a fine way of setting aside the commands of God in order to observe your own traditions!"—Mark 7:9 NIV

Special birthday meals, Christmas Eve services, yearly walks for our favorite charity—we all have some traditions that "make" an occasion for us. Traditions are wonderful as long as they don't take on more meaning than the event or the people they were intended to celebrate.

Over time, the Jewish leaders had developed an oral law of rules and regulations and placed it above the written law of Moses. One of the Jewish leaders' man-made rules concerned elaborate ceremonial washing before eating. The leaders criticized Jesus because His disciples didn't observe the tradition.

Jesus had harsh words for those leaders. He called them hypocrites. Outwardly they seemed devoted to God as they strictly followed the rules they had created. But inwardly, Jesus said, their hearts were far from God. Eating with unwashed hands can never defile a person, He told the crowd gathering around. We are defiled by the attitudes of our hearts.

Are you focused on how you appear to others more than how your heart appears to God? What would Jesus say to you about your heart today?

Lord Jesus, look into my heart today. Free me from a need to impress others with my service and worship. Thank you for cleansing me from every sin that defiles. Amen.

If

MARK 9

Immediately the boy's father exclaimed, "I do believe; help me overcome my unbelief!"—Mark 9:24 NIV

Do you believe in Jesus but also have doubts? What do you doubt? Jesus had given the disciples authority to cast out demons, but they hadn't been able to free this demon-possessed boy. Skeptical teachers of the law argued with the demoralized disciples about their failure but had no help to offer. Hesitantly, the boy's distressed father appealed to Jesus, "If you can do anything, take pity on us and help us" (Mark 9:22 NIV).

Jesus turned the father's "if" around. If *he* could believe, anything was possible. The father realized he did indeed have faith and trust in God. He proclaimed his faith and asked for help to overcome his doubt.

Doubt distrusts God's goodness, power, love, and promises. Jesus invited the father to consider the object of his faith—*who* it was that he believed. Throughout the Gospels, Jesus never condemned honest, seeking doubt but always encouraged doubters to believe.

So do you have doubts? What do you doubt? Focus on who it is that you believe and watch your faith grow as your doubt shrinks.

Lord Jesus, I do believe; help my unbelief! Grow my faith and diminish my doubt as I remember your goodness, power, love, and promises. Amen.

245

Servant of All

MARK 10

"Even the Son of Man did not come to be served, but to serve, and to give his life as a ransom for many."—Mark 10:45 NIV

Do you aspire to lead others? Do you yearn for significance? What motivates you?

James and John had aspirations. In the future when Jesus ruled the world, they wanted to be sitting right next to Him, one on each side of His throne. "You don't really know what you are asking," Jesus said. But James and John believed they were able to face whatever was required to receive the honor they were asking for.

Their bold request rankled the other disciples, who began to argue with James and John. Then Jesus interrupted them all for an important lesson.

Service is the way to greatness, He said. Leaders must be servants. Even He—God in flesh—had come not to be served but to serve, and with everything that He had.

Significance is found in service. We lead others closer to Jesus—children and grandchildren, spouses, colleagues, neighbors, other believers—when we serve them.

What example could be more motivational for us than that of our Savior? How will you follow Jesus' example today?

Lord Jesus, may my only claim to greatness be the people I loved and served for your sake. Amen.

Moving Mountains

MARK 11

"Therefore I tell you, whatever you ask for in prayer, believe that you have received it, and it will be yours."—Mark 11:24 NIV

A fig tree forms leaves and bears fruit simultaneously, so Jesus expected to find figs on the leafy tree near Bethany as He headed into Jerusalem with the disciples. But the fig tree's leaves seemed just for show; the tree had no figs. Jesus cursed the fig tree, and the next time the disciples saw it, the tree had completely withered. What did it mean?

The Old Testament uses the fig tree as a metaphor for Israel. God had formed and blessed Israel to bear fruit for Him, but the people's leaders had turned from true worship and fruitfulness to ritual religion and legalism. Jesus' curse of the fig tree symbolized God's judgment.

But when the disciples noticed the withered fig tree, Jesus surprised them by telling them to have faith. What's the connection between the fig tree and faith? Without faith in God, no one can bear fruit. Obstacles will come, but obstacles can be moved. In Jewish culture, moving a mountain meant accomplishing something that seemed impossible.

Mark 11:24 often is misused. The verse doesn't mean that God is obligated to give us whatever we ask for if we just have enough faith that He will! But when we ask in faith for God to move a mountain-sized problem *His way*, we can count on Him to answer and to act.

Lord Jesus, I want to bear fruit for you. When obstacles come, I'll ask you to accomplish your will your way. Help me trust you! Amen.

247

Free

MARK 14

> While they were eating, Jesus took bread, and when he had given thanks, he broke it and gave it to his disciples, saying, "Take it; this is my body."—Mark 14:22 NIV

Only the blood of a perfect lamb on their doorposts saved the Israelites on the night God set them free from slavery in Egypt. The Passover meal the Israelites observed each year commemorated that night of freedom. In Communion we remember the high cost of our freedom from the power and effects of sin—the life of Jesus, our Passover Lamb.

Jesus celebrated Passover with His disciples on the night before He died. But while they were eating He gave new meaning and significance to two elements of that meal—the bread and the wine. Like a loaf of unleavened bread broken into pieces, Jesus' body would be broken as a once-for-all sacrifice for sin. Like the glistening wine on the Passover table, Jesus' blood would be poured out to initiate a new covenant between God and all who would believe. Incredibly, Jesus freely suffered and died in our place.

My friend Judy visited a church with her nephew, Parker, who was five. As they got in line to take Communion, Parker exclaimed with great excitement, "It's free!"

"Yes, Parker," Judy wrote on Facebook, "more free than you realize."

Lord Jesus, you freely gave your life to set me free. I want to remember and thank you at every Communion observance and every day that I live. Amen.

Joy

MARK 16

And very early on the first day of the week, when the sun had risen, they went to the tomb.—Mark 16:2 ESV

From afar, they watched Jesus die on the cross—Mary Magdalene, Mary the mother of James and Joseph, and Salome—some of the women who had followed Jesus as He ministered in Galilee and who had come with Him to Jerusalem. The two Marys watched as Joseph of Arimathea and Nicodemus hurried to anoint and bury Jesus' body before sundown (John 19:39–42). Then as the Sabbath began, so did the waiting.

Friday night, Saturday . . . on Saturday evening, the Sabbath ended. The women prepared more spices and ointments for anointing Jesus' body and burial clothes. But then, more waiting . . . another long, dark night.

Psalm 30:5 says, "Weeping may last through the night, but joy comes with the morning." But when the sun finally rose and the women went to the tomb, they weren't expecting joy. They were worried about who could roll the stone away so they could enter the tomb and finish burial preparations on a corpse. No, they weren't expecting joy.

But they found it.

The stone? Rolled away. The tomb? Empty. Their assignment? "Go, tell his disciples and Peter that he is going before you to Galilee. There you will see him, just as he told you" (Mark 16:7 ESV).

Trembling. Astonishment. Joy!

Lord Jesus, death couldn't hold you! Such amazing joy! In my dark times of waiting, may I remember this. Amen.

249

Certainty

LUKE 1

> Having carefully investigated everything from the beginning, I also have decided to write an accurate account for you, most honorable Theophilus, so you can be certain of the truth of everything you were taught.—Luke 1:3–4

Do you have a favorite doctor, one who never seems rushed and always listens to your concerns? As a physician (Colossians 4:14), the author of the Gospel of Luke would have learned to observe and listen carefully, and it seems he put that skill to work as a writer too.

Luke's account of Jesus' life is the longest of the four Gospels and the most detailed. A Gentile Christian, Luke wrote with a Greek and Roman audience in mind and based his account on eyewitness reports. It's possible that Luke spoke with Jesus' mother, Mary, given the unique details he includes about Jesus' conception and birth.

Dedicating his Gospel to Theophilus suggests that Theophilus might have been Luke's financial support as he wrote, a common practice because writing by hand on costly parchment was a time-consuming, expensive venture. Even as Luke honored Theophilus, however, he had a greater concern. Luke wanted Theophilus to be assured of the truth of what he had been taught about Jesus—His diety and His humanity; His life, death, and resurrection; and His salvation.

Are you as certain of these truths about Jesus as Luke desired Theophilus to be? Luke invites us all to read his investigative report and be assured.

Dear Lord, thank you for your Word, carefully written, guided by your hand, so I and others can know your Son, Jesus, and believe. Amen.

Surprised by an Angel

LUKE 1

> "The Holy Spirit will come upon you, and the power of the Most High will overshadow you. So the baby to be born will be holy, and he will be called the Son of God."—Luke 1:35

When Zechariah found himself face-to-face with the angel Gabriel in the temple, he asked Gabriel for a sign that what he said was true. But Mary responded much differently to Gabriel's words to her.

Mary could have been a teenager when Gabriel appeared to her with the astounding message that God had chosen her to bear His Son. Mary's betrothal to Joseph—much more binding than a couple's engagement today—meant that being found pregnant before the wedding could result in divorce and much social shame.

But Mary accepted Gabriel's announcement with calm submission. She didn't ask why. She didn't ask for a sign. She only asked for more information. Since she was a virgin, just how would she conceive?

By the power of God, Gabriel said.

Mary's mind and emotions had to be swirling as she considered this. What would she tell her family? What would she tell Joseph?

"'I am the Lord's servant,' Mary answered. 'May your word to me be fulfilled'" (Luke 1:38 NIV).

May you and I always respond to God's direction with such amazing, unwavering submission!

Dear God, what you ask of us, you empower us to do. I want to trust and follow you fully, as Mary did. Amen.

251

Shepherds and Prophets

LUKE 2

But Mary treasured up all these things and pondered them in her heart.
—Luke 2:19 NIV

Gabriel had told Mary that her son would receive the throne of his ancestor David and that He would reign over a kingdom with no end (Luke 1:32–33). After Jesus was born, God gave Mary more insight about the baby's future.

First came the shepherds, looking for a baby wrapped in swaddling clothes and lying in a manger. Finding Mary, Joseph, and the baby exactly as the angel had described to them, the shepherds couldn't stop talking about the angel's message that this baby was the Savior, God's Messiah.

Later, when Jesus was forty days old, two prophets of God spoke to Mary and Joseph when they brought the baby to the temple. Simeon praised God for letting him see the One who would bring salvation to Jews and Gentiles alike. But Simeon also prophesied about the divisions and sorrows that awaited. Anna, another prophet in the temple that day, "gave thanks to God and spoke about the child to all who were looking forward to the redemption of Jerusalem" (Luke 2:38 NIV).

Luke tells us that Mary treasured everything the shepherds told her and stored up their words to ponder in her heart. Surely she added the prophets' words to her treasure store as well. The future would unfold in time, but for now, she had a special boy—a gift from God—to raise.

Heavenly Father, may I seek insight in your Word and strength from your Spirit and confidently face the tasks you give me, as Mary did. Amen.

In My Father's House

LUKE 2

"Didn't you know that I must be in my Father's house?"—Luke 2:49

When Jesus was twelve, He accompanied Mary and Joseph on their yearly pilgrimage to Jerusalem to celebrate Passover there. And when the feast had ended, Jesus' words and actions gave Mary more reason to ponder what the future held for her son—and for herself.

Rather than join the group of family and friends beginning the long walk back to Nazareth, Jesus stayed behind in Jerusalem, at the temple. When Mary and Joseph finally found Him there, He was conversing with the temple teachers, listening to them and asking them questions, and "all who heard him were amazed at his understanding and his answers" (Luke 2:47). But Jesus expressed surprise that Mary and Joseph had to search for Him. Didn't they know He needed to be in the temple, His Father's house?

Mary and Joseph had yet to fully understand what Jesus already knew—He was the Son of God, with a priority to serve His Father in heaven. But Jesus returned to Nazareth and remained obedient to Mary and Joseph, and once again Mary "stored up all these things in her heart" (Luke 2:51).

Have you felt slow to understand who Jesus is and what that means for you? Continue to seek Him and, like Mary, to ponder. He will make the truth clear as you do.

Lord Jesus, help me seek you in the Word and grant me understanding. I want to know you! Amen.

253

Rejection

LUKE 3–4

"I tell you the truth, no prophet is accepted in his own hometown."—Luke 4:24

After His baptism and His temptations in the wilderness, Jesus began teaching in the synagogues throughout Galilee. Synagogue worship on the Sabbath included the reading of Scripture and a time of teaching based on that Scripture. Everywhere Jesus taught, people praised Him.

Until He returned to Nazareth.

There, He went to the synagogue on the Sabbath—as was His custom—and He read aloud a passage from Isaiah about the Messiah. "The Scripture you've just heard has been fulfilled this very day!" He said (Luke 4:21).

But His listeners doubted. "Jesus is the one God has sent to set people free? Isn't this Joseph's son?" They had known Him since He was a child. What kind of Messiah could He be?

Jesus knew their thoughts and their lack of faith. He knew they would demand miracles and signs, and He challenged them not to react to Him as the Israelites had reacted to Elijah and Elisha. Hearing this, the synagogue crowd turned violent and tried to rush Jesus out of town and over a cliff, but He passed through the crowd and slipped away.

If you had been in the synagogue that day, would you have reacted to Jesus' announcement with scoffing and disbelief, or with faith? Have you accepted Him as the Messiah, sent to set you free?

Lord Jesus, I believe you are who you say you are—the Savior sent from God. Thank you for your love and sacrifice. Help me grow in freedom and faith. Amen.

Prayer

LUKE 4–5

But Jesus often withdrew to the wilderness for prayer.—Luke 5:16

In their book *Only One Life: How a Woman's Every Day Shapes an Eternal Legacy*, Jackie Green and her daughter Lauren Green McAfee include the story of Susanna Wesley and her amazing prayer habit. The mother of ten children in the early 1700s, Susanna craved time to meet with God. So she scheduled two hours for prayer and Bible study each day, sitting with her long kitchen apron thrown over her head while her children played quietly around her.

On Sunday afternoons, Susanna taught others what she learned in her private prayer and study times, and two of Susanna's sons, John and Charles, became renowned evangelists and Christian leaders. But as Jackie Green and her daughter write, the great truth in Susanna's story "is how prayer does not occupy the stage of activity. Its power is in the quiet trust of gentle souls who are willing to pull away from the everyday to commune with God."

Perhaps Susanna learned that power of prayer from the example of Jesus himself. Jesus frequently left the crowds clamoring for His attention for time alone with His Father in a wilderness space. If the Son of God needed to pray and made time for it, then surely we need time with God and must make it a priority in our day as well. Have you talked with God today?

Dear Lord, grow in me a longing for time with you, and show me how to make that time a priority in my life. Amen.

255

Disciples

LUKE 5–6

> "Don't be afraid! From now on you'll be fishing for people!"—Luke 5:10

The day Jesus stepped into Peter's fishing boat and taught the crowd gathered on the shore wasn't the first time Simon Peter had met Jesus. Peter's brother Andrew had introduced them earlier (John 1:40–42), and Jesus had visited in Peter's home and healed his mother-in-law (Luke 4:38–39). Peter, Andrew, and their fishing partners James and John had been getting to know Jesus for a while. But the miraculous, great catch of fish Jesus caused that day seems to have convinced them—they would answer Jesus' call and follow Him.

Witnessing the staggering number of fish in his nets and those of James and John, Peter fell on his knees before Jesus. He recognized two things—he was a sinner, and Jesus was Lord. Peter's first response was fear, but Jesus encouraged him not to be afraid and to embrace a new role—fishing for people.

Peter, Andrew, James, and John were the first disciples, or students, Jesus called. A little later, He called the tax collector, Matthew, too (Luke 5:27–28). Later, from among all those following Him, Jesus chose twelve to be apostles (Luke 6:12–16). Except for Judas, who would betray Him, these closest companions of Jesus would be witnesses to the resurrection, and as the church began, the Holy Spirit would send them out with the gospel message.

Do you follow Jesus—are you His student, His disciple? Don't be afraid—start fishing!

Lord Jesus, help me learn from you each day, and show me where and how to "fish." Amen.

New Wine

LUKE 5

"No one puts new wine into old wineskins."—Luke 5:37

According to one wine-industry website, 80 percent of Americans drink wine because they enjoy the taste, and 61 percent say they drink it primarily to relax. But in Bible times, because water supplies could easily become contaminated, people drank wine as a necessity. Israel was home to abundant vineyards, and Jesus' listeners would have been familiar with the wine-making process.

Harvesting the grapes and then treading, or pressing, the juice from the grapes were festive, joyful occasions. The juice was poured into clay jars or new wineskins, made from whole, tanned goat hides, to ferment. Only new wineskins could accommodate freshly trod grape juice. As the juice fermented, it produced gases that stretched the new skins but would have caused previously used wineskins to burst.

Jesus used the image of wine making to challenge the thinking of the religious leaders who viewed Him as a threat to their established ways. His teaching was like new wine, not intended to succeed within the framework they had built. And there was a danger for those who loved the "old wine"—the old ways—and didn't want to consider the new wine or give it time to reach its fullness.

Have you tasted the new wine of the good news about Jesus? And are you giving your relationship with Him the attention and time that's needed for the gospel to do its work in you?

Lord Jesus, may your words and your teaching grow in me and make me to be more like you. Amen.

257

John the Baptist

LUKE 7

"The blind receive sight, the lame walk, those who have leprosy are cleansed, the deaf hear, the dead are raised, and the good news is proclaimed to the poor. Blessed is anyone who does not stumble on account of me."—Luke 7:22–23 NIV

What have you prayed about that didn't turn out the way you wanted?

God sent the man we call John the Baptist to preach and prepare the way for Jesus and His message. John got people thinking about their need for God and for a Savior; he baptized them in the Jordan River as a sign of repentance.

He also publicly called out Herod, the Roman ruler of Galilee and Perea, because Herod had married his brother Philip's wife, Herodias. That got John arrested and imprisoned, and perhaps he began to wonder why God allowed this. He sent two followers to ask Jesus, "Are you the one I thought you were?"

Jesus' answer turned John's focus to the words of the prophet Isaiah, which Jesus was fulfilling. John needed that focus, as Jesus surely knew, because soon Herodias would demand the head of John the Baptist on a plate, and Herod would grant her wish.

Doing God's will doesn't always turn out the way we want. Prayers aren't always answered the way we think they should be. Jesus told John these are not reasons to doubt Him. Is there a situation you are struggling to make sense of? Jesus is still the Savior. Will you trust Him?

Lord Jesus, may I always submit myself to you, praising you, whatever my circumstances. Amen.

Love and Forgiveness

LUKE 7

"I tell you, her sins—and they are many—have been forgiven, so she has shown me much love."—Luke 7:47

An unnamed woman who quietly crashed a dinner party gave us an unforgettable image of the relationship between our love for God and the forgiveness we receive from Him.

Simon, a religious leader, had invited Jesus to dinner at his home. But Simon ignored the ordinary, expected acts of hospitality—water for washing off the dust, a friendly greeting, anointing oil—and he looked on disdainfully as Jesus allowed this woman to touch His feet. Surely, Simon thought, Jesus would know what kind of woman she was if He were truly a prophet. But Jesus did know, and He also knew what Simon was thinking. With a parable about two debtors, Jesus pointed out that greater forgiveness leads to greater love.

As this unnamed woman with a sinful past washed Jesus' feet with her tears, dried them with her hair, and anointed them with a costly fragrance, her great love showed her awareness of God's forgiveness for her many sins. Simon didn't even have awareness of his need to be forgiven.

The love we have for Jesus is an accurate measure of the awareness of our sin and the forgiveness we've received. Would this be a good time to take inventory of all you've been forgiven and how much love you show?

Lord Jesus, help me see how deep and vast your forgiveness is, and help me grow my love to match. Amen.

259

Faith-Filled Women

LUKE 8

"Daughter," he said to her, "your faith has made you well. Go in peace."—Luke 8:48

Besides the twelve who traveled with Jesus, a group of women also followed Him. Some, like Mary Magdalene, had been healed by Jesus. Joanna, the wife of the manager of Herod's household, had a visible social standing. Others had financial means with which they supported Jesus and the disciples as they ministered. First-century Jewish women had a limited role in religious life, but Jesus welcomed these faith-filled women who chose to follow Him.

Another woman, whose name Luke doesn't tell us, bravely sought out Jesus in her need and received healing and compassion. She had experienced bleeding for twelve long years with no relief, a debilitating condition that also made her ritually unclean and therefore cut off socially. She made her way through the crowd and managed to touch the hem of the back of Jesus' robe. Instantly, she was healed.

Jesus asked, "Who touched me?" (Luke 8:45)—an invitation for the woman to make herself known. When she did, He commended what she had done.

Whatever your need, don't be afraid. Reach out to Jesus with faith that He will act. Your life could change as completely as this woman's did, with just one touch.

Lord Jesus, you so kindly invite us and welcome us when we come to you in faith. May I always reach out to you to help me, whatever I need. Amen.

260

Glory

LUKE 9

> As he was praying, the appearance of his face was transformed, and his clothes became dazzling white.—Luke 9:28

I stepped outside as the summer sky grew dark, and looked up. Venus and Mars shone brightly. Watching the sky, I began to see small, quick streaks of light—the beginning of the peak of the Perseids meteor shower. Amazing! "The heavens declare the glory of God," King David wrote (Psalm 19:1 NIV).

But Peter, James, and John experienced a greater glimpse of glory—the event we call the transfiguration. On a mountaintop with Jesus as He prayed, they saw His appearance change and His clothes become as bright as lightning. Elijah and Moses were there too, talking with Jesus about what He would soon accomplish—His death on the cross. Then a cloud covered the entire mountaintop, and a voice came from the cloud, saying, "This is my Son, whom I have chosen; listen to him" (Luke 9:35 NIV).

Peter, James, and John could never forget seeing Jesus in His glory or hearing God's voice give the command to listen to Him. We also need to listen to Jesus and follow Him. Where do you encounter Jesus' words to you, and how closely are you listening?

Lord Jesus, you are the Son of God and my Savior. I want to listen to you and follow you. Help me turn from all that distracts me to spend frequent time with you. Amen.

261

Who Is My Neighbor?

LUKE 10

The man wanted to justify his actions, so he asked Jesus, "And who is my neighbor?"—Luke 10:29

The man knew the commandments—love God, and love your neighbor. But he wanted off the hook, so he asked Jesus, "Who is my neighbor?" That's when Jesus told His listeners the parable about the man we call the Good Samaritan.

The Jewish people treated Samaritans as outcasts because they were a mixed race. But it was a Samaritan who showed kindness to a Jewish traveler in Jesus' parable after a Jewish priest and a temple worker refused to get involved. Who was a neighbor to the Jewish man? The one who showed kindness. So be like the Samaritan, Jesus said.

This parable always challenges me. So many ministries and helping organizations need resources to sustain their work. So many people need encouragement, direction, a friend, a smile, a prayer. How can I extend kindness to them all?

I can't. But a long-ago Sunday school lesson about this parable has stayed with me: my neighbor is the person I can help. It might be the child I sponsor in another country or the family who receives emergency meals through a food bank I support. It might be the elderly widow across the street whom I visit with a plate of cookies. If my heart is bent toward kindness, I'll find the people in need of what I can give.

How about you? Who is your neighbor?

Lord Jesus, fill me with kindness and show me the ones in need of my help today. Amen.

Mary and Martha

LUKE 10

"There is only one thing worth being concerned about. Mary has discovered it, and it will not be taken away from her."—Luke 10:42

Is busyness the newest status symbol? Some researchers say yes. They found that people who post on social media about their busy lifestyles often are perceived as having higher social status than people who post mostly about their leisure activities.

Jesus had a different way of looking at how we use our time.

When Martha invited Jesus to her home, she became consumed with all the details of showing hospitality to her special guest. But her sister, Mary, wasn't interested in that. Jesus was in the living room, talking and teaching! Mary didn't want to miss a minute. Jesus commended her—she had made the best choice.

Ministry should never crowd out the time we spend with God—talking to Him and listening to what He wants to say to us. But if we are honest, serving the Lord often takes priority over spending time with Him. So do our long lists of must-do tasks each day.

Here's the thing: we're not impressing Jesus with all our efforts and all we're accomplishing. He cares about our hearts, and our hearts need time with Him. Choosing to spend time with Jesus is the best choice we can ever make.

Lord Jesus, every day I feel the pressure of all I think I must accomplish. Help me shift my focus to what you say is important. Help me spend time each day with you! Amen.

263

Keep Praying

LUKE 11

"So if you sinful people know how to give good gifts to your children, how much more will your heavenly Father give the Holy Spirit to those who ask him."—Luke 11:13

When a gift-giving occasion approaches and there's a gift you'd love to receive, do you create a wish list? Leave hints around the house? Ask for what you want?

Jesus prayed often. He taught His disciples to pray. And He encouraged them—and us—to pray boldly and with persistence. He promised that God *will* answer. Why?

Because looking to God as a way of life, praying persistently, is a sign of faith, trust, and dependence—heart qualities that please Him.

Because God is a good Father.

And because God loves to give good gifts to His children.

If imperfect human fathers answer their children's requests with good things, Jesus said, how much more will our perfect heavenly Father give good gifts to His children? Not-giving-up prayer for our needs and our desires *will* be answered. We *will* receive—but not necessarily everything we ask for. God may grant some of what we ask if it is His will and part of His best for our lives. But always, we will receive something even better—the gift of himself, the Holy Spirit in our lives.

So go ahead. Ask. Seek God. Knock persistently. Be bold! And be ready to receive the best gift ever!

Dear God, you are a good, good Father! Thank you for all your blessings, and thank you most of all for the gift of yourself. I love you. Amen.

Division

LUKE 12

"Do you think I came to bring peace on earth? No, I tell you, but division."—Luke 12:51 NIV

Jesus offers us peace with God and makes us part of God's family when we put our trust in Him. But in some places of the world, leaving your family's religion to follow Jesus invites anything but peace within *your* family. Instead, a decision to follow Jesus results in being shamed, disowned, and even imprisoned or killed.

Believers in these places understand what Jesus meant when He said He came to "cast fire on the earth" (Luke 12:49 ESV) and to bring division. Perhaps you experienced rejection too when you became a Christian. Sometimes those closest to us feel the most threatened by our relationship to the Savior. Choosing to have faith or to reject it affects relationships like a refining fire separates gold and dross. And Jesus understands the pain this causes.

Jesus also knew that what He had come to do on the cross was essential to God's plan, and even though it meant great suffering, He was ready to see it through. Is your family divided because of Jesus? Pray for the salvation of those who are rejecting Him. But also be willing to accept the necessity of the refiner's fire just as Jesus was willing to accept the necessity of His death on the cross.

Lord Jesus, you willingly suffered so much in order for so many to be saved. Please heal families divided over faith in you, and may I be willing to accept the pain of any divisions that must come. Amen.

265

Lost and Found

LUKE 15

"Let's have a feast and celebrate. For this son of mine was dead and is alive again; he was lost and is found."—Luke 15:23–24 NIV

To have a child walk away from the Lord and choose a sinful lifestyle is painful. But when that child returns, desiring forgiveness and a new life? Joy and gratitude overflow.

The religious leaders couldn't understand why Jesus cared about the people they considered sinners—people like the tax collectors and others who didn't follow the Jewish law and traditions. To answer them, Jesus told three parables.

If you have lost one sheep, He said, you leave the rest of the flock and search until you find it—and gladly carry it home. If you lose one coin, even though you still have nine others, you diligently sweep your house until you find the coin you lost—and then you call your friends together to tell them the good news. And if you are a father with a son who rejects you and goes his own sinful way, you watch for him daily—and when he returns, repentant, you welcome him back and throw a *big* party!

At some point we've wandered away from our Father, and by His grace we returned. He was watching for us—and heaven celebrated when we turned from death to life—because God loves us so.

Heavenly Father, may I never underestimate how you value and love every person and long for each of us to return to you. Thank you for saving and loving me. Amen.

266

Rich and Poor

LUKE 16

> The rich man also died and was buried. In Hades, where he was in torment, he looked up and saw Abraham far away, with Lazarus by his side.—Luke 16:22–23 NIV

Jesus talked often about the use of money and about the reality of hell. In the parable of the rich man and Lazarus, He talked about both.

In the parable, a rich man ignored the desperation of a poor man named Lazarus who lay outside the rich man's gate. In death their situations were reversed. The rich man suffered in Hades while Lazarus enjoyed heaven at Abraham's side. The rich man desired mercy, but it was too late; his hard heart and lifestyle on earth had determined his fate.

"Then send Lazarus back to earth to warn my brothers," the rich man begged.

But the problem wasn't that the brothers needed evidence of hell. As hard-hearted as the rich man, they already had the writings of Moses and the prophets but chose not to listen to them. So not even someone raised from the dead would convince them, Jesus said.

What about us? How do we view the poor, and how do we help? What are we doing to point people to God's Word and the message of the gospel? How strongly do we desire to keep people out of hell?

> *Lord Jesus, your teaching challenges me! May it change me as well. Help me consider the ways my decisions influence others toward heaven or hell. Amen.*

267

Thankful

LUKE 17

> Then one of them, when he saw that he was healed, turned back, praising God with a loud voice.—Luke 17:15 ESV

I was born with just one hip socket, a problem not discovered until I tried to walk. Instead of the formation that should have cupped the ball of my right thigh bone, my right hip was just a stump. (Newborns today are routinely checked for this defect.) My parents were offered a new treatment option. Doctors positioned the ball of my thigh bone against the stump of my hip and put me in a series of body casts to keep the bones in place. The pressure of the thigh bone against the stump eventually caused a hip socket to grow, and I walk normally.

I am so grateful! But I confess that some days—many days—I am more like the nine men with leprosy Jesus healed than I am like the one healed man who turned around, praised God loudly, and fell at Jesus' feet to thank Him.

It's so easy to take our blessings for granted. But it's not right. Jesus asked, "Were not all ten cleansed? Where are the other nine?" (Luke 17:17 NIV).

The man who gave thanks to God looked through eyes of faith. He saw God's hand in his healing. His faith not only made his healing possible, it saved his soul. May we, as women of faith, see God's hand in all our blessings and give thanks.

Dear Lord, how you have blessed me! Even in the difficulties, I see your hand when I look through eyes of faith. Keep me thankful, Lord. Amen.

268

Let the Children Come

LUKE 18

"Let the children come to me, and do not hinder them, for to such belongs the kingdom of God."—Luke 18:16 ESV

When Jesus told the disciples, "Let the children come to me," He meant the words in a literal sense. The disciples had been rebuking parents who brought their little ones to Jesus for Him to bless. But Jesus meant what He said in a broader sense as well: Help children to know Him. Do nothing to hinder their faith. And follow their example—because trusting God the way children trust their parents is the way to receive God's kingdom in our hearts.

It's a joy to introduce children to God. Help them know Him first as the Creator; teach them that Jesus is their friend. Worshiping and praising is telling God we love Him. Prayer is simply talking to God; reading from the Bible is hearing His words and learning what He says is right.

We hinder children when we downplay their capacity for faith and when our own example doesn't create desire in their hearts. We lead them to the Savior when we point the way and join them on the journey. And even if distance or circumstances limit our contact, we can pray. Do the children in your life know Jesus?

Lord Jesus, I want my children, grandchildren, and children everywhere to know you! Help me point the way to you and remind me to come to you with childlike trust and faith. Amen.

269

Changed

LUKE 19

> "I will give half my wealth to the poor, Lord, and if I have cheated people on their taxes, I will give them back four times as much!"—Luke 19:8

Groups like Alcoholics Anonymous and Celebrate Recovery include making amends as an important part of personal growth and change. Desiring to take responsibility for your behavior and acknowledging how your actions have affected others lead to doing what you can to make things right. A tax collector named Zacchaeus understood this well.

Small of stature, Zacchaeus climbed a tree so he could see Jesus over the crowd at the edge of the road when Jesus came to Jericho. Jesus must have known how close Zacchaeus was to the kingdom, because He called Zacchaeus out of the tree and invited himself to the tax collector's home for dinner. Zacchaeus responded joyfully to this sudden turn of events.

Tax collectors were notorious cheaters; it's how they grew rich. As rich as he was, Zacchaeus may have cheated a lot of people. But the first thing he did after coming to faith in Jesus was to declare his intention to make amends—to give half of all he owned to the poor and to pay back four times to anyone he had cheated. Salvation, Jesus said, had come to Zacchaeus's home that day.

Real repentance shows itself in actions. Do you need to make amends to anyone today?

Lord Jesus, may my actions always reflect a changed heart, and may I make amends to others when doing so will cause no further harm. Guide me, I pray. Amen.

270

Agony in the Garden

LUKE 22

"Father, if you are willing, remove this cup from me. Nevertheless, not my will, but yours, be done."—Luke 22:42 ESV

Their celebration of Passover had been intense. Jesus had been talking about His death once again, and now in the dark night they couldn't stay awake. If you've ever been physically and emotionally exhausted in the midst of a difficult situation, then you can identify with the disciples in the garden of Gethsemane. I think we all can.

But can we identify with Jesus at all? A stone's throw from the disciples, Jesus agonized in prayer. Soon He would face humiliation, physical torture, and death on the cross. Even more fearsome, He would feel the guilt of the world's sin—but He himself had never sinned. He would bear God's wrath toward sin—but all He had ever known was His Father's love. He would experience death—but He was the living God. No wonder He asked for a different way to be found. No wonder an angel came to strengthen Him as He prayed.

We *can't* identify with Jesus as He faced the cross. But how amazing that Jesus was willing to identify with us! He submitted to the Father's will and plan, and He faced all the consequences of sin in our place—instead of us, so we don't have to.

He submitted to God and died for us. May we submit to God and live for Him.

Lord Jesus, you steadfastly faced the cross—for me. May I with great determination live each day for you. Amen.

271

Voices

LUKE 23

> But the mob shouted louder and louder, demanding that Jesus be crucified, and their voices prevailed. So Pilate sentenced Jesus to die as they demanded.—Luke 23:23–24

To Herod, Jesus was a curiosity; to Pilate, a serious inconvenience. To the religious leaders, He was a threat to their position; to the Roman soldiers, some crazy guy who thought he was a king.

Jesus said little to any of them, but He prayed to God about them. He said, "Father, forgive them, for they don't know what they are doing" (Luke 23:34).

To the gathering multitude and the women who mourned as they followed Him out of the city, He was their hope, but He was dying. To the women He said, "Don't weep for me. Weep for what's coming."

To one of the criminals crucified with Him, He was a fraud, but to the other, He was the Savior. To him Jesus said, "Today you will be with me in paradise" (Luke 23:43 ESV).

To the Roman centurion overseeing the crucifixion, Jesus was unlike anyone he had ever dealt with. Just before He died, Jesus said, "It is finished" (John 19:30 ESV) and "Father, into your hands I commit my spirit!" (Luke 23:46 ESV). The centurion praised God and said, "Certainly this man was innocent!" (Luke 23:47 ESV) and "Truly this man was the Son of God!" (Mark 15:39 ESV).

Listen to the voices coming from the crucifixion. Consider how people responded to Jesus. Which voice is yours today?

Lord Jesus, help me love my enemies and forgive according to your example. May I always speak with a voice of belief and faith. Amen.

Understanding

LUKE 24

Then Jesus took them through the writings of Moses and all the prophets, explaining from all the Scriptures the things concerning himself.—Luke 24:27

Have you ever worked diligently on a thousand-piece puzzle, only to discover after hours of work that you're missing one piece?

The disciples had known Jesus as a powerful prophet and a great teacher. They had expected Him to deliver Israel from Roman occupation and make their nation strong again. But He'd been crucified. Now they heard that He was risen. The disciples didn't know what to think.

Jesus appeared to two of the disciples and opened their eyes to what Scripture says about God's plan for the Messiah—His plan to make everything right again. He appeared then to the apostles and other disciples in Jerusalem. Once more He explained, "Everything must be fulfilled that is written about me in the Law of Moses, the Prophets and the Psalms. . . . This is what is written: The Messiah will suffer and rise from the dead on the third day, and repentance for the forgiveness of sins will be preached in his name to all nations, beginning at Jerusalem" (Luke 24:44, 46–47 NIV).

The disciples grasped the missing piece and put it in place. All the history of their people fit together, even Jesus' crucifixion. And now, Jesus was alive, and they had a message to share—not just with the Jews, but with the world!

Dear God, may I understand your Word more and more and share with others the message of Jesus' death and resurrection, the good news of forgiveness—and everlasting life with Him for all who believe. Amen.

273

Witness

JOHN 1

The Word became flesh and dwelt among us.—John 1:14 ESV

C.S. Lewis wrote in *Mere Christianity*, "A man who was merely a man and said the sort of things Jesus said would not be a great moral teacher. He would either be a lunatic—on the level with the man who says he is a poached egg—or else he would be the Devil of Hell. You must make your choice. Either this man was, and is, the Son of God, or else a madman or something worse." The apostle John, writer of the Gospel of John, presents his readers with a similar choice.

John was one of the twelve disciples closest to Jesus, and John refers to himself a few times as "the disciple whom Jesus loved." It's believed John wrote his Gospel in the last decade of the first century, toward the end of his life. Rather than give an account of the events of Jesus' life, John presents longer teachings of Jesus and miracles that clearly show and support Jesus' claim to be God in human flesh. He writes as a witness who knew Jesus well. As John presents the evidence, readers have the opportunity to believe and, by believing, to receive life (John 20:31).

Have you considered the evidence? Have you made your choice? Believe, and live!

Lord Jesus, I believe you are who you say you are—the Son of God, the Word made flesh, my Savior! Thank you for the life you give, now and forever. Amen.

Truth for Every Day

JOHN 2

After he was raised from the dead, his disciples remembered he had said this, and they believed both the Scriptures and what Jesus had said.—John 2:22

Has something in the Bible that you've read many times before suddenly seemed especially full of relevance for your life? That's been my experience.

My friend Lynn, a former missionary, says that's also happened to her. For about ten years, Lynn and I, along with other women, read through the Bible every year and met on Monday nights to discuss what we'd read. Lynn had read the Bible many times before, but she said, "As I read through in a given year, Scriptures that relate to the current issues jump out, often as if I'm seeing them for the first time."

The disciples seem to have experienced Scripture this way too. When Jesus cleared the area of the temple intended as the place where Gentiles could pray, the disciples thought of the Scripture "Zeal for your house will consume me" (John 2:17 ESV). But Jesus' words to the religious leaders, "Destroy this temple, and in three days I will raise it up" (John 2:19 ESV)—a reference to Psalm 16:10—didn't connect with the disciples right away. After the resurrection, they understood.

Do parts of Scripture puzzle or confuse you? Don't worry. Stay engaged. Keep reading and searching. The Word of God is living and active (Hebrews 4:12 ESV). At the right time, God will give you the understanding that you need.

Heavenly Father, thank you for your life-giving words that reach me with what I need at every age and stage of my life. Amen.

275

Believe It

JOHN 3

> "For God so loved the world that he gave his one and only Son, that whoever believes in him shall not perish but have eternal life."—John 3:16 NIV

Robert Ripley's *Believe It or Not!* began as an illustrated newspaper panel in the *New York Globe* in 1919. In 1923, Ripley, an artist, moved to the *New York Evening Post* and hired Norbert Pearlroth as his researcher. Pearlroth spent the next fifty-two years hunting down weird and amazing facts for Ripley to include. After the daily feature was syndicated in 1930, more than 80 million people read it every day. Did they all believe the strange and bizarre facts and events Ripley presented? Most likely they did, because they trusted Ripley, but I suspect nobody's life was changed.

Belief that doesn't change behavior is only intellectual assent. John's Gospel is full of references to belief that lead to great change—belief that Jesus is the Son of God. When we truly believe this, we entrust Jesus fully with our past, present, and future. We receive Him and become children of God (John 1:12). We are, as Jesus told Nicodemus, born again.

This kind of believing leads, Jesus says, to life—eternal life that begins right now. Are you a believer?

Lord Jesus, God's Son, I do believe in you. I have entrusted myself to you. Thank you for my new and never-ending life! Amen.

Harvest

JOHN 4

"Look, I tell you, lift up your eyes, and see that the fields are white for harvest."—John 4:35 ESV

On His way to Galilee, Jesus went through Samaria instead of around it—unusual for a Jewish man, but what happened next was even more unusual.

Resting beside a well while the disciples went into the city to buy food, Jesus asked a woman for a drink. She had come to the well alone, in the middle of the day. She was surprised that Jesus, a Jew, would talk to a woman in public, especially a Samaritan woman. Jesus deftly turned the conversation to spiritual thirst and the living water He could provide. Without condemnation, He showed her His knowledge of her life story. Soon He revealed to the woman that she was speaking to the Messiah.

Could it be? The woman left her water jar and hurried to tell everyone to come meet the man who told her everything she had ever done.

The harvest is ready, Jesus told His disciples. The townspeople asked Jesus to stay with them awhile, and He did. Many believed in Jesus first because of the woman's story, but after listening to Jesus himself they chose to believe based on His words.

Some of the people we know or meet are ready to respond and believe in Jesus—they just need an introduction. Whom do you know who might be ready to hear about Jesus from you today?

Lord Jesus, help me learn to introduce others to you, sensitive to the leading of your Spirit. Amen.

277

Bread of Life

JOHN 6

"I am the bread of life. Whoever comes to me will never go hungry."
—John 6:35 NIV

Do you love bread? I do. Sandwich bread loaded with whole grains, nuts, and seeds. Cinnamon raisin bread. Sourdough bread. Corn bread and tortillas. But not the soft white squares I grew up on—I stopped eating that years ago. It's not real bread!

After the miraculous event we call the feeding of the five thousand, the crowd came looking for Jesus again. He knew they were looking for bread—He had fed them all the day before. But He turned their attention to a different kind of food—spiritual food. He turned their attention to himself. "The true bread of God is the one who comes down from heaven and gives life to the world," He said (John 6:33).

"I am the bread of life" (John 6:35) is the first of seven "I am" statements of Jesus in the Gospel of John. No matter how healthful bread is or how good it tastes, after eating it we will eventually be hungry again, and someday our physical bodies will die. But Jesus is bread that satisfies and gives us life forever. If we continue to believe in Him and live in relationship with Him, He will raise us up on the last day. His body was broken—like bread—for us. He *is* our bread of life.

Lord Jesus, show me how to be nourished by you, the bread of life, today and every day. Amen.

Sin No More

JOHN 8

"Let any one of you who is without sin be the first to throw a stone at her."—John 8:7 NIV

Parents trying to get to the bottom of misbehavior when more than one child is involved often hear something like this:

"I didn't do it. He did!"

"I didn't do it. HE did!"

But when the religious leaders dragged an adulterous woman before Jesus as He sat teaching a crowd, the woman didn't fight back. Instead, Jesus stood up for her.

Everywhere He went, Jesus treated women with kindness, compassion, and respect. The religious leaders were only using this woman as part of a trap. They wanted Jesus to say something—anything—against the law of Moses that required stoning as the punishment in certain situations. Jesus forced them to be honest. "Fine. Go ahead and stone her, and whoever among you has never sinned, go ahead and throw the first stone." One by one, the woman's accusers walked away. The woman was left alone with Jesus and the watching crowd.

"Go and sin no more," Jesus told her. He didn't condemn her. He forgave her. But He directed her to make a change. So often we emphasize Jesus' love and forgiveness but neglect His expectation that forgiveness must lead to a changed life.

We *all* need to face the sin in our lives and confess it. No trying to pass the blame; no finger pointing! Be honest with Jesus, then go and sin no more.

Lord Jesus, may your forgiveness always lead me to leave my sin behind. Help me be honest with you. Amen.

279

Light of the World

JOHN 8–9

"I am the light of the world. Whoever follows me will never walk in darkness, but will have the light of life."—John 8:12 NIV

For a class project, my seven-year-old grandson was assigned to report on the Tybee Island Lighthouse near Savannah, Georgia. I visited the lighthouse with him and climbed all 178 steps to the top. What a view! It was easy to imagine the time when ships depended on lighthouses to help them navigate through a dark night and to keep them away from danger.

The Bible associates light with God and darkness with evil and spiritual need. The Old Testament promised the coming of the light of salvation and the light of God, and Jesus fulfilled those promises. As we follow Jesus, we have the light of life—the light of God in our lives, guiding us and giving us understanding and wisdom.

Jesus healed physical blindness and offered spiritual sight as well, but many turned His offer down. When Jesus healed a man who had been blind since birth, the religious leaders could have responded to this display of God at work and acknowledged Jesus as God's Son, but they refused. As a result, they became even more spiritually blind. A note in one of my study Bibles says, "As the light of the world, Jesus came that the blind might see and those who think they can see will be made blind."

So can you see, or are you blind? Don't refuse the light Jesus offers you.

Lord Jesus, you shine in my darkness and show me the way, and I am grateful. Amen.

The Gate

JOHN 10

"Very truly I tell you, I am the gate for the sheep. . . . Whoever enters through me will be saved."—John 10:7, 9 NIV

Hanging in my home for years has been a framed poster of a painting called "Beyond the Gate." The scene looks out from a fenced garden area toward the street, and a gate stands open toward the garden. Has someone just gone out, or just returned? Or has someone left the gate open in anticipation of a loved one's homecoming? Whatever the situation, the gate has great significance.

When Jesus said, "I am the gate for the sheep," His listeners could easily form two pictures in their minds. The first would be the gatekeeper who guarded a town's common sheepfold at night. In the morning, the gatekeeper was responsible for letting the shepherds into the sheepfold to claim their own sheep and take them out to pasture. Anyone who came into the sheepfold another way was a thief or a robber, not a true shepherd. Jesus' listeners also would have thought of improvised sheepfolds—rocks stacked up to form enclosures in an open field. At night the shepherd slept across the opening, forming a "gate" with his own body.

The way to salvation and full, abundant life, Jesus said, is through the gate—himself. Others make similar claims, but they are thieves and robbers whose goal is to destroy. Have you entered the sheepfold, God's kingdom, through the gate?

Lord Jesus, thank you for making a way for me to find salvation and abundant life. Thank you for being the gate. Amen.

281

The Good Shepherd

JOHN 10

> "I am the good shepherd. The good shepherd lays down his life for the sheep.—John 10:11 NIV

Sheep *need* a shepherd. They wander away from the flock without knowing how to get back. They won't drink from moving water but *will* choose still water that's dirty and contaminated. When sheep feel threatened, they tend to huddle together in one place instead of running away to safety.

But there's one thing sheep are very good at—they learn to recognize the voice of their shepherd. And when their shepherd calls them, the sheep respond and follow wherever their shepherd leads.

In New Testament times, hired hands sometimes took care of sheep, but they couldn't be counted on to stay with the sheep when wild animals came around. Jesus is the good shepherd because He laid down His life to save His sheep—all who would believe and follow Him, whatever their nationality.

Sheep know the voice of their shepherd because they spend much time with him and learn to recognize it above the voices of other shepherds. Because we are Jesus' sheep, we need to spend time with Him, listening to Him, in order to know His voice apart from all the other voices that try to persuade us to follow them.

Can you hear the voice of your Shepherd? Are you listening?

Lord Jesus, I'm so grateful to be one of your sheep. Help me listen to your voice and follow you when you call to me. Amen.

282

The Resurrection and the Life

JOHN 11

"I am the resurrection and the life. Whoever believes in me, though he die, yet shall he live."—John 11:25 ESV

Of all the miracles Jesus performed, John included seven in his Gospel. John calls these seven miracles *signs* because each one signals something different about who Jesus is. The final sign in John's Gospel is the raising of Lazarus from the dead.

Jesus and Lazarus had been good friends, but when Jesus got word that Lazarus was gravely ill, He delayed going to see him. When Jesus did arrive in Bethany, the village where Lazarus lived with his sisters Mary and Martha, Lazarus had been dead for four days. The sisters couldn't understand why Jesus hadn't come to heal Lazarus before he died, but Jesus had known all along what He was going to do. He told Martha, "I am the resurrection and the life." When He called, "Lazarus, come out!" and Lazarus walked out of his tomb, Jesus demonstrated His power over life and death in preparation for His own resurrection—and for ours.

In some places, people who have died are buried facing east, in order to greet Jesus face-to-face when He returns and the dead are raised to life (Matthew 24:27). The resurrection of our bodies is the crux of Christian hope. Jesus told Martha, "Everyone who lives in me and believes in me will never ever die," and He asked her, "Do you believe this, Martha?" (John 11:26). Put your name in the place of Martha's. Do you believe what Jesus has promised?

Lord Jesus, I do believe your promise. I do believe you are the resurrection and the life. Amen.

283

Divine Example

JOHN 13

"Now that I, your Lord and Teacher, have washed your feet, you also should wash one another's feet."—John 13:14 NIV

In second grade I said to my teacher, "I know God made the world, but who made God?" She drew a circle on the chalkboard and said, "God is like this circle, with no beginning and no end." This happened a long time ago, but I can still see my teacher drawing that circle and answering my question.

All teachers know the impact of a good visual to aid a lesson—most certainly Jesus, a master teacher, did. Perhaps that's why, on the night before He died, Jesus gave the disciples a visual to impress on them a lesson about serving one another. In a land where people wore sandals and traveled dusty streets, hospitable hosts provided a servant to wash the feet of dinner guests. But at the start of the Passover meal He ate with His disciples, Jesus took on the role of a servant and washed His disciples' feet. They couldn't miss the meaning of His example or His expectation of them.

We aren't more significant than our Savior, the Lord of heaven and earth; He came to be a servant to all. How have you been serving your fellow believers recently? Do you have a servant's heart? Is there an attitude adjustment you need to make, or something you need to begin to do?

Lord Jesus, help me follow your example. Forgive me for ignoring the needs of fellow believers. Lead me to be a servant. Amen.

A New Commandment

JOHN 13

"A new command I give you: Love one another. As I have loved you, so you must love one another. By this everyone will know that you are my disciples, if you love one another."—John 13:34–35 NIV

How should a church increase its visibility and influence? How should a church communicate to visitors and members what the church is all about? Many modern congregations adopt contemporary marketing methods. They create mission and vision statements, design logos, and place coordinated signage and banners around the church building. They shape worship services to appeal to the people they are trying to reach. Members wear matching T-shirts when they reach out to the community with service projects.

None of these are bad things. They work. But sometimes they might seem to take priority over the command Jesus gave us that tells us how His disciples are to be known. "As I have loved you, so you must love one another."

The New Testament teaches us that the church is Jesus' body. Sometimes I fear that believers don't value one another highly enough. Jesus laid down His life for us. Are we willing to sacrifice with that same attitude for others in our local church and even around the world? If we are, and if we do, then the people in our communities will know that we follow the One who first loved us—and them—and proved it by His death.

Lord Jesus, may I and all believers follow your command to love one another. Let others who need to know you see that we love in the way you first loved us. Amen.

285

The Way, the Truth, the Life

JOHN 14

"I am the way and the truth and the life. No one comes to the Father except through me."—John 14:6 NIV

Have you ever been lost in an unfamiliar area? Has an app on your phone ever given you wrong directions to the address you were trying to find? At times, getting where we want to go depends on someone authoritative knowing the way.

Jesus' disciples didn't understand what He was telling them about where He soon would go and where He someday would take them. "We don't know where you're going," they said. "How can we know how to get there?"

"I am the way to the Father," Jesus said. "And now that you know me, you also know the Father." Later on, the writer of the letter to the Hebrews would say of Jesus, "He is the radiance of the glory of God and the exact imprint of his nature" (Hebrews 1:3 ESV). To know Jesus is to know God.

The popular saying "All roads lead to heaven" isn't true. There's only one way to know God, and that's through His Son, Jesus. He's the Way and shows us the way. He's the Truth and teaches us truth. He's the Life and gives us life. Do you know where you are going, and do you know how to get there? Follow the Way, the Truth, and the Life, and you will reach your destination.

Lord Jesus, thank you for coming to show me the way. Help me follow you throughout life to my home in heaven with our Father. Amen.

Come, Holy Spirit

JOHN 14

"I will ask the Father, and he will give you another advocate to help you and be with you forever—the Spirit of truth."—John 14:16–17 NIV

Do you have a best friend, a sister, a mentor, perhaps an aunt—someone you turn to for a listening ear, for comfort, for advice? Someone you can count on to always come alongside you, to be there for you? That person's role illustrates the meaning of the Greek word for *advocate* or *counselor*—other terms the Bible uses for the Holy Spirit.

As the Son of God, Jesus had every power of God to guide and help the disciples. Our best friends, however, are limited in their ability to help us, because they are human. As Jesus talked with His disciples about the fact that He would be leaving them, He promised to send them "another advocate" like himself—with unlimited ability. The Holy Spirit would soon come to live *in* the disciples, to teach, guide, and strengthen them and to help them love and obey God.

Is the Spirit alive in you? Do you need the help of a divine advocate to navigate challenges and live a holy life? The Holy Spirit comes to live with and in all who trust Jesus as their Savior. He is with you, and His help is always available—just ask!

Lord Jesus, thank you for the gift of the Holy Spirit and the help and peace He brings. Amen.

287

The True Vine

JOHN 15

"I am the true vine, and my Father is the gardener."—John 15:1 NIV

The Old Testament symbolizes Israel as a vine. But in this last of the seven "I am" statements of Jesus in John's Gospel, Jesus says *He* is the true vine. God's plan for all who become His children is that we stay attached to the vine, accept His pruning, and produce much fruit. And Jesus tells us how to do that.

Stay attached. Branches receive their nourishment from the vine. Let Jesus' words dwell in you (John 15:7). Recognize and accept your need for Jesus in order to fulfill God's purpose for your life. "Apart from me you can do nothing" (John 15:5).

Accept pruning. Dead branches are cut away in order to make room for new growth. But even living branches need pruning in order to produce a greater abundance of fruit. Much of the pruning God does in our lives comes from the influence and effect of the Word. That's why it's so important to allow Scripture to fill our hearts.

Produce fruit. Abiding in Jesus, the vine, and accepting God's pruning through the Word leads to fruitful living because we grow in love for God. Then because we love more, we want to obey more. And as we obey more, God produces His fruit—we live holy lives that please Him and make His glory known throughout the world.

Lord Jesus, help me abide in you—to listen closely to your teaching, to allow your Word to direct me daily, and to produce the fruit the Father desires to see in me. Amen.

In the World, Not of It

JOHN 15–17

"Here on earth you will have many trials and sorrows. But take heart, because I have overcome the world."—John 16:33

During and after their last Passover meal together, Jesus poured into the disciples His final messages before His death. Judas had already left to betray Him, and Jesus knew how the night would end. He sought to prepare and comfort the disciples for what was coming, and in His words to them we can find many lessons for ourselves as well. One of those concerns our relationship as believers to the world—to the system of life lived without reference to God.

- *We no longer belong to the world* (see John 17:14). We have answered God's call to come out of the world, and we now belong to the kingdom of God.
- *The world hates Jesus and those who belong to Him* (see John 15:18–20). We shouldn't be surprised by rejection and persecution when it comes.
- *Jesus has overcome the world* (see John 16:33). The evil one who rules the world has already been defeated.
- *We are called to live in the world* (see John 17:15). Jesus prayed for our unity with God and one another to make Him visible to the people of the world, that they might also believe.

Sometimes the pull of the world is strong. Are you living in the world but not of it? Are your values, actions, and relationships part of the answer to Jesus' prayer?

Lord Jesus, help me live in the world as one who is free from the world, that others might see you and believe. Amen.

289

Examine the Evidence

JOHN 20

"Because you have seen me, you have believed; blessed are those who have not seen and yet have believed."—John 20:29 NIV

We call him Doubting Thomas. And when something good seems a bit farfetched, we tell ourselves and others not to emulate his example. But Jesus didn't criticize Thomas. Jesus helped him to believe by encouraging Thomas to examine the evidence—the wounds in Jesus' hands and side.

Thomas missed seeing Jesus in the upper room in Jerusalem when Jesus first appeared to the disciples after the resurrection. When he heard the news, Thomas wanted proof. Why he felt this way we don't know.

Eight days later, Jesus appeared to the disciples again, and Thomas was there. Jesus spoke directly to Thomas: "See and feel the wounds." He wanted Thomas to have faith and believe.

And Thomas did. Sometimes seeing is believing.

But Jesus knew that most who would believe in Him would have to do so without such proof, including you and me. And He said we are blessed because we do.

We don't have the resurrected Jesus standing physically beside us, encouraging us to believe. But we do have evidence—the cohesiveness and unity of the Bible, the prophecies Jesus fulfilled, God's promises kept, the miracles of Jesus, the resurrection, and the testimony of the Spirit within us. John wrote his gospel to affirm Jesus as God's Son, that all who read his words might believe (John 20:30–31).

"Don't be faithless!" Jesus told Thomas—and us. "Believe!"

Lord Jesus, I believe you are God's Son and my Savior. Help me stay strong in faith each day I live. Amen.

Peter

JOHN 21

> Jesus said to Simon Peter, "Simon son of John, do you love me more than these?"—John 21:15 NIV

In the courtyard of the high priest on the night Jesus was arrested, Peter denied knowing Jesus three different times. Just hours earlier, Peter had announced he would follow Jesus anywhere and even die for Him. It's not hard to imagine the shame Peter felt as the rooster crowed and he realized Jesus' prediction about him (John 13:38) had been true.

After the resurrection, at a breakfast on the beach with some of the disciples, Jesus asked Peter three times, "Peter, do you love me?" Peter felt grieved by the questions—"Lord, you know everything!"—but Jesus was assuring him that he was forgiven, that his role as an apostle was intact, and that one day Peter would indeed lay down his life for Jesus.

Peter wondered what would happen to John. The important thing, Jesus told him, was not what would happen to John, but what Peter would do. "You follow me!" Jesus said (John 21:22).

And Peter did. Soon he would be preaching the gospel on the day of Pentecost to the thousands gathered in Jerusalem for the feast of Pentecost (Acts 2:14–36) and leading the early church. May we each be faithful all our days as he was, accepting the tasks Jesus has for us and trusting Jesus for the results.

Lord Jesus, increase my trust and help me follow you. I love you. Amen.

Encountering
GOD'S HEART
for YOU
in the
NEW TESTAMENT

The Book of History

291

The Holy Spirit Comes

ACTS 1–3

Each day the Lord added to their fellowship those who were being saved.—Acts 2:47

The Acts of the Apostles is part two of the account Luke wrote for his friend Theophilus. (The first part is the Gospel of Luke.) Acts relates the ways the Holy Spirit empowered the apostles and other believers to take the good news of Jesus to both Jews and Gentiles as the church began.

After Jesus had ascended into heaven (Acts 1:9–11), the apostles and other disciples were together in an upper room in Jerusalem. Suddenly the Spirit came upon them with the sound of a strong wind and what looked like tongues of fire resting on each one. Then, led by the Spirit, they began to speak in other languages—languages that could be understood by those who had come from other nations for the Festival of Pentecost. The noise brought a crowd, and Peter preached his first sermon, outlining for his Jewish audience the proofs that Jesus was God's promised Messiah and their Lord.

Three thousand people believed Peter's message and were baptized. The church had begun! They worshiped and ate together and sold their possessions to meet one another's needs, and God added new believers to the church daily. Signs and wonders by the apostles—like the healing of a man who was lame by the temple gate—gave opportunity to tell people about Jesus and call them to believe and repent.

What is your faith story? Spend some time today thanking God for the gospel and for the Holy Spirit who lives in you.

Heavenly Father, how grateful I am for the gospel, for my Savior, and for the Holy Spirit! Amen.

292

Emboldened

ACTS 4–5

After they prayed, the place where they were meeting was shaken. And they were all filled with the Holy Spirit and spoke the word of God boldly.—Acts 4:31 NIV

What's the bravest, boldest thing you've ever done? The apostles quickly learned to be bold by depending on the Spirit.

As the number of believers grew, the religious leaders became "greatly annoyed" (Acts 4:2 ESV)—they thought they had gotten rid of Jesus. After the healing of the man who was lame, the leaders arrested Peter and John, demanding an explanation. Peter boldly proclaimed the power of Jesus' name, and to the leaders' command that they stop speaking of Jesus, Peter replied, "We cannot but speak of what we have seen and heard" (Acts 4:20 ESV).

After their release, Peter and John and the church prayed for continued boldness to speak God's Word. They would need it. Soon the high priest and other leaders arrested all the apostles.

Miraculously released by an angel during the night, the apostles were brought back before the Jewish council the next day. The leaders decided to let them go but first had them flogged. Yet the apostles rejoiced that they could suffer for Jesus' name, and they continued teaching and preaching that Jesus, the Messiah, had come.

How boldly do you speak of Jesus to your family, friends, neighbors, co-workers, or others God brings across your path? Do you need to ask God for the power and courage to be bold for Him?

Dear Lord, grant me boldness to speak of Jesus according to your plans and purposes, today and every day. Amen.

293

Ananias and Sapphira

ACTS 5

"How could you do a thing like this? You weren't lying to us but to God!"—Acts 5:4

Have you ever felt pressure to make yourself look good in front of other believers?

Many of the believers in Jerusalem sold property and gave the money to the apostles for the needs of others in the church. Ananias and his wife, Sapphira, did the same, but they agreed ahead of time to keep back some of the money for themselves. There would have been nothing wrong with this, except they said the money they gave was the entire amount of the sale. Their swift and severe consequence emphasized the need for the community of believers to allow the Holy Spirit, not Satan, to fill their hearts and lead their actions.

Scripture doesn't tell us why Ananias and Sapphira acted as they did. Perhaps the couple wanted to be seen as measuring up to the actions of others in the church. Peter said their deception came from Satan, the father of lies (John 8:44). The lie, rather than keeping some money back, was their sin.

So what about us? Speakers, authors, teachers, programs, and studies can help us grow, but growing as Christians is not one size fits all. God is not looking for Christian clones. Our ultimate guide is the Holy Spirit, working through the Word to make each of us the best version of ourselves we can be—and more important, to make us more like our Savior, conforming us to His image (Romans 8:29).

Dear God, thank you for the freedom to become the woman you created me to be, as I follow the Holy Spirit's leading in my life. Amen.

294

Stephen

ACTS 6–7

"You stiff-necked people! Your hearts and ears are still uncircumcised. You are just like your ancestors: You always resist the Holy Spirit!"—Acts 7:51 NIV

How well do you know your family history, the stories of your ancestors? Most of us probably can name only our grandparents and perhaps our great-grandparents. But within our Christian family—the church—our history over thousands of years matters a lot. Stephen, a Greek-speaking Jewish believer who became the first Christian martyr, certainly understood the history of the Jews.

The apostles approved Stephen as one of seven chosen to oversee the daily distribution of provisions to widows within the church. Stephen also performed miracles and taught the Word. But persecution began again, this time not from the Jewish leaders but from among the people. Members of a synagogue falsely accused Stephen of blasphemy and arranged for false witnesses to testify against him before the Jewish council.

As Stephen began to make his defense, his face shown brightly like that of an angel. He decisively reviewed the Old Testament history of the Jews and declared that like their ancestors, the current generation was guilty of refusing to listen to God and obey, because they would not turn to Jesus.

The Old Testament shows us how God prepared the way for Jesus—the Messiah, our Savior—to come to die for sin. It's the history of the Jews, but it's our history too as people of God from every place. Let's not neglect it.

Heavenly Father, deepen my understanding of your Word as I read it day by day, year by year. Amen.

Scattered

ACTS 8

The believers who were scattered preached the Good News about Jesus wherever they went.—Acts 8:4

After Stephen's death, persecution of all the believers began. Saul, a zealous young Jewish man who stood by approvingly as Stephen died, took part in the widespread persecution. "He went from house to house, dragging out both men and women to throw them into prison" (Acts 8:3).

Many Christians fled Jerusalem. It might have looked like defeat . . . but everywhere they went, these believers talked about Jesus! The gospel began to spread exactly as Jesus had said it would. As examples, Luke tells us that Philip the apostle preached in the city of Samaria, in a region whose people the Jews despised. People there believed with joy. Peter and John preached throughout the region as well. Led by the Spirit, Philip then introduced an Ethiopian to Jesus and baptized him on the desert road to Gaza.

I don't want to face persecution. You probably don't either. But Jesus said we should expect it (John 15:20). In 1956, Jim Elliot and four other young missionaries attempted to take the gospel to the Aucas, a dangerous tribe in the thick jungle of Ecuador. Jim and the others were speared to death. But two years later, Jim's wife, Elisabeth, and their young daughter, along with the sister of one of the other men, were able to live among the Aucas, and many of the tribe became believers. In God's economy, persecution is never the end of the story.

Dear Lord, if persecution does come to me, I pray to be able to accept it and embrace it boldly. Amen.

296

On the Damascus Road

ACTS 9

"Saul is my chosen instrument to take my message to the Gentiles and to kings, as well as to the people of Israel."—Acts 9:15

When you hear that someone who has committed crimes or antagonized Christians has become a Christian himself, do you believe what you hear?

The disciples in Jerusalem knew Saul's reputation as a persecutor of the church. And now *he* was a disciple? Impossible!

But it was true.

Saul, a Roman citizen by birth, also was known by his Jewish name, Paul. On the way to Damascus with letters from the high priest, intending to find and arrest any believers in the synagogues there, Saul encountered the risen Lord in a blinding light, and Jesus spoke to him. Three days later, after God sent a believer named Ananias to Saul, Saul regained his sight and was baptized. Soon he was preaching in the Damascus synagogues that Jesus is the Son of God. His life had changed forever.

About three years after his conversion, Saul went to Jerusalem, but the believers there were afraid of him. Barnabas brought Saul to the apostles and vouched for him. Saul spent time with Peter, and he met James, the brother of Jesus. But a plot by some of the Jews to kill Saul was discovered, and the disciples sent Saul away to Tarsus, where his ministry was based for about the next eight years.

God had a special purpose for Saul. Meeting Jesus was just the beginning.

Dear God, you specialize in making us different and new. Mold and make me according to your will! Amen.

Rise and Eat

ACTS 10–11

"I see very clearly that God shows no favoritism. In every nation he accepts those who fear him and do what is right."—Acts 10:34–35

God arranged dramatic events to emphasize that salvation is open to all and to begin to send the gospel throughout the non-Jewish world. God had given the Israelites dietary laws that set them apart from other people groups, but by New Testament times, Jewish customs and traditions had forbidden associating with Gentiles and especially eating with them. Peter's extraordinary vision from God and meeting with the Roman centurion Cornelius showed Peter it was time for change. God wanted Cornelius and his household to hear the gospel and have the opportunity to respond to it with faith—and they did. The Holy Spirit was poured out on these new Gentile believers as Peter spoke to them.

When he returned to Jerusalem, Peter had some explaining to do. But after he told his story, the Jewish believers there "stopped objecting and began praising God" (Acts 11:18).

Peter had been appalled at the direction God gave him in his vision; he even refused to follow it at first. Peter wasn't perfect, but he obeyed the Spirit's leading. God can use us too for His good purposes when we keep our hearts open to Him.

Heavenly Father, keep me open to those in my community who are different from me but need to know you! Show me how to share the gospel with all I meet. Amen.

298

Prayers for Peter

ACTS 12

"It's really true!" he said. "The Lord has sent his angel and saved me from Herod and from what the Jewish leaders had planned to do to me!"—Acts 12:11

Have you ever been surprised by the answer to your prayers?

The Roman ruler Herod Agrippa I began persecuting the Jerusalem church, perhaps to ingratiate himself to the leaders of his Jewish subjects. He executed the apostle James (the brother of John), and he arrested Peter. A squad of Roman soldiers guarded Peter at all hours, and the church constantly prayed for him.

Herod planned to wait for the completion of the Jewish holy days that followed Passover before he dealt with Peter. But on the night before Herod intended to execute Peter, God sent an angel to free him. Peter thought he was dreaming until he found himself standing alone on a street outside the prison. And the Christians who had gathered to pray for Peter that night? They didn't believe it at first either. But Rhoda, who answered Peter's knock at the door and recognized his voice, insisted it was true.

Confounded, Herod searched for Peter but couldn't find him. Herod executed the soldiers, and eventually he died an inglorious death (Acts 12:20–23). But "the word of God continued to spread, and there were many new believers" (Acts 12:24). God's power and purposes couldn't be stopped—not even today. And when we pray for His will to be done, God *will* answer—and we just might be surprised and filled with joy.

Dear Lord, may I be faithful to pray and faithful to expect your answers. Amen.

Paul and Barnabas

ACTS 11, 13–14

The Holy Spirit said, "Appoint Barnabas and Saul for the special work to which I have called them."—Acts 13:2

Barnabas had introduced Saul to the apostles in Jerusalem, and later, after learning that believers in Antioch in Syria were reaching out to Gentiles, Barnabas went to Tarsus looking for Saul. He brought Saul to Antioch, where they both stayed for the next year, meeting with the church and teaching. In Antioch, followers of Jesus became known as Christians, and about AD 46 the Antioch church sent out Saul, also known as Paul, on his first missionary journey.

Barnabas accompanied Paul on his travels. Wherever they went, Paul sought out the Jewish community to hear the gospel first. But once rejected or opposed, he turned immediately to the Gentiles.

In Lystra, Paul survived being stoned and left for dead by an angry Jewish contingent from Antioch. He and Barnabas continued their travels the very next day. They revisited some of their earlier stops, encouraging the believers and appointing elders in every church. "With prayer and fasting, they turned the elders over to the care of the Lord" (Acts 14:23), just as they themselves had been "entrusted . . . to the grace of God" (Acts 14:26) by the believers in Antioch. We can learn from their example and trust God to care for those we love and for all those who serve.

Dear God, your care for your children never dims or wavers. Help me trust you for the well-being of those I love. Amen.

300

The Jerusalem Council

ACTS 15

"It seemed good to the Holy Spirit and to us to lay no greater burden on you."—Acts 15:28

When you have an important decision to make, how do you go about it? Jewish believers had come to Antioch teaching that Gentiles must be circumcised according to the law of Moses before they could be saved. The church sent Paul and Barnabas to Jerusalem to meet with the apostles and elders to settle the question. At the meeting:

- *They considered all sides of the issue.* Luke tells us there was "much debate" (Acts 15:7 ESV) but also that the council "listened quietly" to Paul and Barnabas (Acts 15:12).
- *They considered what God had already done.* Peter spoke about his vision and how the Holy Spirit was first given to Gentile believers at the home of Cornelius. Paul and Barnabas told about miracles God had done through them among the Gentiles.
- *They considered what Scripture says.* Jesus' brother James recalled the writings of the prophets about a time when God's people would include the Gentiles.
- *They were prayerful and depended on the Spirit.* The letter they wrote with their decision affirmed this (Acts 15:28).

There was no reason for Gentiles to be burdened with the Jewish ritual of circumcision. But to avoid offending the Jews, whether believers or not, the Gentiles were to act in culturally sensitive ways, avoiding food offered to idols and meat containing blood, and avoiding all sexual immorality.

The next time you must make a decision, try following the pattern of the Jerusalem council.

Heavenly Father, I want your purposes to prevail in all my decisions. Help me to seek you always. Amen.

Disagreement

ACTS 15

> And there arose a sharp disagreement, so that they separated from each other.—Acts 15:39 ESV

Ministry and service, like the rest of life, sometimes include conflict with those who serve with us. How should we view this, and how should we respond?

After the meeting in Jerusalem, Paul and Barnabas returned to Antioch with the apostles' letter. Two leaders from the Jerusalem church, Judas (called Barsabbas) and Silas, accompanied them and remained in Antioch for some time before returning home. Paul and Barnabas stayed in Antioch and continued teaching and preaching.

Then Paul proposed that he and Barnabas travel back to all the places they had previously established churches. Barnabas agreed but wanted once again to take his cousin John Mark as their assistant. Paul balked, because John Mark had left them and returned to Jerusalem before their first missionary journey had been completed. They couldn't agree so they decided to separate. Paul chose Silas to travel with him, while Barnabas took Mark.

As a result, their impact doubled. Both Mark and Silas eventually ministered on their own as well—and Mark later wrote the Gospel of Mark. Paul and Mark apparently reconciled, for Paul later wrote from prison in Rome, "Get Mark and bring him with you, for he is very useful to me for ministry" (2 Timothy 4:11 ESV).

Sometimes a turn of events seems to be an ending, when under God's sovereignty it is only a beginning.

> *Dear Lord, when I don't understand the missteps and twists in the road, help me trust you that your good purposes will be accomplished. Amen.*

302

Doors

ACTS 16

They headed north for the province of Bithynia, but again the Spirit of Jesus did not allow them to go there.—Acts 16:7

In Lystra, in the region of Galatia (part of modern Turkey), Paul met Timothy, a young believer spoken highly of by others in the church, whose father was a Greek. Paul invited Timothy to join him on his travels, but first, to avoid any controversy among the Jewish people they would meet, Timothy was circumcised. At each stop, Paul and his companions delivered the apostles' decision regarding Gentile believers, and the churches were encouraged and continued to grow.

Continuing west and north toward areas he had not visited before, Paul would have expected to preach the gospel, but the Holy Spirit did not allow him to go where he intended (Acts 16:6–7). What was the meaning of these closed doors? Paul didn't know just yet. He continued on another route until he came to the coastal city of Troas, and there he received a vision. He saw a man from Macedonia (now northern Greece) pleading, "Come and help us." Paul and his companions concluded that God was calling them to preach the gospel in Macedonia. After the closed doors, a different door had opened.

What "doors" have opened and closed for you as you have followed Jesus? You can always trust that God is working out His purposes.

Dear God, may your wisdom always guide my life as I follow the leading of your Spirit. Amen.

303

Belief and Opposition

ACTS 16

Then he brought them out and asked, "Sirs, what must I do to be saved?"—Acts 16:30

Wherever the gospel goes, it meets both belief and opposition.

In Macedonia, Paul and Silas came to Philippi, a Roman colony. Looking for a place of prayer on the Sabbath, they found some women gathered near the river and sat down to speak with them. Lydia, a Gentile businesswoman who worshiped God, believed the gospel as she listened, and the Lord opened her heart. She was baptized along with all her household.

Others in the city opposed Paul's message, including the owners of a slave girl with a spirit of divination. When Paul cast the spirit out of the girl, her owners lost the fortune-telling income she had earned for them. They dragged Paul and Silas before the city's magistrates with charges of disturbing the peace. Paul and Silas were stripped, beaten with rods, and imprisoned with their feet in stocks.

But that night as they prayed and sang hymns together, with the other prisoners listening, an earthquake shook the prison. Everyone's chains fell off and all the cell doors opened, but no one tried to escape. Overcome, the jailer asked Paul, "What must I do to be saved?" (Acts 16:30). Hearing the gospel, the jailer and all his household believed and were baptized.

Despite opposition, the gospel continued to be heard and believed as the Spirit led and God's servants followed. Are you following God's direction in your service for Him today?

Heavenly Father, help me follow your lead today so my words and actions will point others to Jesus. Amen.

304

Searching the Scriptures

ACTS 17

They searched the Scriptures day after day to see if Paul and Silas were teaching the truth.—Acts 17:11

The leaders of the Jewish community in Thessalonica reacted to Paul's gospel message, especially the resurrection of Jesus, with resistance and a mob mentality.

In the city of Athens, full of idols and an altar with an inscription to an unknown god (Acts 17:23), the civil and religious leaders listened to Paul with curiosity, but the message didn't touch their hearts.

Only in Berea, between these two locations, did the leaders give serious consideration to Paul's message.

According to his custom, Paul always sought out the Jewish community first in any location he visited. In Berea, the members of the synagogue received Paul's message eagerly. More than that, they wanted to verify it for themselves, so they searched the Scriptures—the Old Testament—every day, finding there the evidence Paul presented for God's plan to send the world a Savior through His people. Many of the Bereans, both Jews and God-fearing Gentiles, believed the gospel. Then a mob from Thessalonica arrived and the believers arranged for Paul to travel to Athens for his safety.

The Bereans examined Scripture to learn truth, and we can do the same. God reveals himself and His truths when we turn to His Word with open hearts and a desire to understand.

Dear Lord, help me know you better and understand your purposes more as I open your Word to hear your truth. Amen.

Keep Learning

ACTS 18

They took him aside and explained the way of God even more accurately.—Acts 18:26

Never make the mistake of thinking you're too old to learn something new. Just ask any students who head back to school in their retirement years to earn college degrees and receive their diplomas.

Or ask Apollos.

After leaving Athens, Paul traveled to Corinth. He met Priscilla and Aquila, a Jewish couple who possibly were already believers and had recently come from Rome. Like Paul, they were tentmakers, and Paul worked with them to support himself while he preached and taught. Then Paul left Corinth and sailed with Priscilla and Aquila to Syria. He left his friends in Ephesus and continued on, making his way back to Antioch, where his long journey had begun.

In Ephesus, a well-spoken Jewish believer named Apollos came and spoke boldly in the synagogue, but he knew only about the baptism taught by John the Baptist. Priscilla and Aquila went to Apollos privately and provided the instruction he was missing. Apollos must have received their teaching well, because when he wanted to move on to another place, the believers in Corinth encouraged him and wrote a letter to introduce him. In Achaia, Apollos powerfully used the Scriptures to show the Jewish leaders that Jesus was the Christ.

No matter our age or how long we have been a believer, we can always learn more of the way of the Lord. Every encounter with God's Word can yield new wisdom, knowledge, strength, and power if our hearts are open.

Dear God, I want to keep learning to know you better and share the good news of Jesus more! Amen.

306

Ephesus

ACTS 19–20

"Now I entrust you to God and the message of his grace."—Acts 20:32

In 1983, Michael W. Smith released the recording of his now-classic song "Friends." When friends have Jesus as Lord, he sang, those friendships are forever. We know that on earth, however, there are times we have to say good-bye.

Paul set out from Antioch once again, traveling back toward Ephesus, where he spent the next three years (about AD 52–55) teaching both Jews and Gentiles. Paul's miracles and influence plus his preaching against idolatry threatened the business of the silversmiths who made shrines to the goddess Artemis for homes of the city's residents. One of them, Demetrius, instigated a riot, but Paul was unharmed. When the uproar had quieted, he left Ephesus and again visited churches in Macedonia and Achaia (northern and southern Greece).

From Miletus, south of Ephesus, Paul called for the Ephesian elders to come and meet with him—so he could say good-bye. The Holy Spirit was compelling Paul to go to Jerusalem even though a time of trouble and imprisonment would begin there, and Paul knew he would not see these beloved friends again. He reminded them to take good care of the believers, and he warned them to be on alert against false teachers who would try to mislead the church. Then he knelt and prayed with these friends, and everyone wept.

Even when friends in Christ must separate, the bond of love in Christ continues. Do you have friends like this? How has God used them in your life?

Heavenly Father, how I thank you for the gift of friends who love you and encourage me! Amen.

307

In Jerusalem

ACTS 21–23

"Just as you have been a witness to me here in Jerusalem, you must preach the Good News in Rome as well."—Acts 23:11

On his way toward Jerusalem, Paul met disciples who tried to change his mind about continuing, but they could not persuade him, and in Jerusalem the church leaders received him gladly. They also proposed that Paul perform a purification ritual to prove to Jews who opposed him that rumors about his teachings were false.

When the seven days of purification were almost over, Jews who had come from Asia (Turkey) saw Paul in the temple and stirred up a crowd against him. The appearance of the Roman tribune and his soldiers saved Paul's life, and the tribune granted Paul's request to speak to the mob. Speaking in the Hebrew language, Aramaic, Paul told the story of his conversion, but the mob began agitating again when Paul spoke about his mission to the Gentiles.

In the Roman barracks, where the commander took Paul to "interrogate" him by flogging, Paul made known his Roman citizenship. A citizen could not be flogged if no charges had been made against him. The next day Paul spoke before the Jewish council, where more dissension broke out, and soldiers had to remove Paul from the council by force.

The Spirit's warnings about what Paul would experience in Jerusalem were coming true. But Jesus appeared to Paul and encouraged him: as Paul had testified to the facts about Jesus there in Jerusalem, he would also do in Rome.

Dear Lord, may I follow your direction for my life with the strong faith and determination of Paul. Amen.

308

An Appeal to Caesar

ACTS 23–26

"Now I am on trial because of my hope in the fulfillment of God's promise made to our ancestors."—Acts 26:6

Some of the Jews plotted to ambush Paul, but Paul's nephew heard the plan and told Paul and the Roman commander. Paul was sent at night to the Judean governor, Felix, in Caesarea, accompanied by nearly half the commander's Roman forces. Five days later, the high priest and some of the Jewish elders came to press charges against Paul. Felix listened to Paul's defense but refused to decide his case immediately; he kept him in custody and sent for him often to converse with him, hoping for a bribe.

After two years, Festus became governor and the Jews tried again to bring charges against Paul. This time Paul appealed to Caesar, the Roman emperor. But before Paul could be sent to Rome, Festus received a visit from the Jewish King Herod Agrippa II. Festus asked for Agrippa's advice about Paul, and Agrippa asked to hear Paul for himself.

Paul spoke boldly to King Agrippa, explaining the way he had persecuted Christians, his own conversion, and his work to share the gospel. Agrippa cut Paul short when Paul presented him with the choice to believe in Jesus. But he and Festus agreed that Paul had done nothing deserving of death or imprisonment. "And Agrippa said to Festus, 'This man could have been set free if he hadn't appealed to Caesar'" (Acts 26:32).

Dear God, may I take every opportunity to make your goodness known, as Paul bravely did. Amen.

Shipwrecked

ACTS 27

"Don't be afraid, Paul, for you will surely stand trial before Caesar! What's more, God in his goodness has granted safety to everyone sailing with you."—Acts 27:24

Remember Jonah? His presence threatened a ship and its crew. Paul's presence on a ship had a different effect.

Under the custody of a Roman centurion named Julius, who treated him kindly, Paul began his journey to Rome on a small trading vessel. Luke traveled with him. At Myra, they transferred to a larger ship sailing for Italy. Weather slowed their journey, and by the time they reached the south of the island of Crete, Paul advised harboring for the winter. The ship's crew wanted to find a better harbor farther north, and the centurion sided with them.

But Paul was correct. Late fall and winter were dangerous seasons on the Mediterranean Sea. A northeaster blew the ship off course and across the open Adriatic Sea. As the storm wore on, God encouraged Paul—who encouraged the crew—with a message delivered by an angel: the ship would run aground but no one would be killed. Paul *would* arrive safely in Rome to testify.

After two weeks, the ship finally broke apart on the tiny island of Malta, but everyone survived, including all the prisoners. When spring arrived and it was safe to sail again, Paul's journey continued, ending in Rome about AD 62. Once again, God's purposes and promises had proved true.

Heavenly Father, whatever our circumstances, you work your good in our lives as we trust in you. May I trust you with courage! Amen.

310

In Rome

ACTS 28

He welcomed all who visited him, boldly proclaiming the Kingdom of God and teaching about the Lord Jesus Christ. And no one tried to stop him.—Acts 28:30–31

Sometimes as you wait for situations to resolve, does your patience waver?

Christians in Rome met Paul when he arrived, encouraging him. He was allowed to live in private quarters, although guarded by a soldier. Soon after his arrival Paul called the local Jewish leaders to meet with him so he could explain why he was in Rome. He also spent a day with the leaders and other Jews, sharing with them from Scripture the proofs that Jesus was the Messiah. Some believed, but most did not, and once again Paul turned his primary attention to the Gentiles. For the next two years, Paul preached and taught unhindered about Jesus and the kingdom of God.

The book of Acts ends here, but what else do we know about what happened to Paul?

His burden and care for the well-being of the churches continued. During his two-year imprisonment, Paul wrote his letters to the Ephesians, Philippians, Colossians, and to Philemon that we find in our Bibles. Later non-biblical writers indicate that Paul was released and traveled farther west, perhaps to Spain, before he was arrested again, imprisoned, and executed.

Paul gives us an example of willingness to wait patiently for God when circumstances are not in our control. When have you needed to wait patiently for God to act? Are you waiting on Him right now?

Dear Lord, help me trust and wait for you with patience. Amen.

Encountering GOD'S HEART for YOU in the NEW TESTAMENT

The Letters

All Have Sinned

ROMANS 1–3

For everyone has sinned; we all fall short of God's glorious standard.
—Romans 3:23

Paul had not yet been to Rome when he wrote his letter to the church in Rome. He wrote from Corinth, during the year and a half he spent there on his second missionary journey, anticipating that one day he would visit Rome and eventually take the gospel from there to Spain. Rome had a large Jewish population, and the Roman church included Jewish and Gentile believers. Paul wrote to assure them that the goal of the gospel—the righteousness that comes by faith—was not a new idea but was rooted in the Old Testament and in all of God's dealings with His people.

Everyone needs the gospel, Paul wrote, because everyone sins. The Jews had received God's law and had been entrusted with the revelation of God through the Old Testament Scriptures. From the beginning, however, God's standard has been righteousness; none of us have any of our own.

The more we encounter God's heart in the Bible—discovering His power, wisdom, and character—the more we can see our own sinfulness. What quality of God are you aware of today that shows you your great need for the gospel?

Dear God, you are ___________ . And I am not! How I need you and thank you for the gospel of Jesus, my Savior! Amen.

312

By Faith

ROMANS 4

People are counted as righteous, not because of their work, but because of their faith in God who forgives sinners.—Romans 4:5

We have no righteousness of our own, but God has always been willing to give right standing with Him to those who have faith in Him. The Jews believed that God would do this only for good people who kept God's law. But God's dealings with Abraham show us that God *justifies* us (makes us "just as if I'd never sinned") on the basis of our faith, not on what we do.

Sometimes we humans make promises we don't intend to keep or promises we find impossible to honor. The promises God made to old, childless Abraham might have seemed outlandish and impossible to him, but Abraham believed God could and would do what He said. Because of Abraham's faith—not anything good that he had done—God "counted him as righteous" (Romans 4:3), and Paul says Jews and Gentiles can be assured that faith in Jesus operates the same way.

If you've been trying to earn God's favor, you can stop now. We can't earn forgiveness. Our right relationship with God comes only one way—by faith in the One who was "handed over to die because of our sins, and . . . raised to life to make us right with God" (Romans 4:25).

Heavenly Father, thank you for your gift—righteousness and relationship with you through faith. Amen.

Friends and Enemies

ROMAN 5

So now we can rejoice in our wonderful new relationship with God because our Lord Jesus Christ has made us friends of God.—Romans 5:11

Think of a good friend. What qualities do you love about your friend? How have you benefitted from being her friend? Jesus has made us friends with God, and this new relationship is cause for great rejoicing.

- *We have peace with God because of our faith in what Jesus has done for us.* We can "confidently and joyfully look forward to sharing God's glory" (Romans 5:2).
- *We can find purpose in the problems and trials we face.* They develop our endurance, strength of character, and confidence in our salvation.
- *The Holy Spirit fills our hearts with God's love*, telling us "how dearly God loves us" (Romans 5:5).

Adam's sin in the garden set sin loose in the world and brought death to everyone. But God loved us even when we were His enemies, opposed to Him. "God showed his great love for us by sending Christ to die for us while we were still sinners" (Romans 5:8). Jesus never sinned and didn't deserve death, but He willingly died so God could offer us His gifts of grace and righteousness and make us His friends.

Are you treasuring the blessings of being God's friend?

Dear Lord, how amazing that you love me and sent Jesus to die for me so I could be your friend! Amen.

314

Life in the Spirit

ROMANS 6–8

And because you belong to him, the power of the life-giving Spirit has freed you from the power of sin that leads to death.—Romans 8:2

Got any bad habits? Any struggles with sin? I'm not surprised. I do too. Our fallen human nature makes us slaves to sin. But the good news is that the gospel is about much more than forgiveness. The Spirit gives us power to rely on God and live righteous lives.

Before we come to Christ, Paul says, we often find ourselves doing what we know is wrong even when we want to do what's right. That's the power of sin over us. But now another power has come into our lives and set us free—the power of the Holy Spirit. We aren't controlled by our sinful natures any longer. We let the Holy Spirit take control. We no longer have any obligation to do what our sinful nature wants us to do (Romans 8:12).

The Holy Spirit in you is proof of God's love, and nothing can separate you from His love. God is *for* you, His adopted child, and you can walk through every day, every temptation, every trial with confidence and reliance on the Spirit of God in you. Are you walking with the Spirit?

Dear God, I confess that I don't always rely on the power of your Spirit to help me live for you. Today, may I turn from what my sinful nature wants and follow the Spirit instead. Amen.

Grafted In

ROMANS 9–11

Dear brothers and sisters, the longing of my heart and my prayer to God is for the people of Israel to be saved.—Romans 10:1

What about Israel? The recipients of Paul's letter to the Roman church must have had questions much like many do today. What *was* God's plan for Israel after the nation rejected Jesus as the Messiah?

Paul first reminded his readers that salvation had never been determined by nationality, but always by faith (Romans 9:6). No one, Jew or Gentile, was entitled to God's grace, as Paul had written earlier in his letter. But the gift of salvation was open to all, and each person has a responsibility to choose to believe or not. Israel had made the wrong choice, and the unbelief of Israel opened a door for the Gentiles to believe.

But God has not rejected His people and still has a plan for Israel. God's family is like a special olive tree, Paul says, with Abraham and the other patriarchs as the roots. Some of the branches—the people of Israel—had been broken off, and the Gentiles had been grafted in. But at the right time the people of Israel will be grafted back in, because God is faithful to His promises and rich in mercy.

Paul looked forward to that day with thanks and praise. "Oh, how great are God's riches and wisdom and knowledge! How impossible it is for us to understand his decisions and his ways!" (Romans 11:33).

Heavenly Father, you are worthy of my praise! Your ways are mysterious but loving and just. Help me always trust in you. Amen.

316

True Worship

ROMANS 12–16

I urge you, brothers and sisters, in view of God's mercy, to offer your bodies as a living sacrifice, holy and pleasing to God—this is your true and proper worship.—Romans 12:1 NIV

Have you ever had a disagreement with another believer about how something should be done?

Paul ended his letter to the believers in Rome with instructions about living by the Spirit's power as a community of people whom God had declared righteous. Those instructions are for us as well. The starting point? Laying down our demands and allowing God to transform us into new people by changing how we think. Then using our gifts to serve one another, keeping our focus on the Lord and our hope in Him, doing all we can to live in peace with everyone, and conquering evil by doing good.

The disagreements the Christians in Rome were experiencing about when to worship and what to eat or drink could be solved by following the principle of the commandment "Love your neighbor as yourself." There was to be no judging and condemning believers with weak faith and no insistence they do things in ways they believed were wrong. Instead, a spirit of living to please others and to build them up in the Lord should prevail. "Accept each other just as Christ has accepted you so that God will be given glory" (Romans 15:7).

What person or situation has come to mind as you read this? How will you put Paul's guidance to work in your relationships today?

Dear Lord, where I'm experiencing disagreement and strife with other believers, show me how you want me to respond instead. Amen.

Unity

1 CORINTHIANS 1–4

Let there be no divisions in the church.—1 Corinthians 1:10

Paul had established the church in Corinth on his second missionary journey, and he lived and taught in Corinth for a year and a half. About five years later, while he was in Ephesus, Paul learned of serious problems in the Corinthian church and wrote this letter. The problems of the mostly Gentile church in Corinth sound like problems we face, and Paul's instructions and his problem-solving methods are for us too.

In some ways, the beginning of Paul's letter to the Corinthians sounds like a continuation of his instructions to the church in Rome. But the divisions in the Corinthian church seem to have been deeper. The believers had separated into factions, some claiming special knowledge unavailable to others and some following one leader or apostle over another. Paul challenged them to turn from such worldly "wisdom" to the wisdom of God, displayed in the cross and the gospel, just as he had taught them earlier.

Jealousy and quarrels proved those in the church were living like people of the world, acting out of their sinful natures rather than listening to the Spirit. Paul urged them to stop being arrogant. "The Kingdom of God is not just a lot of talk; it is living by God's power" (1 Corinthians 4:20).

Do you have a favorite Christian teacher or leader? Learn from that person, but keep your focus on what God has done. "As the Scriptures say, 'If you want to boast, boast only about the Lord'" (1 Corinthians 1:31).

Dear God, help me keep unity in the church by keeping my attention on you. Amen

318

Changed

1 CORINTHIANS 5–6

You do not belong to yourself, for God bought you with a high price. So you must honor God with your body.—1 Corinthians 6:19–20

Besides disunity, Paul had learned of other problems in the Corinthian church. Believers were taking each other to court and having sex with prostitutes, and a man in the church was living with his stepmother. Rather than being ashamed, the church was proud of its "enlightened attitude," but Paul was shocked—even the pagans in Corinth wouldn't tolerate that, he said. The church needed to stop all association with this man in order to bring him to repentance.

Our bodies are made for the Lord, Paul said, and God cares about them. He purchased us with the blood of His Son, and He will raise our bodies just as He raised Jesus from the dead. Our bodies are temples of the Holy Spirit, who lives in us. For all these reasons, Paul said, "Run from sexual sin!" (1 Corinthians 6:18).

And if we haven't? Then the beauty of forgiveness and the power of God to change us goes to work. Within the Corinthian church were believers who had previously lived sexually immoral lives and committed other sins. "Such were some of you," Paul wrote. "But you were washed, you were sanctified, you were justified in the name of the Lord Jesus Christ and by the Spirit of our God" (1 Corinthians 6:11 ESV).

Heavenly Father, help me live the kind of life you look for in your children, a life that honors you and gives you glory. Amen.

Marriage and Singleness

1 CORINTHIANS 7

Each person has a special gift from God, of one kind or another.—1 Corinthians 7:7

Paul had apparently written to the Corinthians prior to this letter (1 Corinthians 5:9), and they also had written to him with questions about marriage, singleness, and divorce. Within contemporary culture, our own churches seek answers to these issues too.

Paul wrote that marriage between one woman and one man is the proper place for sexual intimacy. Some in Corinth had been teaching that all sexual relations should be avoided, even in marriage, and that marriage itself was wrong, but Paul refuted these wrong ideas. God gives some the ability to be married and some the ability to live a celibate life. Both are gifts. Paul had the gift of celibacy and found it advantageous to his ministry, but neither gift is better or more spiritual than the other.

Believers with unbelieving spouses who agree to stay together should do so, but if the unbelieving spouse chooses to leave the marriage, the believing spouse is free to remarry. "God has called you to live in peace" (1 Corinthians 7:15).

Paul looked at life with an eternal view. The things of this world, he said, including marriage and singleness, should not absorb us. Are you looking at your life with the same eternal view as Paul?

Dear Lord, your will and your plans for me are good. Help me trust you always! Amen.

320

Flee Idolatry

1 CORINTHIANS 8–10

> You cannot drink the cup of the Lord and the cup of demons. You cannot partake of the table of the Lord and the table of demons.—1 Corinthians 10:21 ESV

Meat from sacrifices made to idols at Corinth's many pagan temples was served at temple restaurants and sold in city markets. Some of the Corinthian Christians thought eating this meat was terribly wrong, while others had no problem with it, and they had asked Paul what to do.

Because an idol was really nothing, Paul said, Christians who understood this could eat meat sacrificed to idols, but they shouldn't do so when it would cause another believer without this understanding to stumble and sin. Love must take priority over exercising our own rights.

Paul had more to say. Finishing our lives of faith well means being willing to bear up under temptation, and idolatry tempts everyone. The people of Israel had not finished well because they gave in to the temptation of idolatry. Paul asked the Corinthian Christians to consider what was actually taking place during the feasts at the pagan temples, although the physical idols had no power, "what pagans sacrifice they offer to demons" (1 Corinthians 10:20 ESV). Therefore, Paul advised the Corinthians to "flee idolatry," counting on God to provide the way of escape against this temptation (1 Corinthians 10:13) and not eating at the pagan temples.

Faced with popular practices like yoga, mantra meditation, reiki, or the enneagram, be wise. Consider what's really going on and be cautious about proceeding.

Dear God, help me flee idolatry and avoid participating in practices that don't please or honor you. Amen.

See the Body

1 CORINTHIANS 11

"Do this in remembrance of me."—1 Corinthians 11:24

What do you think about as you participate in Communion? Sometimes I look around the room and think about the fact that all of us partaking together are part of Jesus' body, the church. The emblems representing Jesus' body and blood remind me not only that He died, rose, and is coming again, but also that the new covenant He established is for *all* believers:

- The people I like . . . and those with personalities that grate on me.
- The people I admire . . . and those I think who "just don't get it."
- People I've known forever . . . and people I don't know yet.
- People who are doing well and people who are struggling.
- People who are young and old, healthy and sick, rich and poor.

The Corinthians gathered for a meal before the Lord's Supper—but not everyone got to eat. The wealthy believers had a feast; those who were poor came without any food, and no one shared with them. Paul wrote that they dishonored the Lord's body by acting this way. Jesus sacrificed His life for them, but they acted selfishly. Jesus thought of others, but they thought only of themselves.

The next time you observe Communion, be sure you see the body—the body of Christ.

Dear Jesus, what a price you paid to free me from the power of sin! May I always remember your broken body and your spilled blood. Amen.

322

Gifts

1 CORINTHIANS 12–14

There are different kinds of spiritual gifts, but the same Spirit is the source of them all.—1 Corinthians 12:4

We don't always like what we see when we look in a mirror, do we? There's usually something we'd like to change. But in fact we need all the parts of our bodies—those we can see and those we can't. In God's amazing and intricate design of the human body, every part has a role. Every part matters.

The church is like that too. God designed the church to function like a body. Every person in the body has a role. Every believer has a spiritual gift to use in service to keep the whole body healthy and strong. Some are "up front" gifts like preaching or teaching, and others are "backstage" gifts like helping others, but all are necessary. We need to use whatever gifts we've been given, without worrying about the gifts we *don't* have.

But over and above every gift, Paul says, is love. Without love, nothing else we do matters. "Three things will last forever—faith, hope, and love—and the greatest of these is love" (1 Corinthians 13:13). To love should be our highest goal.

Heavenly Father, may I discover and use the gifts you've given me for the good of Christ's body, the church, and no matter what, may I always act in love. Amen.

323

Imperishable

1 CORINTHIANS 15

When the trumpet sounds, those who have died will be raised to live forever. And we who are living will also be transformed.—1 Corinthians 15:52

As I'm writing, autumn beckons. I know the season will be lovely, but after autumn . . . winter. I already dread the cold, gray days that seem to immobilize me. I have to start reminding myself now that spring and summer *will* return, with warmer temperatures, sunshine, color—new life!

Some of the Corinthians had been teaching that there is no resurrection of the dead. If that were true, Paul wrote, then Christ had not been raised either. "And if our hope in Christ is only for this life, we are more to be pitied than anyone in the world" (1 Corinthians 15:19). But Christ *has* been raised—and those who place their faith in Him will be raised also, when Christ returns.

What kind of bodies will we have? As a seed planted in the ground becomes something quite different, Paul wrote, our resurrected bodies will be different than our worn-out earthly bodies. We will have transformed, glorious bodies that will never die. When Jesus returns and the dead are raised, that is when death will be swallowed up by the victory of Jesus over sin (1 Corinthians 15:54–56).

This is our true hope of heaven. "Thank God! He gives us victory over sin and death through our Lord Jesus Christ" (1 Corinthians 15:57).

Dear Lord, as spring follows winter, new life—eternal life in an imperishable body—will follow death. How I praise you! Amen.

324

Hardship and Comfort

2 CORINTHIANS 1–7

God is our merciful Father and the source of all comfort.—2 Corinthians 1:3

The Corinthian church didn't respond well to the letter we call 1 Corinthians, nor to a visit Paul made to them afterward. So Paul wrote again, this time a stern rebuke. That letter has been lost, but we know it was effective (2 Corinthians 7:5–8). Hearing of the repentance of most in the church, Paul responded with the letter we call 2 Corinthians.

Paul had not enjoyed having to write so harshly, but because he greatly loved the Corinthian believers, it had been necessary. Now he and the church could be reconciled, and Paul could comfort them. "He comforts us in all our troubles so that we can comfort others" (2 Corinthians 1:4).

Some in the church were still unhappy and critical of Paul. So in this new letter he included a defense of his apostleship, his integrity, and his ministry, letting his readers see how difficult and dangerous his life often was. The comfort he could offer was the comfort God provided for him.

What experiences has God led you through that allow you to provide comfort to others in need?

Dear God, you have often comforted me. Help me offer understanding and comfort to others who are suffering. Amen.

Live Generously

2 CORINTHIANS 8–9

Each one must give as he has decided in his heart, not reluctantly or under compulsion, for God loves a cheerful giver.—2 Corinthians 9:7 ESV

Paul planned to take a monetary gift from the Gentile churches to the church in Jerusalem, which was suffering under a famine. The Macedonian churches had already presented Paul with their gift, and their generosity had overflowed. Their ability to give beyond their limited means was due to God's grace in their lives, Paul said. They had committed themselves first to the Lord and then to however they could assist Paul in ministry.

The Corinthian church had begun collecting their offering earlier, and now Paul encouraged them to have the gift ready when his co-worker Titus came to receive it. Paul's instructions can help us when we want to be generous but hold our money or possessions too tightly.

- "Give in proportion to what you have. Whatever you give is acceptable if you give it eagerly" (2 Corinthians 8:11–12).
- "Whoever sows sparingly will also reap sparingly, and whoever sows bountifully will also reap bountifully" (2 Corinthians 9:6 ESV).
- "God will generously provide all you need. Then you will always have everything you need and plenty left over to share with others" (2 Corinthians 9:8).

Do you find it easy to be generous, or difficult? Let God's grace in your life overflow.

Lord Jesus, you gave everything for me. Help me give as generously. Amen.

326

Adopted

GALATIANS 1–4

And because we are his children, God has sent the Spirit of his Son into our hearts, prompting us to call out, "Abba, Father."—Galatians 4:6

Gotcha Day—it's a way to celebrate with your adopted children the day they officially became part of your family. Do you remember the day that God adopted *you*?

Paul and Barnabas established churches in Galatia on their first missionary journey. Not long after they had traveled on, Jewish Christians came to those same churches preaching the Gentiles' need to be circumcised before they could be saved. When Paul heard of it, he wrote this letter in response.

Anyone who wanted to be made right with God by following the law was required to keep the entire law perfectly, Paul said, which no one could do. The law was given to show us our sin. The blessings God had promised to Abraham and his descendants had always been based on faith, not on keeping the law.

Paul tells us that the law can't make us right with God. Jesus does that when we put our faith in Him. Then we become God's adopted children and He sends His Spirit into our hearts. All who belong to Christ are God's true children, whether Jew or Gentile, and as His children we are heirs to all He has promised.

And God is glad He's gotcha!

Heavenly Father, you are a good, good Father! Thank you for making a way for me to belong to you. Amen.

Free to Love

GALATIANS 5

Don't use your freedom to satisfy your sinful nature. Instead, use your freedom to serve one another in love.—Galatians 5:13

I always keep a bowl of fruit on my dining table, within easy reach. Depending on the season, you might see peaches, plums, grapes, and pears nestled in with the usual bananas and apples. Different fruits, with different colors and tastes, some appealing to one person and some to another.

The fruit of the Spirit isn't like that. The fruit the Spirit produces in our lives is *one* fruit with many manifestations: "love, joy, peace, patience, kindness, goodness, faithfulness, gentleness, and self-control" (Galatians 5:22–23). When we let the Spirit lead us, our actions will flow from this fruit. We won't be trying to get right with God by keeping the law, but we'll find that we *are* obeying the moral standards in Scripture, because the Spirit sets us free to love God and to love one another. That's what our freedom in Christ is for.

So it doesn't matter if you like peaches more than pears, or grapes more than apples. But it does matter that you live by the Spirit—follow the Spirit, keep in step with the Spirit, obey the Spirit—and the fruit that the Spirit develops in your life will be the tastiest ever!

Dear Lord, thank you for setting me free through Christ to love you and to love others. Let your Spirit lead me in all I do. Amen.

328

Doing Good

GALATIANS 6

So then, as we have opportunity, let us do good to everyone, and especially to those who are of the household of faith.—Galatians 6:10 ESV

Christian psychologists Henry Cloud and John Townsend distinguish between the "burdens" (Galatians 6:2) and "loads" (Galatians 6:5 ESV) we all carry. Every person bears a load—the responsibilities of adulthood, such as working, paying bills, maintaining a home, caring for family members, and contributing to the good of the community. We are required to carry this load ourselves. At times, however, temptations and circumstances in our lives become larger and heavier than we can bear alone. These are burdens, and we need other believers to pull alongside us and shoulder some of the weight—with their presence, resources, encouragement, prayer, and other helpful acts of service.

At times, loving others and doing good by bearing burdens can be wearying. But Paul encouraged the Galatians—and us—not to give up. Because we sow what we reap, "those who live to please the Spirit will harvest everlasting life from the Spirit. . . . At just the right time we will reap a harvest of blessing if we don't give up" (Galatians 6:8–9).

Do you need help bearing a burden today? Do you know someone who does? Ask God for direction and reach out.

Dear God, keep me open to the opportunities to do good that you have for me, to help fellow believers and others too. Amen.

329

God's Plan Is the Church

EPHESIANS 1–3

Even before he made the world, God loved us and chose us in Christ to be holy and without fault in his eyes.—Ephesians 1:4

Sometimes we think we can follow Jesus on our own without being part of the church, but Paul would say that's a bad idea.

Paul loved the people of the Ephesian church. He had planted it and spent nearly three years with them, preaching and teaching and working as a tentmaker. During his first Roman imprisonment, he wrote this letter to encourage the Ephesians to understand and live out God's plan for the church.

God had made a way to reconcile sinners to himself through Jesus' death and resurrection. "By grace you have been saved through faith. . . . It is the gift of God, not a result of works" (Ephesians 2:8–9 ESV). God also reconciled believing Jews and Gentiles with one another, bringing them together in one body, the church, with Christ as the head. "Through him we both have access in one Spirit to the Father" (Ephesians 2:18 ESV), and God dwells in the church with all His people through His Spirit. This was God's plan even before creation!

Maybe you haven't been participating in a church community. Maybe you are but something or someone there displeases or annoys you. Don't decide to just go it alone. Work it out. God's plan is the church—Jesus plus all of us.

Heavenly Father, may I find my place in the church and be an influence there for the unity you desire. Amen.

330

Alive in Christ

EPHESIANS 2

We are his workmanship.—Ephesians 2:10 ESV

I remember the day I learned to read: first grade, sitting in our reading circle, looking at an oversized primer set on a large easel. Suddenly I understood—the letters on the page and the sounds they made became words I could read! You could say that until that moment, the letters and words were dead to me, but at that moment, they came alive.

Before we placed our faith in Christ, we did what we wanted and took our cues from Satan. We were "dead in trespasses and sins" (Ephesians 2:1 ESV). God intervened and saved us. He "made us alive together with Christ" (Ephesians 2:5 ESV). Before and after . . . dead and alive. "He raised us from the dead along with Christ and seated us with him in the heavenly realms because we are united with Christ Jesus" (Ephesians 2:6). Raised with Christ . . . seated in heaven . . . united with Christ. Alive!

Why did God do this? Because of His mercy, kindness, and great love for you and me. We didn't earn our transfer from death to life. It is pure gift.

"We are his workmanship," Paul wrote (Ephesians 2:10 ESV). Some translations use the word *masterpiece*. God saved you and made you new in Christ because He loves you. He's got good things for you to do. You're alive now . . . so start living!

Dear Lord, thank you for my life in Christ and for your love and mercy. Thank you for saving me! Amen.

Children of Light

EPHESIANS 4–5

Once you were full of darkness, but now you have light from the Lord. So live as people of light!—Ephesians 5:8

When summer sputters and fall looms ahead, I pull out my cool-weather clothes and try them all on to see what still fits. Put on . . . and take off. Keep what works, discard what doesn't, and buy what I need. What a process! And as winter thaws and spring peeks in, I'll do this all again to be ready for warmer temperatures.

Paul urged the Ephesian believers to do something similar. "Put off your old self . . . and . . . put on the new self, created to be like God in true righteousness and holiness" (Ephesians 4:22, 24 NIV). Our old selves answered to the dark side. God has made us new, but our old sinful nature still lies packed away like out-of-season clothes. It's up to us to put that old nature off by refusing to wear it any longer.

Choose to put on "new clothes" from the Spirit instead. "Let the Spirit renew your thoughts and attitudes" (Ephesians 4:23). God's light will show you what to put off and what to put on. "This light within you produces only what is good and right and true" (Ephesians 5:9).

Are you putting the Spirit in charge of your "wardrobe" in this season of your life?

Dear God, I want to do the things that please you and leave behind the things that don't. Give me understanding and power through your Word and your Spirit. Amen.

332

Filled with the Spirit

EPHESIANS 5

> Look carefully then how you walk, not as unwise but as wise, making the best use of the time, because the days are evil.—Ephesians 5:15–16 ESV

Stephen Covey, author of *The 7 Habits of Highly Effective People*, famously taught about priorities with a glass bowl, a container of pebbles, and some larger rocks. In Covey's demonstration, the bowl represents our lives, the pebbles represent the myriad small activities of life, and the rocks represent our important priorities. In order to get both the rocks and the pebbles to fit in the bowl, the rocks must be put in first. More than just an illustration of effective time management, Covey's lesson shows us the necessity of being *thoughtful* about how we spend our time.

Paul said the same thing. Be wise. Understand God's will. Don't waste your time—which is your life—on pursuits with no positive effects. Instead, "Be filled with the Spirit" (Ephesians 5:18). How? By making God your focus. The Spirit dwells in you if you belong to Christ. Give Him your attention—every day, throughout the day. Sing to the Lord—with others, by yourself, and quietly in your heart. Give Him thanks—gratitude and praise will keep your thoughts on Him.

The darkness of the world would like to snuff out the light and the power of the Spirit within you. Don't let that happen. Use your time wisely. Put in the big rocks first.

Heavenly Father, may your Spirit fill me daily as I put my focus on you and learn to walk by your light and power. Amen.

Mutual Submission

EPHESIANS 5–6

Submit to one another out of reverence for Christ.—Ephesians 5:21

A friend calls them pseudo-scriptures—the maxims we hear that people say come from the Bible that actually *aren't* found there. "God helps those who help themselves." "God is my copilot" is another. If God is your copilot, that puts *you* in the captain's chair. You're in charge, and God is second in command, just helping you out. But Spirit-filled believers don't live that way. God is in charge. The Spirit leads us, and we follow.

That's the framework for the instructions Paul gave to the Ephesians about mutual submission within the church, Christ's body. Christ is the head, and *everyone follows Him*. Husbands love their wives with the same sacrificial devotion that Jesus showed on the cross. Wives show respect for their husbands and their husbands' decisions for the family. Parents nurture and teach their children, and children obey their parents. (Because slaves comprised more than half the population of Ephesus, Paul included similar instructions for slaves and masters too.)

The command to submit to one another doesn't allow us to abuse another person. Abuse is wrong and needs to be confronted and stopped. If abuse is part of any of your relationships, you must reach out to others who will help you. The mutual submission that marks Spirit-filled relationships creates well-being, never abuse.

Dear Lord, help me submit to the Spirit's leading in my life and in my relationships in healthy ways that please you always. Amen.

334

The Armor of God

EPHESIANS 6

> Put on the whole armor of God, that you may be able to stand against the schemes of the devil.—Ephesians 6:11 ESV

You wouldn't go deep-sea diving or mountain climbing without the right equipment. And you wouldn't simply *carry* your gear, you'd *wear* it, right? The same is true for any battle, whether an athletic contest or a confrontation in war. If you expect to win the fight, you must be well prepared and well equipped. Did you know that God provides you with the gear you need to stand firm as Satan fights against you?

Paul used the image of a Roman soldier's armor—a belt, a breastplate, shoes, a shield, a helmet, and a sword—to represent the protection God has given us: knowledge of truth, right standing with Him, the peace of the gospel, faith, salvation, and the Word of God. And like the Roman soldier, we are meant to *wear* our armor every day and use it in our daily battles.

What battles? "We are not fighting against flesh-and-blood enemies, but against evil rulers and authorities of the unseen world, against mighty powers in this dark world, and against evil spirits in the heavenly places" (Ephesians 6:12). Satan wants to keep the gospel from spreading, and he wants to tear down your faith. He's already been defeated, but he's still fighting.

Don't let Satan take you out. "Be strong in the Lord and in his mighty power" (Ephesians 6:10). Put your armor on—and use it!

Dear God, help me see and stand firm in the battles in my life, wearing and using the armor you provide. Amen.

The Attitude of Christ

PHILIPPIANS 1–2

When he appeared in human form, he humbled himself in obedience to God and died a criminal's death on a cross.—Philippians 2:7–8

Every ten seconds, one thousand selfies are posted on Instagram. Ninety-three million selfies are taken every day. (These U.S. statistics are several years old, so the numbers must be even greater now.) I'm only a teeny-tiny part of those statistics, but I'm not opposed to selfies. I do wonder, though, if Jesus would be taking selfies if He were here today.

Paul wrote his letter to the Philippians during his first imprisonment in Rome. Despite his circumstances, Paul experienced joy, and he wrote to encourage the church to rejoice as well. One reason for Paul's joy was the Philippians' faith and unity, and he urged them to remain unified by developing humility. "Don't be selfish; don't try to impress others. Be humble, thinking of others as better than yourselves. Don't look out only for your own interests, but take an interest in others, too" (Philippians 2:3–4).

As a model of humility, Paul said, look to Jesus. Even though He was God, He willingly left heaven and came to earth in human form and humbly obeyed the Father by dying on the cross for us. Our attitude toward God and others should be the same as His.

Having the attitude of Christ in my relationships—now that's a selfie worth taking for everyone to see!

Lord Jesus, help me choose to follow you with the humility you lived out for me. Amen.

336

Pressed Forward

PHILIPPIANS 3–4

Keep putting into practice all you learned and received from me—everything you heard from me and saw me doing.—Philippians 4:9

As a zealous young Pharisee, Paul had harshly persecuted Christians. He was a man with a past, but he pressed forward, anticipating a future with God in heaven. He made knowing Christ his life's goal.

Paul had suffered great hardships as an apostle, yet he was full of joy. He had learned to be content whether he had little or much in the way of material possessions and provisions—because Christ gave him strength whatever his circumstances. Paul understood that our thoughts affect how we feel, so he had learned to focus his thoughts on things that are "excellent and worthy of praise" (Philippians 4:8). He knew that worry is useless but prayer with thanksgiving brings peace.

Paul had started the church in Philippi and spent time with the believers there. They had benefitted not only from Paul's teaching but from seeing how he lived. Now, although he was under house arrest in Rome for the sake of the gospel, he called on them to remember and to follow the pattern of his life.

Who are the Christians you admire, and what have you learned from them? How are you putting into practice what you see in their lives of faith?

Heavenly Father, help me press forward in faith to know Christ, my Savior, following Paul's example and the example of mature believers in my life today. Amen.

Christ Is Supreme

COLOSSIANS 1–2

Christ is the visible image of the invisible God.—Colossians 1:15

Paul had never been to Colossae, a city east of Ephesus. But a Colossian named Epaphras probably became a believer when Paul was in Ephesus and returned home to start the church there. Now, Paul was under house arrest in Rome, and Epaphras told him of false teachings infiltrating the Colossian church. We don't know exactly what the false teaching was, but Paul does make references to asceticism (treating one's body harshly) and worshiping angels. Paul wrote this letter (along with Timothy, who was with him in Rome) to combat the false teachings and encourage the Colossian believers to remain true to Christ.

Paul began with a prayer asking for spiritual wisdom for the Colossians, and then he wrote about the absolute supremacy of Christ over all other powers:

- He is the visible image of God, who is invisible.
- He existed before anything was created.
- Everything was created through Him and for Him and He holds all creation together.
- He is the head of the church, His body.
- He is first in everything, including those who rise from the dead.
- God was pleased to live in Him and reconciled all things to himself through Christ's blood on the cross.

Jesus, therefore, is everything we need. "Continue to believe this truth and stand firmly in it," Paul wrote (Colossians 1:23).

So be discerning. Don't fall for deceptions and drift away from the assurance of the gospel. In Christ you have everything you need.

Lord Jesus, you alone are to be worshiped, and everything I need is found in you. Amen.

338

Devoted to Prayer

COLOSSIANS 2–4

> Devote yourselves to prayer with an alert mind and a thankful heart.—Colossians 4:2

"Do you have any singles?" my husband, Ed, asked as we came near a vending machine at the garden store on a hot, humid southern Ohio afternoon. I handed him my cash and continued to load up my cart with the bird food we had come to buy. Ed stopped to talk with one of the store's employees, and he handed the man a bottle of water.

Back in our car, my husband said, "I've seen him before. He works harder than anyone else here."

My husband's kind action didn't surprise me. He frequently notices people who might need a little encouragement. He looks for them. He's alert to opportunities to be of help.

Paul tells us to be alert to needs for prayer, and not just to take note but to actually pray. A threatening hurricane, a friend's medical diagnosis, a local election, an international crisis, a church conflict, a grandchild's report card—our days can become ongoing conversations with God if we stay alert to the needs around us and commit ourselves to bringing those situations to our loving Father for His care.

Dear Lord, I confess that so often I take a pass on prayer. Help me make talking with you a consistent habit of each day, and keep me alert to the needs around me. Amen.

Reward and Crown

1 THESSALONIANS 1–4

> What is our hope, our joy, or the crown in which we will glory in the presence of our Lord Jesus when he comes? Is it not you?—Thessalonians 2:19 NIV

Paul's letters to the church in Thessalonica, the capital city of Macedonia (northern Greece), are some of the earliest New Testament writings. Paul had visited Thessalonica on his second missionary journey and preached the gospel there. Some of the Jewish population believed, as did some Greek worshipers of God. But before Paul could thoroughly teach the new Christians, persecution by some of the Jews in the city began, and Paul was sent away at night for his safety.

Paul tried to make a return visit several times, but Satan prevented it. The new believers were precious to Paul, however. "Just as a nursing mother cares for her children, so we cared for you" (1 Thessalonians 2:7–8 NIV). So later, from Athens, Paul sent Timothy to Thessalonica to see how the church was doing. He was filled with joy and thanks to hear back that their faith remained strong. He prayed for their love for one another and all people to continue to grow.

Who are the people who will be your joy and crown when Jesus returns? Whose faith have you influenced? Thank God for them and pray for their faith to remain strong and their love to grow.

Dear God, what a privilege and joy to share the gospel and teach new believers to follow you! Bless those who are such a blessing to me. Amen.

340

Resurrection Hope

1 THESSALONIANS 4–5; 2 THESSALONIANS 1–2

The day of the Lord will come like a thief in the night.—1 Thessalonians 5:2 NIV

The believers in Thessalonica had remained faithful to the Lord, but they did have questions. One of their questions concerned some in the church who had died. Would they miss the day of Jesus' return?

Paul wrote that believers have reason to grieve when loved ones die, but with hope. Because Jesus died and was raised to life again, we have assurance that our loved ones will rise again. "When Jesus returns, God will bring back with him the believers who have died" (1 Thessalonians 4:14). First, those who have died will rise from their graves, and then along with them, those who are still alive will be "caught up in the clouds to meet the Lord in the air" (1 Thessalonians 4:17).

The church also had questions about *when* Jesus will return. Paul said His coming will be unexpected, like a thief in the night. But first there will be signs, including a time of deception and the revelation of the "man of lawlessness" (2 Thessalonians 2:8–10). Paul encouraged his readers to stay watchful and alert but not to worry—instead, to have confidence in God's protection and their salvation (1 Thessalonians 5:8).

Resurrection hope is called hope only because we don't have it yet, not because we're unsure it will actually happen. It *will* happen, Paul assures us. "Therefore encourage one another with these words" (1 Thessalonians 4:18 NIV).

Heavenly Father, thank you for my sure hope, the promise of Jesus' return and my resurrection to live with you forever. Amen.

Stay True

1 TIMOTHY 1–2

Timothy, my son, here are my instructions for you.—1 Timothy 1:18

Paul had no children, but Timothy became Paul's "true son in the faith" (1 Timothy 1:2). Timothy began traveling with Paul on his second missionary journey and remained a trusted friend and co-worker throughout Paul's life. Paul wrote his first letter to Timothy from Rome while under house arrest, when Timothy was ministering to the church at Ephesus. Paul encouraged Timothy to stay true to his calling to provide the church with sound teaching and an example of godly living.

One of Paul's concerns was order within the church. Men were to avoid anger and controversy and be devoted to prayer. Paul's instructions for women in this letter are often debated, but it's wise to keep in mind the Gentile culture from which these new believers had come. Women were to avoid getting caught up in excessive focus on fashion and appearance (as their wealthy Roman neighbors likely did) and let their good deeds make them attractive. Women were encouraged to learn the Word (unusual because women in the culture generally were uneducated), but they were not to take on an authoritative role in the church.

"The purpose of my instruction," Paul wrote, "is that all believers would be filled with love that comes from a pure heart, a clear conscience, and genuine faith" (1 Timothy 1:5).

Dear Lord, may all I do come from a heart filled with love for you. Amen.

342

Never Too Young

1 TIMOTHY 4

Don't let anyone look down on you because you are young.—1 Timothy 4:12 NIV

Age should never be a barrier to serving God.

Katie Davis Majors was a senior in high school when she traveled to Uganda for three weeks over Christmas break. After graduation, she felt a call to return to Uganda and signed on to teach kindergarten in an orphanage for one year. Many of the children in the orphanage had parents but their families were financially unable to pay for their schooling and support. Katie remained in Uganda and began a ministry to assist families with child sponsorship. By the time she was twenty-three, she had adopted thirteen young Ugandan girls as her daughters. Katie wrote about her experiences in the 2012 bestseller *Kisses from Katie.*

Paul advised Timothy not to let anyone discount his leadership because of his age. Instead, like Katie Davis, Timothy was to "set an example for the believers in speech, in conduct, in love, in faith and in purity" (1 Timothy 4:12 NIV).

Are you a young believer who needs to take Paul's advice to heart? Are there young believers and leaders in your life who would benefit from your encouragement or mentoring today?

Dear God, as I mature, may I be a blessing and encouragement to those in the faith who are coming after me. Amen.

Unafraid and Unashamed

2 TIMOTHY 1

God gave us a spirit not of fear but of power and love and self-control.
—2 Timothy 1:7 ESV

We can have strong faith yet be timid about using our spiritual gifts or telling others about Jesus. Timothy had strong, genuine faith yet needed a reminder not to neglect the gift he had been given for ministry.

Paul's second letter to Timothy was written near the end of Paul's life. He had been imprisoned again and now was awaiting execution (2 Timothy 4:6). He hoped to see Timothy one last time and poignantly wrote, "Do your best to come before winter" (2 Timothy 4:21 ESV).

Paul told Timothy to fan his spiritual gift into flames, and just as fire requires a spark, fuel, and oxygen to ignite and burn, using our spiritual gifts requires willingness, effort, and practice. We don't need to fear or be timid about developing and using our gifts—God gives us power, an attitude of love, and the self-discipline needed to do so.

Paul also urged Timothy never to be ashamed of the gospel or the suffering it may bring. Paul himself was suffering in prison but not ashamed. Have you ever wanted to tell someone about Jesus but held back because you weren't sure what they would think of you? Paul reminded Timothy to be ready to suffer for the gospel with the strength that God would give him. That's a reminder and a promise that we can hold on to as well.

Heavenly Father, help me claim the power, love, and self-control you give so I can serve you unafraid and never be ashamed of the gospel. Amen.

344

All Scripture

2 TIMOTHY 3

> All Scripture is God-breathed and is useful for teaching, rebuking, correcting and training in righteousness, so that the servant of God may be thoroughly equipped for every good work.—2 Timothy 3:16–17 NIV

Christians sometimes wonder about the value of the Old Testament for their lives, but Paul sets our thinking right about that. *All* Scripture comes to us from God himself. If the most important person in your life sent you a letter, I'm pretty sure you would open it and read it. Why wouldn't you want to read messages of love and truth from the most important Person in the universe, especially prepared for *you*? Among the things the Old Testament teaches us is God's plan to redeem us.

Timothy's father was Greek, but his mother and grandmother were Jewish, and they had taught Timothy the Old Testament Scriptures throughout his childhood. As a result, Timothy recognized Jesus as the Messiah when he heard the gospel. Paul reminded Timothy of this: "You have been taught the holy Scriptures from childhood, and they have given you the wisdom to receive the salvation that comes by trusting in Christ Jesus" (2 Timothy 3:15).

Jesus told the Jewish leaders, "The Scriptures point to me!" (John 5:39). All believers need the whole Word of God. We need to read it and teach it to our children, to one another, and to ourselves.

Dear Lord, may your whole Word always be precious to me, and may I listen well to what you say to me there. Amen.

Mentors

TITUS 1–3

Older women must train the younger women.—Titus 2:4

My sister, Faye, served as a mentor to two younger women during her first year with an empty nest. "I was nervous at first," she says, "but I did feel confident that I have always been good at listening and encouraging." One of Faye's mentoring relationships became a strong friendship. "I can see God's hand over both of these relationships. One was for a season, and one has stretched into its third year now."

The apostle Paul had left Titus on the island of Crete to shepherd the new churches there. Crete was known for immorality, and Paul's letter to Titus emphasizes guidelines for godly living the new believers needed to be taught to follow. One of those was the command for older women to train, or mentor, the younger women—in their relationships with their husbands and their children, in caring for their homes, making good decisions, and doing good for others.

In all of Paul's instructions for Titus and the churches in Crete, Paul had one objective: that no one would bring shame upon God's Word or the gospel message. When Christians behave in love toward one another, we make God attractive to outsiders, and those opposed to our faith can't find anything to criticize.

Do you need a mentor to encourage you through this season of life? Do you have wisdom gleaned over the years to offer to someone younger? We can help one another grow in love and faith!

Dear God, may your good purposes prevail in my life and in the lives of other women I can share with and learn from. Amen.

346

Now a Brother

PHILEMON 1

It seems you lost Onesimus for a little while so that you could have him back forever.—Philemon 1:15

While Paul ministered in Rome under house arrest, a slave in Colossae named Onesimus stole from his master, Philemon, and ran away. In Rome he met Paul and became a believer. He was a helpful friend to Paul, but Paul faced a dilemma. Under Roman law, slaves were property of their masters (and escaped slaves could be killed), so Paul was required to send Onesimus back to Philemon. And he did—but with this short letter appealing to Philemon's faith.

We can't control what others do, but we can make our wishes known. Paul asked Philemon to forgive Onesimus just as Jesus had forgiven him. He reminded Onesimus that though he had lost the service of his slave for a time, he was now receiving both his slave and a brother in Christ.

Paul also implied his hope that Philemon would free Onesimus so he could return to Rome to continue assisting Paul. He asked Philemon to receive Onesimus as he would receive Paul himself, and added, "I won't mention that you owe me your very soul!" (Philemon 1:19). How like Jesus that is, who says to God the Father about us when we put our faith in Him, "Receive this one as you receive me. She is mine."

Lord Jesus, in difficult situations when I can't see any good, may I remember Onesimus and Philemon and praise you for your life-transforming work on the cross. Amen.

Hold On

HEBREWS 1–3

At many times and in many ways, God spoke to our fathers by the prophets, but in these last days he has spoken to us by his Son.—Hebrews 1:1–2 ESV

God spoke to His people, the Israelites, through the prophets and their writings until the coming of His Son, Jesus. With the death and resurrection of Jesus, the old covenant between God and Israel ended and a new agreement—salvation by faith in God's Son—began. When the letter to the Hebrews was written (sometime before AD 70), Jewish believers were facing persecution and wondered if leaving Judaism had been the right decision. Whoever penned this letter wrote it with a two-fold message: Hold on; don't go back. Jesus is now the only way—and He is completely superior to angels, to Moses and the prophets, to any priest, to the old system of sacrifices, to the old covenant.

Our answering machine holds a message from eight years ago that we hope we never accidentally erase. Our only grandson at the time, who was three, left the message, asking us to make a video call to him on Skype. He and his parents had suddenly moved seven hundred miles away, and we replayed his phone message often to encourage ourselves as we adjusted to our new circumstances.

Hearing words of encouragement is important in any stressful situation. As one commentator has said, Jesus *is* the message. In these last days, we need to listen and hold on.

Heavenly Father, thank you for Jesus, higher and better and above all. Help me listen to Him and hold on. Amen.

348

Grow!

HEBREWS 2, 5–6

Let us move beyond the elementary teachings about Christ and be taken forward to maturity.—Hebrews 6:1 NIV

Pediatricians monitor their patients' height and weight by charting them against the measurements of other children in their age group. My little grandson who just turned two is in the 75th percentile for height and the 37th percentile for weight. (He's tall and thin!) If you and I were measured for spiritual maturity against others who have been believers for the same amount of time, I wonder where on the charts we would place.

The letter writer to the Hebrews chided his readers, "You have been believers so long now that you ought to be teaching others. Instead, you need someone to teach you again the basic things about God's word" (Hebrews 5:12–13). Ouch!

We're expected to grow in Christ. Not doing so can have a destructive effect. We might drift away. We won't learn to fully discern right from wrong. We might stop meeting together. We might become indifferent and deliberately keep on sinning.

So don't allow your faith to plateau. Let the prayer at the end of Hebrews be answered in your life: "Now may the God of peace . . . equip you with all you need for doing his will. May he produce in you, through the power of Jesus Christ, every good thing that is pleasing to him" (Hebrews 13:20–21).

Pay attention. Keep growing!

Dear God, show me what I need to do now to stay on your path and grow in faith and maturity. Amen.

Our High Priest

HEBREWS 4–5, 7–10

Our High Priest offered himself to God as a single sacrifice for sins, good for all time.—Hebrews 10:12

The theme of Jesus as the high priest of all believers flows throughout Hebrews.

Under the law of Moses, once each year the Jewish high priest made atonement for himself and the people for all the sins they had committed during the year. Only the high priest was allowed to enter the Most Holy Place in the temple to stand before God. First he made a sacrifice for himself and all the people. Then he brought the blood of the sacrifice into the Most Holy Place and sprinkled it on the cover of the ark of the covenant, also known as the mercy seat.

Jesus' willing sacrifice on the cross of His own sinless life ended the sacrificial system of the old covenant. It had been only a shadow, a foretelling, of the perfect sacrifice to come. Rather than a high priest who could enter God's presence only once a year, on the Day of Atonement, Jesus opened the way to God for us. Because of His perfect sacrifice, we can "come boldly to the throne of our gracious God. There we will receive his mercy, and we will find grace to help us when we need it most" (Hebrews 4:16). We can "go right into the presence of God with sincere hearts fully trusting him" (Hebrews 10:22). Don't let anything keep you away!

Dear Lord, may I never neglect to come boldly to you with every need and sin, since Jesus, my high priest, has opened the way. Amen.

350

By Faith

HEBREWS 10–11

Faith is confidence in what we hope for and assurance about what we do not see.—Hebrews 11:1 NIV

Blind faith" is an oxymoron, a combination of contradictory words, when it's applied to faith in God. We find too much evidence in Scripture and in the experiences of people who have lived by faith for our faith to be unfounded.

The writer of Hebrews says faith is confidence and assurance that what God says is true. Famously called the faith chapter of the Bible, chapter 11 contains a long list of people who believed God and obeyed Him. Some accomplished great and good things and others suffered and died, but all had faith—confident assurance in the better, future life God has promised. That's the kind of faith we're commanded to have. "It is impossible to please God without faith. Anyone who wants to come to him must believe that God exists and that he rewards those who sincerely seek him" (Hebrews 11:6).

The recipients of the Hebrews letter had experienced that same confident assurance when they had suffered as new believers, and they needed to hold on to it. "Do not throw away this confident trust in the Lord. Remember the great reward it brings you!" (Hebrews 10:35).

Think back over your faith story. Have your confidence and trust in God and His promises increased or decreased? Do you need to remember, renew, and hold on?

Heavenly Father, thank you for your promises of resurrection, hope, and life with you forever. Increase my faith, my trust in you. Amen.

Divine Discipline

HEBREWS 12

> My child, don't make light of the LORD's discipline, and don't give up when he corrects you.—Hebrews 12:5

Actor Ricardo Montalban said about his mother and father, "There couldn't be better parents than mine, loving yet strict. They disciplined with love. . . . You cannot have freedom without discipline." Not every child has such good parents. But as children of God, we have the perfect Father, and He disciplines us for our good.

Life is like a race—there's a finish line to cross, and getting there requires perseverance through obstacles along the way. Sin is our biggest obstacle, and to keep us from getting tangled up in it, our Father disciplines us. He wants us to have the freedom we need to finish the race well.

Discipline is training, not punishment, though it may include punishment at times. Sometimes it is the natural consequences of our actions. Sometimes it is having to make our way through hard circumstances we didn't choose. Discipline can be painful. "But afterward there will be a peaceful harvest of right living for those who are trained in this way" (Hebrews 12:11).

Is your heavenly Father disciplining you right now? God's goal when He disciplines us is to see us end our race with our faith not simply intact but enlarged. He is training and teaching us to live a holy life. His discipline is meant to encourage us—it means He loves us!

Dear Lord, you are a good, good Father, and I am glad you discipline me for a holy life with you forever. Amen.

352

Hospitality

HEBREWS 13

> Do not forget to show hospitality to strangers, for by so doing some people have shown hospitality to angels without knowing it.
> —Hebrews 13:2 NIV

As a stay-at-home mom for several years when my daughters were young, I loved visiting my friend Debby, who lived down the street. Debby spent her time playing with her children and making sure they and her husband were well fed and cared for; she didn't worry much about what the house looked like. Even though visiting Debby might have appeared to be stepping into chaos, in truth her home was warm, welcoming, comfortable, and relaxed—because she was.

Hospitality among Christians should be an expression of sisterly love—a deep sense of friendship, family, and partnership. In New Testament times, traveling Christian teachers needed homes to stay in when other accommodations were unavailable or unsafe. Although they might be strangers, they were family. Today, we might host a visiting missionary or even make a habit of inviting church members we don't know home for lunch on a Sunday afternoon.

Whenever I think about true hospitality, I think of my friend Debby. She always gladly shared her time, her space, her resources; she focused on her guests, not herself. She was a true friend. In the family of faith, let's be like Debby. And who knows—we might even discover we brought an angel home for lunch. Is there someone you should call or text with an invitation soon?

Dear God, teach me to be truly hospitable to all in the family of faith as an expression of love for you and for them. Amen.

Faith and Works

JAMES 1–2

Faith by itself, if it is not accompanied by action, is dead.—James 2:17 NIV

I put my key in the ignition and turned it enough to be able to roll down the windows while I cleaned out the car. Then I got distracted and left the key in that position for hours. Later, when my husband went out to lock up the car as he usually does—surprise!—the battery was dead. Oops.

Faith that doesn't find expression in deeds of love is just as useless as the dead battery in my car, according to James, Jesus' half-brother, a son of Mary and her husband, Joseph. Although Jesus' brothers opposed Him during His early ministry, at some point James believed, and he eventually became the leader of the church in Jerusalem. His letter in the New Testament, one of the earliest New Testament writings, is written to "Jewish believers scattered abroad" (James 1:1). It's a short course in living effectively as people of faith.

Faith must show itself in our actions to be faith at all. Our good deeds and acts of obedience don't save us—the apostle Paul wrote clearly about that. But James isn't contradicting Paul; he's giving us a way to evaluate our faith: What difference is it making in our lives and in the lives of others?

Heavenly Father, may my faith be living and active, showing my love for you in all I do. Amen.

354

Ask!

JAMES 3–5

The earnest prayer of a righteous person has great power and produces wonderful results.—James 5:16

If you've got something to say, you've never had more opportunities to say it. In 2017 there were an estimated 440 million blogs and microblogs online. In 2015, users uploaded four hundred hours of video to YouTube every minute. So go ahead, speak up. But heed James's advice before you do: "Be quick to listen, slow to speak, and slow to get angry" (James 1:19).

We probably all remember hurtful words spoken to us years ago that still sting when we think of them, or words we spoke that we would banish from someone else's memory if we could. Learning to listen more than we talk and choosing to wait before we speak helps us manage what James calls "a restless evil, full of deadly poison"—our tongue (James 3:8 ESV).

But James gives very different advice about how we should talk to God—jump in and pray! When we're experiencing trouble, when we're happy, when we're sick, when we've sinned—we don't need to hold back. We can pray alone, and we can—and should—pray with others.

Have you underestimated or underutilized the power of prayer in your life? Is it time for you to start talking?

Dear Lord, may I use words that reflect my love for you. Help me listen to others and not rush to speak—yet be quick to pray in every circumstance. Amen.

In His Steps

1 PETER 1–4

To this you were called, because Christ suffered for you, leaving you an example, that you should follow in his steps.—1 Peter 2:21 NIV

In His Steps by Charles Monroe Sheldon, published in 1896, is one of the best-selling books of all time. In the novel, a pastor challenges the members of his congregation to do nothing without first asking themselves, "What would Jesus do?" Those who accept the challenge to follow in Jesus' steps find their lives transformed.

Peter, fisherman turned apostle, wrote this letter to believers facing opposition and persecution in Asia Minor, around AD 62. In it he gives his readers, and us, a similar challenge—to follow Jesus' example of suffering. Peter offers three distinct suggestions that can help us endure suffering when people oppose or persecute us because of our faith in Christ:

- *By remembering who we are*—living stones in a new temple with Jesus as the cornerstone and "a chosen people, a royal priesthood, a holy nation, God's special possession, that you may declare the praises of him who called you out of darkness into his wonderful light" (1 Peter 2:9 NIV).
- *By remembering how Jesus suffered for us.* "By his wounds you are healed" (1 Peter 2:24).
- *By keeping our focus on our inheritance in heaven*, not on our temporary home here on earth where we are "sojourners and exiles" (1 Peter 2:11 ESV).

Are you suffering as a Christian? "Praise God for the privilege of being called by his name!" (1 Peter 4:16).

Dear God, may I never be ashamed to suffer for the name of the One who suffered and died for me. Amen.

356

He Cares for You

1 PETER 5

> Humble yourselves, therefore, under the mighty hand of God so that at the proper time he may exalt you, casting all your anxieties on him, because he cares for you.—1 Peter 5:6–7 ESV

Corrie ten Boom, author of *The Hiding Place*, said about worry, "Worry does not empty tomorrow of its sorrow. It empties today of its strength." Why is it so difficult to stop worrying?

Some of us suffer from anxiety disorder, a medical condition. The anxieties Peter wrote about, however, are different—worries and fears based in the facts of our circumstances. Could it be that this type of worry is a sign of pride—a sign that we're not trusting God the way He wants us to, the way He deserves to be trusted?

The believers Peter addressed had plenty they could worry about, but Peter advised them to give up every anxiety and let God take care of them. Giving up worry is an act of humility, he said. When we throw all our anxieties onto God, we are placing ourselves under His mighty hands. We're not in charge anymore; He is. And whatever the outcome, we couldn't be more secure.

God cares for you—He loves you! So take your worries in your hands right now and cast them all on God.

Heavenly Father, I confess I do worry. Forgive me. Help me place all my anxieties on you because you are powerful and trustworthy. Amen.

Be Patient

2 PETER 1–3

> The Lord is not slow to fulfill his promise as some count slowness, but is patient toward you, not wishing that any should perish, but that all should reach repentance.—2 Peter 3:9 ESV

When our oldest child was just four (she's forty now), my husband played the part of Herbie the Snail in our church's production of the children's musical "The Music Machine." Slow-moving Herbie sang about having patience (a perfect role for my husband!), and we still sing Herbie's song aloud when one of the grandchildren needs to wait patiently for something.

Peter's second letter, written near the end of his life, also encouraged patience. After warning about the need to stand firm against deceptive false teaching and opposition *inside* the church, Peter advised how to react to scoffers. They would challenge the idea that Jesus would ever return to judge the world—because if He were coming, what was He waiting for? Peter advised patience, because God's view of time is not like ours. "With the Lord a day is like a thousand years, and a thousand years are like a day" (2 Peter 3:8 NIV). But even more important, Jesus' delay shows us God's great heart of love. His desire is for everyone to repent and believe.

The Lord's patience means salvation for others and for us. We too can wait patiently for His return.

Dear Lord, may I wait with trusting patience for Jesus' sure return. Thank you for your patience and desire for all to repent. Amen.

358

Live in the Light

1 JOHN 1–2

If we walk in the light, as he is in the light, we have fellowship with one another, and the blood of Jesus his Son cleanses us from all sin.
—1 John 1:7 ESV

I live in southern Ohio, where winter brings long stretches of cold, gray days, and the lack of sunlight quickly lowers my mood. If the clouds happen to clear for a moment and the sun shines through, I'm immediately drawn outside into the light.

Sometime before the Romans destroyed Jerusalem in AD 70, the apostle John is believed to have moved to Ephesus and settled there. His three letters in the New Testament were written to the churches in the region to encourage and strengthen them. "God is light," John wrote, "and in him is no darkness at all" (1 John 1:5 ESV). God moved us out of Satan's kingdom of darkness into the kingdom of His Son when we put our faith in Jesus (Colossians 1:13). Now our job is to walk in that light—living according to His ways and following His Spirit.

Jesus said He is the light of the world, and that we, His followers, are too (John 8:12; Matthew 5:14). How can we know that we are shining brightly? John tells us to check our relationships with one another and whether we are choosing to sin less and less—leaving the darkness behind and running toward the light.

Dear God, help me live in your light, according to your truth. Thank you for rescuing me from the darkness through Jesus Christ, your Son. Amen.

Hearts at Rest

1 JOHN 2–5

If our hearts condemn us, we know that God is greater than our hearts, and he knows everything.—1 John 3:20 NIV

Who knows you better than any other person? Maybe it's your spouse, a sister, or a best friend. God knows you even better than that. He knows everything about you, and He loves you—with the love that took Jesus to the cross.

Jesus' sacrifice for us is how we know what true love is, John says in this letter, and the way Jesus loved us is how we should love one another. Our love for others is one of the surest signs that the Spirit of God lives in us.

So don't just talk about loving other believers—actually do it, John says, because that's one way we know that we "belong to the truth and how we set our hearts at rest in his presence" (1 John 3:19 NIV). And when we try but fail to love like Jesus? God is greater than our hearts, and we still have His forgiveness and love.

Heavenly Father, thank you that my heart can always rest in you because of your great love and Jesus' sacrifice on the cross. May His love fill my life and overflow to others. Amen.

360

Deceivers and Deniers

2 JOHN; 3 JOHN

Many deceivers, who do not acknowledge Jesus Christ as coming in the flesh, have gone out into the world.—2 John 1:7 NIV

Like other New Testament writers, John addressed the issue of false teachers. Some he warned about may have been the Gnostics, whose influence began growing toward the end of the first century AD.

That Jesus was fully God and fully human is one of the most basic Christian teachings, but it was opposed by the Gnostics, who saw the material universe as evil and the spiritual world as good. They believed human beings hold a divine spark within themselves that special, secret knowledge could awaken. Having been made aware of their essential self, these awakened individuals would escape the material world completely upon their death. Some Gnostics were drawn to ascetism, harshly treating their bodies to build up their inner selves. Others promoted sensuality, believing nothing the body did could affect the true self inside.

Confronted with anyone promoting these or other ideas opposed to the truth, what should believers do? John's answer: Watch yourselves and be discerning. Even more, "Do not receive him into your house or give him any greeting, for whoever greets him takes part in his wicked works" (2 John 1:10–11 ESV). Serious advice.

Have you encountered teachers, pastors, authors, or bloggers whose ideas feel a little "off" to you? Check it out and then take action. Harsh criticism isn't required; just stay clear. Keep walking in the truth.

Dear Lord, I want to hold to the truth and share it with others. Help me know your Word well and walk in it always. Amen.

Made Perfect

JUDE

Keep yourselves in God's love as you wait for the mercy of our Lord Jesus Christ to bring you to eternal life.—Jude 1:21 NIV

Jude's short but urgent letter ends the section of letters in the New Testament. Jude, brother of James and half-brother of Jesus, probably wrote this letter at about the same time Peter also was writing to warn churches about the dangers of false teaching. Jude has harsh words for those who distort true faith, and he calls on believers to "contend for the faith that was once for all delivered to the saints" (Jude 1:3 ESV).

Did you know you are a saint? It's true! Throughout the Bible, saints are people who belong to God. In the New Testament, saints are people set apart—made holy—because of their relationship with God through their faith in Jesus. And we "contend for the faith" and counter false teaching most effectively by living fully as followers of Christ every day.

So commit yourself to the simple things that help you grow, becoming more and more like Jesus. Study God's Word. Pray. Show love and mercy to others. Take Jude's beautiful message to heart and live it out, remembering God's love for you. He is the one who is "able to keep you from stumbling and to present you before his glorious presence without fault and with great joy" (Jude 1:24 NIV).

Dear God, how wonderful that you love me and that I will stand before you made perfect because of Jesus my Savior! I want to be faithful until that day. Amen.

Encountering GOD'S HEART for YOU in the NEW TESTAMENT

The Book of Prophecy

Visions on Patmos

REVELATION 1

This is a revelation from Jesus Christ, which God gave him to show his servants the events that must soon take place.—Revelation 1:1

From AD 90–95, the Roman emperor Domitian demanded to be worshiped and persecuted Christians, and the apostle John was sent to live in exile on the small island of Patmos for preaching about Jesus. On Patmos, John received a series of visions from Jesus and wrote the book of Revelation as a record for the churches in Asia Minor.

John wrote in the *apocalyptic* style of literature, full of symbolic images and language that seem strange to us. We don't quickly grasp the symbols and images—but John's first readers did. They would have easily understood the comfort and encouragement the book intended for them—and that it now intends for you and me.

Some Christians today read Revelation as telling us primarily about events that are yet to happen, and others see a more historical record looking back as well as forward. Either way, the key message in both views is the same: God still reigns, no matter what evil is taking place on earth, and Jesus will return to conquer evil forever and set up His kingdom rule over a new heaven and earth.

Don't be afraid to read Revelation. "God blesses the one who reads the words of this prophecy to the church, and he blesses all who listen to its message and obey what it says" (Revelation 1:3).

Lord Jesus, as I wait for your return, may your revelation of encouragement to stay strong and trust you always resonate in my heart. Amen.

363

To the Churches

REVELATION 2–3

"Anyone with ears to hear must listen to the Spirit and understand what he is saying to the churches."—Revelation 2:7

Jesus gave John seven messages to write as letters, one to each of seven churches for which John had oversight from his base in Ephesus before his exile. All the churches are commanded to listen to all the messages—and we need to hear and heed them as well.

The messages contain descriptions of Jesus, commendations and rebukes directed to the churches, instructions for dealing with the churches' situations, and promises to faithful believers. Some messages contain consequences for continued disobedience, and one church received no commendation at all. The messages warn us about losing our first love of Christ, tolerating false teaching and sexual immorality, going through the motions as Jesus' followers, and becoming comfortable and complacent. Jesus commended the churches for guarding right teaching, enduring persecution, remaining faithful, growing in love and service, and keeping His Word.

To the church at Laodicea, Jesus urged repentance and offered an invitation: "Behold, I stand at the door and knock. If anyone hears my voice and opens the door, I will come in to him and eat with him, and he with me" (Revelation 3:20 ESV). As you evaluate yourself in light of Jesus' letters to the churches, remember—Jesus cares about your life, and He is always the answer.

Lord Jesus, I want to persevere and be faithful to you. Help me hear what you are saying to the churches and heed your words. Amen.

A New Heaven and Earth

REVELATION 19–21

Then I saw a new heaven and a new earth.—Revelation 21:1

We talk about living with God in heaven forever after we die, but did you know that heaven is not our *final* destination? Instead, God has something more for us. Heaven is our waiting room, until God creates a new heaven and a new earth where He can live among His people, which has always been His plan.

After Satan has been utterly overthrown, after Jesus returns and the dead are raised, after the final judgment before God's throne, it will be time for the wedding supper of the Lamb and His bride, the church. Heaven and earth as we know them will have disappeared. In John's vision, the image of a gleaming city represents the church, all those who have followed Jesus faithfully. "I saw the holy city, the new Jerusalem, coming down from God out of heaven like a bride beautifully dressed for her husband" (Revelation 21:2).

And on the new earth, God will dwell among His people—everyone whose name has been written in the Lamb's Book of Life. No evil or sadness will ever disturb them. The nations will walk in the light of the Lamb and the glory of God.

Think about the best days of your life, the endeavors that give you joy, the people you love to be with. Haven't you said, "I wish this would never end"? One day, in the new heaven and earth where we will live with God, nothing ever will.

Dear Lord, how amazing it will be to live with you in a world without endings, without sorrow, without pain. I can only imagine it and thank and praise you for it. Amen.

365

Come, Lord Jesus!

REVELATION 22

> The Spirit and the Bride say, "Come." And let the one who hears say, "Come."—Revelation 22:17 ESV

The Bible closes as it began, in a perfect creation where God lives with His people. Life will be what it was always meant to be, and even more wonderful than we can possibly know now. "No eye has seen, nor ear heard, nor the heart of man imagined, what God has prepared for those who love him" (1 Corinthians 2:9 ESV).

Jesus promises to come soon. He is God and lives forever. "I am the Alpha and the Omega, the First and the Last, the Beginning and the End" (Revelation 22:13). He is the Anointed One of God who brings us salvation. "I am both the source of David and the heir to his throne" (Revelation 22:16). When He comes, those who have trusted in the blood of the Lamb to cleanse and transform their lives will eat from the Tree of Life and drink freely from the Water of Life—freely, without price, because of the love and grace God showed us in His Son.

Are you ready for sin and sorrow to end? Are you ready for Jesus to return? The creation around us and the Spirit within us beckon . . . there is more ahead.

Come, Lord Jesus!

Lord Jesus, until you come again, may I hold tightly to the hope you bring me, the grace you give me, the love you show me every day. And come soon, Lord Jesus! Amen.

Acknowledgments

I owe heartfelt thanks to numerous people who supported me as I wrote and who influenced the development of this book:

- My editor at Bethany House Publishers, Andy McGuire, who surprised me one day with an email asking if I might be interested in writing a book of devotions through the Bible for women. (My first reaction: Yes!) Thank you for the opportunity and also for your prayers and flexibility when circumstances upset my schedule.
- Janet Kobobel Grant, my agent and the founder of Books and Such Literary Management. It's an honor to be represented by someone with so much expertise, wisdom, and commitment to your authors. And you always find time to listen when that's what's needed!
- My patient husband, Ed. You never complained about all the hours I disappeared into my office to write; you consistently cheered me on. I love you.
- My prayer team: Cheryl Savageau, Marina Bromley, Sherry Grooms, Lynn Pratt, Judy Johnson, Linda Long, Faye O'Neil, Brook Gumm, Judy Dye, and Jill Nutter. Thank you for your emails, cards, flowers, requests for updates, and most of all for

everyone's prayers from start to finish—I *know* they carried me through!

- My proofreader and beta reader, Lu Ann Nickelson. Thank you for your careful reading, correcting, suggesting, and tracking *all* the Scripture references!
- Beth Neuenschwander, who nearly twenty years ago invited me to join a group to read through the Bible in a year. Thank you for that life-changing adventure! You welcomed a group into your living room every Monday night for many years after that, and now your influence has spread to thousands more women through this book and *A Woman's Guide to Reading the Bible in a Year.*
- All the women of the Monday night Bible study groups at LifeSpring Christian Church in Cincinnati, Ohio. Thank you for such wonderful community, discussion, and prayer times! You proved the value and the joy of ordinary women reading the whole Bible to get to know God, encountering His heart on every page and shaping our hearts for Him.

Diane Stortz is author of *A Woman's Guide to Reading the Bible in a Year* and coauthor of *Parents of Missionaries*. Her children's books include the bestselling *I AM: 40 Reasons to Trust God* and *Say & Pray Bible*.

Diane and her husband, Ed, a retired juvenile court probation officer, have two married daughters and five young grandchildren—all boys! When she's not writing, Diane enjoys walking, gardening, and planning her next trip to visit her grandchildren.

Visit DianeStortz.com for free downloadable resources, to sign up for Diane's newsletter, and for more information about all her books.

You May Also Like . . .

God put the Bible together for you. Reading it through in a year helps create a rich experience and a focused understanding of what God wants to reveal about Himself. And with week-by-week reading plans, easy-to-use reference material, and stories of encouragement from women like you, this is the perfect companion for this life-changing practice.

A Woman's Guide to Reading the Bible in a Year